Dance Movement Psychotherapy with People with Learning Disabilities

This book provides an overview of dance movement psychotherapy for young people and adults with learning disabilities. Contributors from a variety of backgrounds examine their work with clients from across the disabilities spectrum, ranging from mild to complex needs. The book chapters present theory and practice relating to the client group and subsequent therapy processes. This comprises psychotherapeutic interventions, dance movement interventions, theoretical constructs, case study material, practitioner care and practitioner learning and development related to individual and group therapy work. The logistics of a dance movement psychotherapy intervention, the intervention itself and the ripples of influence into the clients' wider socio-cultural context are discussed. This stance speaks to current research and practice discourse in health and social care.

The book champions acceptance of difference and equality in the health and social care needs for people with learning disabilities whilst emphasising the importance of dance movement psychotherapy for people with nonverbal communication.

Dance Movement Psychotherapy with People with Learning Disabilities: Out of the Shadows, into the Light will provide a practical and theoretical resource for practitioners and students of dance movement psychotherapy as well as allied health professionals, service providers and carers.

Geoffery Unkovich has extensive dance movement psychotherapy (DMP) experience through eleven years' practice with adults with learning disabilities. Geoffery was on the ADMP UK council for four years, and is currently on their Professional Development Committee. He is a senior lecturer in DMP at the University of Roehampton, and has taught on DMP training programmes at Goldsmiths, University of London, in Croatia and Romania.

Céline Butté has been practising DMP for fifteen years. She works within Merton Arts Therapies Team for People with Learning Disabilities and in private practice. A core member of the teaching team on the Creative Approaches to Supervision training with the London Centre for Psychodrama, she also teaches DMP/T internationally. Céline has provided DMP within NHS adult Mental Health services and for refugees and their children.

Jacqueline Butler has been practising as a DMP for eighteen years. Her DMP work is with adults with learning disabilities for a Local Government Direct Service and for private care-providers in a therapeutic community for those with mental health issues and she also has a private practice for individuals and supervisees. She is a visiting lecturer in Dance Movement Psychotherapy at the University of Roehampton, London.

'This is a beautiful book that takes us on a rich and varied journey connecting us deeply to the many shapes that Dance Movement Psychotherapy in practice can take. We are invited to experience from different perspectives the Dance Movement Psychotherapist in their many ways of 'being with' people with learning disabilities. A strong theme that emerges is how DMP aims to accommodate diversity rather than fix difference and for some people the DMP becomes an interpreter of emotional response between their client and the other significant people within their supportive network. I particularly enjoyed hearing about how DMP enhanced communication for three young men and how their experience led their mother to train to become a DMP herself.'

Dr Noelle Blackman, CEO of
www.respond.org.uk

'This thoughtful, informative and accessible book reflects current dance movement psychotherapy practice with people with learning disabilities. It is an essential resource for anyone working or training in the field of learning disability or therapy. Writers share their experience and their own learning with moving personal honesty and sensitivity to existentially challenging themes.'

Anna Chesner, UKCP registered psychodrama and group analytic psychotherapist and supervisor. She is co-director at the London Centre for Psychodrama Group and Individual Psychotherapy and programme lead of its cross-professional Creative Supervision Diploma training

'I strongly recommend this thought provoking book to therapists of all therapeutic backgrounds who work with people with learning difficulties. Through a vivid range of case studies and vignettes the authors apply dance movement psychotherapy theory and demonstrate clearly the wide range of benefits their clients experience through this wonderfully creative method. This rich book adds significant insights into the lives of people with learning difficulties and the ways in which therapy can reduce isolation and enrich lives.'

Richard Curen, MBACP (reg), MIPD, MIAFP

'In this moving, informative and seminal book dance movement therapy has come of age. It has always had its own longstanding rigorous professional history, but this book is for all professionals and citizens concerned for the therapeutic development and treatment of learning disabled children and adults. From the invitation for us to recognise the position in which we read this book both literally and metaphorically and try a different position now and again, we enter an authentic dialogue with the authors, who cover a wide range of settings, personal and professional experiences, themes of loss, identity, joy, sexuality and death with respect and transparency. The authors have applied many of the major theoretical advances in verbal therapies to their work and as a result of this book, other professionals will now reference and have a greater understanding of what dance movement therapy offers.'

Valerie Sinason, PhD, MACP, M Inst Psychoanal,
President of the Institute for Psychotherapy and Disability

Dance Movement Psychotherapy with People with Learning Disabilities

Out of the Shadows, into the Light

Edited by Geoffery Unkovich,
Céline Butté and Jacqueline Butler

LONDON AND NEW YORK

First published 2017
by Routledge
2 Park Square, Milton Park, Abingdon, Oxon OX14 4RN

and by Routledge
711 Third Avenue, New York, NY 10017

Routledge is an imprint of the Taylor & Francis Group, an informa business

© 2017 selection and editorial matter Geoffery Unkovich,
Céline Butté & Jacqueline Butler individual chapters, the contributors.

The right of the editor to be identified as the author of the editorial material, and of the authors for their individual chapters, has been asserted in accordance with sections 77 and 78 of the Copyright, Designs and Patents Act 1988.

All rights reserved. No part of this book may be reprinted or reproduced or utilised in any form or by any electronic, mechanical, or other means, now known or hereafter invented, including photocopying and recording, or in any information storage or retrieval system, without permission in writing from the publishers.

Trademark notice: Product or corporate names may be trademarks or registered trademarks, and are used only for identification and explanation without intent to infringe.

British Library Cataloguing in Publication Data
A catalogue record for this book is available from the British Library

Library of Congress Cataloging in Publication Data
A catalog record for this book has been requested

ISBN: 978-1-138-96331-3 (hbk)
ISBN: 978-1-138-96332-0 (pbk)
ISBN: 978-1-315-18327-5 (ebk)

Typeset in Times New Roman
by Deanta Global Publishing Services, Chennai, India

 Printed in the United Kingdom
by Henry Ling Limited

Contents

Foreword by Yeva Feldman	vii
List of contributors	xi
Preface	xiii
Acknowledgements	xiv

Introduction   1
GEOFFERY UNKOVICH, CÉLINE BUTTÉ AND JACQUELINE BUTLER

1 Entering the world: Dance Movement Psychotherapy and the complexity of beginnings with learning disabled clients   9
CAROLINE FRIZELL

2 A reflexive account of significant changes in learning disability values: A parent/practitioner story   22
JACKIE EDWARDS

3 DMP assessments for children and young people with learning disabilities and special needs   36
FIONA HOO

4 Dance Movement Psychotherapy as part of a holistic intervention team in a SEND school   52
JENI WILSON

5 Using video to increase sensitivity and attunement with caregivers of children with a disability: A Dance Movement Psychotherapy perspective   66
BETHAN MANFORD

vi Contents

6 On becoming a Monkey   81

SUE CURTIS

7 Finding a place of collaboration, co-created by clients, staff and therapist   94

JACQUELINE BUTLER

8 I will dance with you, all that you have been, all that you are, and all that you can become: An exploration of the application of a Person-Centred Dance Movement Psychotherapy approach with nonverbal clients in a group context   109

LINSEY CLARK AND AND VICTORIA SMITH

9 Men shaping men: Gender discoveries in a Dance Movement Psychotherapy men's group   121

GEOFFERY UNKOVICH

10 How can I meet Syon where he is today?   136

CÉLINE BUTTÉ

Closing reflections: Our body stories are real   148
Index   151

Foreword

As the parent of a child with Down's syndrome, I have discovered that I am an amateur, not in the modern sense of the word, but in the original French/Latin usage – 'a lover' of people with learning disabilities. Through necessity, I have also become an advocate. I have battled for my daughter to be included in mainstream education with the necessary support, navigated the numerous agencies and professionals involved in her care, despaired at the lack of inclusivity and understanding from organisations that should know better, yet celebrated her many incredible achievements (like winning two British Gymnastics National Acrobatic disability championships). I have developed a passion, both personally and professionally, for improving the lives of people with learning disabilities, and I am therefore delighted to have been asked to write the foreword to this book.

My daughter often says 'I was brave' when she does something difficult or new (which is often); she has to be brave every day to do what most of us take for granted. The editors of this book, Geoffery Unkovich, Céline Butté and Jacqueline Butler, were brave to bring this subject to life. It takes courage, determination and resilience to shine a light on what has been kept in the shadows. This is the first book that focuses on dance movement psychotherapy (DMP) with people with learning disabilities in the United Kingdom. It encompasses clinical expertise, embodied relational approaches and DMP resources that have been practised for many years but without acknowledgement or discourse until now. The poignant stories recounted by the authors gives voice to the voiceless. They are ambassadors, who at times must go into 'battle' to fight for those who cannot advocate for themselves. They ask important questions about the kind of society we want to live in. Who decides who should be included? Does an individual have a disability, or is society 'disabled' when it cannot meet the needs of all? These questions have huge impact for someone like my daughter, who does not fit into society's definition of 'normal'. These questions need to be asked. The editors remind us that therapy is also a socio-political act, 'fighting for the rights of people with learning disabilities to be seen, heard, included in our communities and society' (editors). This book inspires me and gives me hope. In its pages, the voices of the wordless are heard, the hidden are seen and the isolated are included through movement and words.

Unkovich, Butté and Butler are founding members of DMPLD Network, a special interest group for DMPs who specialise in learning disability, with between them forty-four years of clinical practice in this area. They are educators and supervisors, as well as clinicians, and this has had a profoundly positive influence on their book. They instil a deep respect for clients, families, care staff and fellow authors. They, along with all the authors, have a great wealth of experience, skills and knowledge in the craft of working with people with learning disabilities, which they share in a number of important ways:

- *Collaboration is essential.* Each author's approach has been developed in collaboration with and in response to clients, families, carers and staff, in combination with setting and system. These approaches have evolved over many years of practice and encourage collective reflection on systemic strengths and difficulties. Collaborative working promotes understanding and awareness, which leads to increased support and additional opportunities for individuals with learning disabilities.
- *Trust your embodied experience.* When working with nonverbal clients, sensations, thoughts and questions arise that resonate with their experience. Trusting one's own body-felt sensations and intuition is crucial to developing embodied listening, listening with one's whole body, to the authenticity of each person. This includes sitting in silence or using touch as a 'natural extension of dialogue' (Butté). Physically placing oneself within the experience of the client, listening and communicating through the body, the authors demonstrate how they are able to see and work with their client's abilities rather than their disabilities.
- *Unconditional acceptance and contact.* The authors illustrate the importance of unconditional acceptance for this client group and its role in promoting a unique sense of self. On numerous occasions in the book, I was moved by the DMP's determination and commitment to see, hear and respond to their clients' authentic voice, regardless of their ability to use language or movement. Poignant moments of contact demonstrate real human connection, fostering an intimacy that touches and transforms both client and therapist (and reader). They do this through learning the client's language, entering his/her world without trying to change or fix it (Curtis).
- *Choice is power.* With the ability to choose comes a sense of power. Choices are the building blocks of self-identity and authentic individual expression. The authors demonstrate numerous examples of how they promote choice making, even if the choice the client makes is to leave the group (Butler). The smallest movement, gesture, breath and sound by the client are received as communication and accepted as self-expression. It is the DMP's propensity for embodied listening, flexibility and resourcefulness that enables this client group to experiment, make choices and experience their power.
- *Reflexivity: Integrating the personal and professional.* I was struck by the authors' intimate stories, how they integrate these into their work and how the

work influences them. They demonstrate how personal experience combined with years of clinical experience shapes their approaches and interventions. Reflexivity weaves throughout each author's story, acknowledges that uncertainties, insecurities, transference and countertransference are very much part of this work, making supervision a necessary component for effective and safe practice. There is mutuality in the impact of the relationship between therapist and client. The quality of transformation embedded in these stories is contagious.

This book brings something new to the field of DMP with people with learning disabilities. It identifies complex and vital issues that should be discussed, but are often avoided, such as learning disability and sexuality, coping with death and grief, working with clients outside the therapy room and practising in non-clinical settings. This book will be useful to trainee DMPs and will become an important entry on reading lists. As a supervisor, this book relates to experiences of DMP trainees and the questions they raise when starting placements with people with learning disabilities. This is as close to a manual on DMP in these settings that we have. But it is much more profound than this. A reality is presented where individuals, who are denied a place in our society, are 'seen, heard, and respected for their amplified individuality' (Unkovich).

The editors ask, 'what is your world view on people with learning disabilities?' Whatever it is you feel at the start of reading this book, I guarantee that your view will be shaped and transformed by the end. I have been touched by the stories of the DMPs and their clients. I have been impacted on personal and professional levels. I have been reinvigorated to continue advocating and 'battling' for my daughter and others like her. I have deep appreciation and respect for the incredible DMP work that is being practised in the United Kingdom with this client group. I am confident that this book will inspire you to become, if you aren't already, amateurs, 'lovers of', people with learning disabilities and DMP.

Yeva Feldman, UKCP
Senior Lecturer
MA Dance Movement Psychotherapy
Roehampton University, London

Contributors

Jacqueline Butler: Jacqueline has been practising as a DMP for eighteen years. She works with adults with learning disabilities for a Local Government Direct Service and for private care-providers. Jacqueline also provides DMP in a therapeutic community for those with mental health issues and has a private practice for individuals and supervisees. She is a visiting lecturer in DMP at the University of Roehampton, London. Jacqueline was treasurer of the ADMP UK when serving as a member of council for three years. She is a current member of the Professional Development Committee of ADMP UK and a founding member of the DMPLDNetwork.*

Céline Butté: Céline has been practising DMP for fifteen years. She works within Merton Arts Therapies team for People with Learning Disabilities and in private practice. A core member of the teaching team on the Creative Approaches to Supervision training with the London Centre for Psychodrama, she also teaches DMP/T internationally. Céline has provided DMP within NHS adult Mental Health services and for refugees and their children. Her practice is informed by somatic movement practices and sensorimotor psychotherapy, and underpinned by psychodynamic and social-constructionist theories. Céline is a co-founder of the DMPLDNetwork* and of the aRTSjAM.** She was on council of the ADMP UK for several years, and the UK Delegate and Treasurer of the European Association for Dance Movement Therapy. Website: www.heartofmovement.com.

Linsey Clark: Executive Director of Dance Voice, Private Practitioner and Clinical Supervisor. Linsey has consistently been interested in the body's ability to communicate that which cannot be spoken and is attracted to the freedom of true expression and meaningful connection within DMP. Linsey has experience in one-to-one and groups with people with learning difficulties, elderly, adults, young people, children and babies in different settings with a variety of needs. Linsey is involved in tutoring and supervising on a DMP MA training and has built up her clinical supervision practice. Linsey is enjoying the challenge of her new role as Executive Director of a charity specialising in DMP called Dance Voice.

Sue Curtis: Sue originally trained as a dancer and teacher before practising DMP for nineteen years within mainstream and special education, particularly with clients suffering loss, trauma and abuse. She has lectured and supervised on MA DMP training courses since 1993, currently on the Goldsmiths, University of London, MA DMP training and guest-lectured in the Ukraine, Spain, Latvia and Poland. She supervises privately and has also been engaged in the work of the ADMP UK. Sue has recently lived through three years of serious illness and treatment for cancer, which left her disabled, but gave rise to exploring 'body mapping' as a way of the body telling its story. She is developing this approach within her private practice of supervision.

Jackie Edwards: Jackie is a Person-Centred DMP currently employed part time by her local NHS Adult Secondary Mental Health Service and part time as a DMP working with adults with learning disabilities living in the community. Jackie is currently a PhD candidate, exploring approaches to DMP for children with autism and is also the parent of two adult sons with learning disabilities, one with a diagnosis of autism and severe learning disabilities and the other with a diagnosis of Asperger syndrome.

Caroline Frizell: Caroline's career began in the 1970s as dancer, teacher, choreographer and community artist, subsequently going on to train as a dance movement therapist. From 1986, Caroline has worked closely with learning disabled children and adults and their families in education and community settings. She draws on her personal experience as the parent of a learning disabled daughter, who is now an adult. In the 1990s, she was the founder member of a number of community and self-help initiatives, one of which was 'Including You', an activist organisation that promoted inclusive practice for learning disabled children. Caroline is currently programme convenor for the MA in DMP at Goldsmiths, University of London, and runs a private practice in rural Devon. Website: http://www.movingdifference.co.uk.

Fiona Hoo: Fiona works in public and private practice with a focus on working with children and young people in a variety of education settings, including autism, learning disabilities and mainstream. She also works in acute settings within adult mental health. Fiona teaches in the MA DMP programme at Goldsmiths, University of London, and is a Clinical Supervisor in London.

Bethan Manford: Bethan works as a DMP with people who have learning disabilities, neurodevelopmental disorders and mental health conditions. She has experience with adults, children, young people and families in a range of settings including forensic inpatient, community and education. Bethan is interested in embodiment in relation to attachment and attunement, particularly in child–caregiver relationships. Bethan practises Iyengar yoga, which supports her in her personal and professional life.

Victoria Smith: Executive Director of Dance Voice. Private practitioner and clinical supervisor. Victoria's passion for movement expression and the belief that everyone has a voice that deserves to be heard led her to become a DMP. Now with over a decade of experience, Victoria has worked in a variety of settings with people of all ages, from pre-school children to elderly. Her experience includes learning and physical difficulties, acquired brain injury, addiction recovery, eating disorders, mental health, Alzheimer's and dementia. Alongside her therapy work she is also involved in tutoring on an MA DMP training programme and provides clinical supervision for both DMP and play therapy trainees and practitioners.

Geoffery Unkovich: Geoffery has extensive DMP experience through eleven years' practice with adults with learning disabilities and complex needs. Other DMP has included work with elders in a residential setting, for teenagers with special needs, in LGBT adult mental health, and short-term therapy for adults in dance performance education. Geoffery was on the council for the ADMP UK for four years, and is currently on the Professional Development Committee for the association. He is a senior lecturer in DMP at the University of Roehampton, and has taught on DMP training programmes at Goldsmiths, University of London, in Croatia and Romania. He is co-founder of the DMPLDNetwork* and a co-founder of aRTSjAM.** Website: www.g-moves. info.

Jeni Wilson: Jeni began her journey in 2003 when she started her BA Hons Degree in Dance at the University of Chichester. On completion of her degree she went on to work at an SEN school as a full-time teaching assistant. She always had a passion for dance and psychology, and was tutored and inspired by the late Dr Jill Hayes to train as a DMP. On completion of her MA in DMP at the University of Roehampton, she was offered a full-time role as a DMP at her SEN school, which she was dedicated to throughout her training.

---

* *The DMPLD Network is a special interest group for dance movement psychotherapists who specialise in learning disabilities.*

** *The aRTSjAM is an Arts Therapies improvisation collaborative.*

Preface

The seed for this book was planted quite a few years ago, when Geoffery and Céline were researching client material in their dance movement psychotherapy (DMP) learning disability practice. Our co-working relationship provided an opportunity for regular co-leading, discussion, writing and presentation of our practice for parents, carers and other health and social care professionals. Our curiosity on wanting to know more led to the development of the Dance Movement Psychotherapy Learning Disabilities Network (DMPLDNetwork) in 2012. This circle of Association for Dance Movement Psychotherapy UK (ADMP UK) registered practitioners working in learning disability contexts, has broadened the discussion on this area of psychotherapy practice in the United Kingdom in particular, although the network has recently welcomed UK-registered practitioners living and practising in other countries.

Jacqueline became part of the editorial team through the DMPLDNetwork.

As dance movement psychotherapists working with people with learning disabilities, we seek to create, open, hold and nurture a space where our clients can experiment with different ways of experiencing and expressing themselves, where we can all explore and learn through the gritty uneasiness of enlivened relationships. What is it like to be human and to find a place in this world with all that we are?

In this book, we privilege practitioner authenticity that emerges through DMP practice in learning disability contexts, authenticity that invites the body and movement relationships as primary storytellers. Our task is to see and state the obvious and the near invisible, to recognise and tell some of the small and hardly visible events that are brought to therapy over and over again and that are milestones in our clients' story, as well as the bolder moving tales we witness.

Our intentions with this book are to incite the curiosity of DMPs and to provide DMP trainees with informative resources so that they feel a little less blind when starting to work with this client group. We invite the wider community of carers, service providers, arts therapists and other health professions colleagues to know more about what DMP is and how it can contribute to the welfare of people with learning disabilities.

Hopefully we can all step towards improving the quality and range of therapy services for people with learning disabilities. We hope that with being more informed about DMP in learning disability services, those that read this book can champion DMP as a valuable intervention.

Acknowledgements

Collaboration was a core principle for this book and as co-editors we found our rhythm and traversed a new path together. With gratitude we would like to honour those authors who responded to the challenge of writing about their practice. Their tremendous effort and good grace is evidenced throughout.

We thank our places of employment, managers and staff who have supported our work and the development of this book. We especially thank our DMP mentors and our clinical supervisors who gave much valued constructive criticism, support and guidance.

We are indebted to families and friends who have accompanied us on this exciting venture, offering invaluable emotional and practical support.

We offer our appreciation and thanks to our clients for the rich experiences and profound opportunity for growth our work with them have generated.

Introduction

Geoffery Unkovich, Céline Butté and Jacqueline Butler

The aim of this book is to make visible the practice of dance movement psychotherapy (DMP) with people with learning disabilities. Our intent is for each page to echo dance movement psychotherapists' practical and lived experience of being with people with learning disabilities and/or complex needs. In the spirit of inquiry and appreciation of difference, we have invited all authors to tell their 'story' from their perspective. We are all aware of strong discrepancies around terminology used to define the client group this book is focusing on: are we to use 'learning disabilities', 'intellectual disabilities', 'learning difficulties', 'learning disabled'? Are we talking about clients, service users or patients, pupils or even customers (as more recently encouraged in some local authorities' services)? We have invited each author to use the terminology of their choice, reflecting their preference as well as that of the setting within which they practise. This choice of language/label is a sensitive issue that raises valuable contention and highlights our society's challenge in successfully accepting the differences presented by people with learning disabilities. Depending on the perspective we take, one word might be 'better' than another. We all know that a single word can have a profound impact on someone for the rest of their life. People with learning disabilities must be included in conversations regarding language and labels and must be listened to and responded to with positive action.

This essential service user voice is evident in the Researchnet group at St George's Hospital Tooting, London, which was founded in the summer of 2011 by art psychotherapist Ami Woods and psychologist Paula Manners. The purpose of this group is for the learning disability service users' experience and voice to improve health care in a hospital setting. The group continues to have an impact through service user teaching roles at the medical school along with conference presentations and ongoing research. Although this is an excellent example of a very positive initiative, the necessity for improved, effective and appropriate services for people with learning disabilities is a continuing concern for adults and children services alike (Jacobs *et al.*, 2015; Walker *et al.*, 2014).

The authors/practitioners in this book all live and work in the United Kingdom. This well-considered decision to have only UK practitioners provides a focus on a territory 'known' by the editors to present a truthful account of UK practice.

We hope that the book's contents, authors' words and client material inspire others to write of their work in a learning disability context. Through this book, we see the emergence of a dialogue amongst practitioners in this field and of a language for the practice of DMP with people with learning disabilities.

The material in this book covers what can be 'termed' mild to profound and complex learning disabilities with either verbal or nonverbal people. This is inclusive of those people with a learning disability and who are on the autism spectrum, with an autism spectrum condition, or autism spectrum disorder. These varying terms echo what we have highlighted above regarding the use of terminology that best fits the person or context. We are very aware that autism is not defined as a learning disability, however, there are many people with a dual diagnosis of learning disability and autism spectrum condition and who access the same range of services. For this reason it is important that they too have a presence in this book, as there is very productive work being done with people on the autism spectrum.

The acronym 'DMP' is used for dance movement psychotherapy and dance movement psychotherapist. Robust consent and ethical considerations have been adhered to by each author. Our professional stance in this editorial context has brought us to complex personal and professional discussions with authors around consent, best interests, capacity and familial ethics. This falls in line with the robust collaborations in the work place with other health professionals, carers and/or family members to choose how best to meet the needs of those in our care. Accountability and ethical considerations regarding capacity and consent are paramount for those less able to choose for themselves. Choice is integral to all our work as DMPs in the learning disability context where we are sometimes called upon to be an 'advocate' for our clients. Those clients who in therapy sessions ask us to speak for them at their clinical/social service reviews; those clients who ask us to be with them as they share some difficult, new or negative news to peers, parents, carers or support workers. Sometimes we champion being an advocate in a verbally dominated culture, supporting clients through our movement interactions, posture and gesture to find the words they need in a group context.

When reading each chapter, we invite you to consider which perspective you are taking. What is your worldview on people with learning disabilities? Can you come closer to the work from a position of curiosity and openness to difference? Feel free to sit, lie or stand as you read this book; recognise the position you choose, literally and metaphorically, and try a different position now and again; experiment and let yourself be surprised and moved. We invite you, the reader, on a journey into the somatic and sensorial experience of this embodied relational experience and on to a deeper journey that delves into the flesh of therapeutic relationships, before surfacing to a reshaping of your relationship to this encounter of DMP with people with learning disabilities.

Through our own writing process, we are reminded and touched by the intimacy of our work with this client group, and humbled by the task of editing this much-needed book. Each chapter is a vital contribution to the profession and the wider context; each chapter presents a vibrant fibre of experience and contributes to the life tapestry that makes our psychotherapy practice so rewarding. Some authors look from within the therapy space, others present more intimate and reflective accounts of their personal journey with people with learning disabilities, whilst others look at what methods of practice can be achieved and integrated into the work of the DMP, to better serve or support both our clients and those who care for them.

The authors' authentic voices demonstrate the complexity of facilitation and approach in the practitioners' holding of relationship in themselves and clients. In our therapy practices and during this editorial process we have debated the use of many words and labels which colour the life experience, personal and professional relationships, individual and collective identities, opinions and truths of clients and ourselves.

Each chapter unravels threads of embodied relationships, giving voice and language to personal and political aspects of the learning disability DMP context. Our intent is for the writing to colour the readers' experience through language that reflects the work and stimulates the senses. Working with people with learning disabilities provides a valuable opportunity to work in and with the idiosyncratic; the idiosyncratic person, space, dialogue and relationship. In this work we immerse ourselves in people's individual and symptomatic communication, clothing, eating, drinking, dancing, singing and vocalising that are not tied to rules or socio-political precedents. This work calls us to be open to change and to the unexpected or to be bound by a person's safety in their ritual and precise repetitions. Sound, sight, taste, smell and touch are alive in the work and in the embodied experience of being amongst those people who challenge society's ideals on what it is to be 'normal'. People with learning disabilities provide new, different, challenging, rewarding and pleasurable shaping of our embodied relationships and interactions, where we can find ourselves in extraordinary circumstances of communication: laying on the floor, shouting across the room, cradling each other with gentle whispers, crying with laughter, making up words and sounds or communicating with whatever sounds emerge.

DMP practice with this client group has been taking place for several decades in the United Kingdom, being informed by people such as Veronica Sherborne (1975, 1990) with her developmental movement for children and Walli Mieir (2008) with her work in special needs schools in the 1970s and at the Nordoff Robbins Music Therapy Centre in the 1980s. We also acknowledge the formative work in learning disability contexts of UK DMPs Marie Ware and Hillary Barratt. Marie Ware's work in community education and long-stay 'mental handicap' institutions in the 1970s led to her development of 'Dance Voice' in Bristol, a community-based charity offering DMP to people with learning disabilities. Hillary Barratt's experience began with her 1940s-childhood experience of exploring Laban's concepts of weight, time, space and flow in relationship to gymnastic apparatus. She later went on to work with children with physical and cognitive disabilities at the Meldreth Manor School and eventual DMP training at Roehampton University (Barratt, 2008). Professional trainings specifically related to learning disabilities and dance began in the late 1970s with the Laban Centre's one-year course in dance and special education.

This book is written at a time of great contradictions in the United Kingdom, where there is a heightened awareness of the vulnerable and of those in need, a heightened awareness of disability, a heightened awareness of a need to do more, and yet funding to learning disability services is being slashed (BILD, 2016). Unfortunately, most people with learning disabilities do not have a loud voice in the socio-political arena so remain marginalised and silenced.

The emergence of community, person-centred based services for adults with learning disabilities with a 'personalisation' -based political agenda has and has not worked. 'The Winterbourne View – Time for Change' (Transforming Care, 2014) report highlights the continuing need for much greater work to be done in taking people out of long stay hospitals and into more personalised living situations (Leaning and Adderley, 2015: 168). Without this move to community living and care, people with behaviour that appears to challenge services and staff remain marginalised with 'those aspects of the person's life which do not fit within the dominant, problem-saturated story' being negated. The introduction of Personalised Independent Payment (PIP) in 2013 in the place of Disability Living Allowance (DLA) itself introduced in 1992, received (and continues to receive) significant media coverage, denouncing PIP as a way of hiding an agenda to reform how much financial support those with disabilities or long-term ill-health actually receive (Sandhu, 2016; Marsh and readers, 2016). The Care Act (DoH, 2014) stipulates the importance of safeguarding and the Care and Support statutory guidance (DoH, 2016), that recently followed suit, made it a legal requirement for all organisations to have a robust safeguarding structure in place and recognised, in a much broader sense, what constitutes abuse and neglect. However, the person-centred ethos brought forward by these governing documents, research and numerous services continues to be overshadowed by a focus on cost-saving. Consequently, service user interests of people with learning disabilities continue to be squashed and unheard, and inequality prevails. Advocacy services, for example, deemed too costly, are extremely hard to access, thereby leaving a gap in the genuine support of individuals with learning disabilities and their families, at times of great vulnerability and litigation (Lawrence, 2016).

There is so much more that can and should be done socially, politically and therapeutically. This book touches on what can be done as we navigate the DMP practice territory with our spyglass focused on the sessions themselves, what happens between the client/s and the therapist/s and how the therapist uses this to make sense of the client's story. We look at how DMP can contribute to the emotional well-being of the community within which it operates. We consider what DMP with people with learning disabilities looks like from the point of referral, through the assessment process, and as an intervention embracing specific methodologies to address the particular needs of the clients and the setting. Our aim is to speak the life of the practice and in so doing, to bring it a little closer to the heart of the reader.

Introduction 5

We begin our journey with *Caroline Frizell*, who offers a very moving mother's story of discovering their child is learning disabled. She discusses 'how individual subjective experience of parents can bring into focus the uncomfortable and mixed feelings that confront us as we face learning disability as a lived reality'. A challenge all practitioners will face every time they meet a new client. Through her chapter, Caroline offers some direction and begins to answer a most important question asked by the novice practitioner: 'what do I do with them?' Like Caroline, this book seeks to offer some answers to this question.

Some of the ongoing complexities of learning disability lives are eloquently discussed by *Jackie Edwards*, who shares her story of becoming a DMP, incorporating the personal and the professional. She speaks of her own children's learning disabilities and their experience of DMP that forged her path to becoming a therapist. Jackie's chapter offers insight into several decades of socio-political changes in familial and social care understanding of learning disabilities. It illuminates the profound impact that DMP can have on a family system's methods of communication.

DMP with children with profound and multiple learning disabilities (PMLD) in specialist and mainstream schools can be significant in recognising and integrating nonverbal communication as a meaningful language for building successful relationships. *Fiona Hoo* tells us of the importance of establishing robust ethical assessment procedures in a school setting. In her chapter, Fiona describes her assessment process and offers a model of assessment she has developed through her research and practical experience in a range of school settings.

The complexities and tensions of being a psychotherapist in a school setting provide particular challenges in regards to educational laws and measuring outcomes. *Jeni Wilson* writes of her transition from being a teaching assistant to becoming a DMP and her consequent integration of DMP and educational outcome measures to provide evidence of engagement and attendance to DMP sessions in a school setting. The publication of SEND (Special Educational Needs and Disability – 1 September 2014) by the Department of Education advocates a holistic approach to the health, care and education needs of children and young people with learning disabilities. DMPs working with young children provide valuable consideration on the ripples of impact into and out of the therapeutic space, ripples of impact that necessitate change for parents, carers and the school and social service systems.

Systemic change often arises out of profound experience and this is amplified with *Sue Curtis*, who provides a compassionate and very real account of her experience of life, death and loss on a personal and professional level. She discusses the role of DMP in a school context when loss and bereavement strike. What is the scope and value of the creative, nonverbal and therapeutic aspect of DMP in providing a space where children can grieve the loss of a peer, where staff can reflect on their experience of loss and where families can engage with services to gain the necessary support? In her poignant chapter, Sue invites us not to just dip our toe in, but to really let our self be taken by the work so we can genuinely meet those individuals in her care. When we can understand and appreciate the support that is needed we can all support systemic initiatives that offer positive change in the best interests of those we care for in social, educational, psychological, medical or community settings.

It is apparent from these practitioners' experience that the complexities of being a DMP require skills appropriate to working with parents, carers, siblings, educators and related health professionals. *Bethan Manford*, whose chapter on the use of video for supporting caregivers in seeing, understanding and attuning to the children and young people in their care, offers an innovative way of integrating DMP within parenting programmes. She highlights the value of using video to help families attune to each other in their goals and relationships. Bethan's innovative work demonstrates the importance of developing context-specific interventions for raising awareness on how nonverbal communication supports various aspects of a young person's development.

This first part of the book tells us of the beginning of life with a learning disability and how DMP in particular offers a means to accompany these infants and their parents, children and their carers, into a life in which they are entitled to thrive. As these young people move into adulthood, services continue to play an essential role in the life of the learning disabled person and need to continue to address their needs.

Jacqueline Butler introduces us to her work in an adult learning disability community setting where collaborative working relationships with support workers and other professionals require particular attention. She discusses some of the tensions and successes in developing her work, in what she describes as a 'non-clinical setting'. Jacqueline offers valuable discussion of the flexibility and spontaneity needed in this therapy context. Her story brings our attention to the person in the room and to questions regarding what is the best practice and/or theoretical modality in our particular place of employment.

This notion of the person is amplified by *Linsey Clark* and *Victoria Smith,* as their chapter discusses the person-centred approach that is integral to the educational and therapy setting where they work. Their chapter provides vivid vignettes of one man's DMP journey from his initial hesitation to step into the setting, to his participating in a shared performance in a therapy context. Their story demonstrates the potential for individual growth and interpersonal relationships when we put the person before the label of disability.

Despite striving to see the person first, the label, the diagnosis and the system all have an impact on a person and their identity. Who can we be in a world where we are bombarded with images, words, music, art, sport, dance, religion, faith, family, community and a government that want us to 'fit' their model of being human? *Geoffery Unkovich* leads us into his work with a group of men who explore their understanding and experience of their gender, sexuality and sexual orientation. He discusses the significance of posture and gesture as a way of amplifying understanding for this group of men. At this work's core is Geoffery's life experiences of what it means to be a man and his chapter demonstrates the necessity for gender-specific therapy relationships in certain contexts.

Finally, beginnings, endings and the intimacy of therapy resonate loudly in our final chapter by *Céline Butté*. Her understanding of DMP, of meaning making, and personal investment in the psychotherapy context was stretched as she worked one to one with a man living with chronic pain, loss of mobility, increased dependency on family and carers, and faced the irreversible turn his life took. Céline's personal and professional compassion is evident as she describes her work with Syon until his passing, where her belief in DMP practice and contextualised facilitation demonstrates the significance of DMP in palliative care.

As you delve into this book and into the world of DMP and learning disability, we invite you to take care of yourself, to consider the impact of the words that we share here. Notice where this 'reading' journey takes you. What do you notice in your body, what thoughts come and go and what thoughts, memories or sensations remain?

This book gives a voice to the voiceless and speaks of a profession that operates with and without words; it offers words on paper that represent a multi-dimensional, interpersonal, alive reality. We hope that each author's authenticity touches you with their words and brings the practice alive, as they share concrete examples of the reality and scope of DMP with people with learning disabilities.

References

Jacobs, M., Downie, H., Kidd, G., Fitzsimmons, L., Gibbs, S. and Melville, C. (2015) 'Mental health services for children and adolescents with learning disabilities: a review of research on experiences of service users and providers'. *British Journal of Learning Disabilities*, 44: 225–232.

Leaning, B. and Adderley, H. (2015) 'From long-stay hospitals to community care: reconstructing the narratives of people with learning disabilities'. *British Journal of Learning Disabilities*, 44: 167–171.

Sherborne, V. (1975) 'Movement for retarded and disturbed children'. In Jennings, S. (ed.) *Creative Therapy*. London: Pitman Publishing.

Walker, C., Beck, C. R., Eccles, R. and Weston, C. (2014) 'Health inequalities and access to health care for adults with learning disabilities in Lincolnshire'. *British Journal of Learning Disabilities*, 44: 16–23.

Online resources

Barratt, H. (2008) 'The road from Barkhill'. *e-motion*, XVIII(2). ISSN: 1460–1281 (Accessed 26/09/16).

The British Institute of Learning Disabilities (BILD) (15 September, 2016) *News on What's on. News on Learning Disabilities. DWP slashes funding for disability supported housing and homeless hostels.* Available at www.bild.org.uk (Accessed 30/09/16).

Care Act (2014) Available at www.legislation.gov.uk (Accessed 08/11/16). *Care and Support Statutory Guidance* (2016) Available at www.gov.uk/government (Accessed 08/11/16).

Lawrence, C. (22 August, 2016) 'Lord Rix was told to put his daughter into a home. Instead he fought for people like me'. *The Guardian*. Available at www.theguardian.com (Accessed 7/10/16).

Marsh, S. and readers (26 September, 2016) '"I feel ashamed in a way I never did before": Your stories of PIP assessment'. *The Guardian.* Available at www.theguardian.com (Accessed 7/10/16).

Meier, W. (2008) 'Dance Movement Therapy: My story'. *e-motion*, XVIII(2), ISSN: 1460–1281 (Accessed 26/09/16).

Sandhu, S. (16 March 2016) Budget 2016. 'Caroline Lucas accuses Georges Osborne of "hypocrisy" over disability cuts'. *The Independent.* Available at www.independent. co.uk (Accessed 7/10/16).

Chapter 1

Entering the world

Dance Movement Psychotherapy and the complexity of beginnings with learning disabled clients

Caroline Frizell

This chapter explores the significance of beginnings in relation to working as a dance movement psychotherapist (DMP) with learning disabled clients. I explore the nature of 'beginnings' for the learning disabled infant, illustrating that experience with one mother's story as she faces the news that her child has Down's syndrome. I am not suggesting that subjective experience can validate generalisations about learning disability and I have no wish to reinforce a zeitgeist that seeks to theorize through personal experience rather than empirical research, mistaking 'personal belief ... for public knowledge' (Anastasiou and Kauffman, 2011: 369). In this chapter I explore how individual subjective experience of parents can bring into focus the uncomfortable and mixed feelings that confront us as we face learning disability as a lived reality. Through an analysis of that individual experience in relation to relevant literature, I identify issues that can help us to think about the implications for the transference when working as a DMP with learning disabled clients, in particular in relation to beginnings. I will finish with vignettes from my therapy practice to illustrate how the complex dynamics embedded in a client's psychic infrastructure might manifest symbolically in the therapeutic relationship. I have full permission to share the stories in this chapter. Pseudonyms are used and some details have been changed to protect confidentiality.

A note on language

Throughout this chapter I use the term 'learning disabled person' (rather than people with a learning disability) to reflect discourses around discrimination and a 'political expression of the fight for rights' (Slorach, 2016: 24) regarding disability. This use of language supports a social model of disability and locates the disabling factors in the social and cultural contextual constructions (see for example Sinason, 1992; Slorach, 2016), rather than belonging to the person. The term 'disabled people' has been campaigned for and promoted by the disability movement (Slorach, 2016).

Beginnings

Beginnings, like endings, play a crucial role in therapy and our entry into this world is characterised by relational transactions that are nonverbal. Daniel Stern

10   Caroline Frizell

(2010: 110) notes how 'the primacy of movement and its dynamic features' forms the basis of our 'developmental infrastructure'. As a DMP, I remain aware of the subtle nuances of beginnings as I meet with the particular developmental infrastructure of any particular client, the history of which becomes enacted in the intersubjective space from the moment he or she enters the orbit of my awareness. I pay close attention to my embodied felt-sense throughout the assessment and consultation process leading to the first encounter. I invest in my skills of observation and remain open to the way the client's relationship with beginnings is characterised and evolves throughout the therapeutic process. Beginnings, like endings, hover continuously in the psychic space of the therapeutic process.

As a practitioner working with learning disabled people, I remain open to the inconvenient and uncomfortable truth of how many have experienced being welcomed into the world. These early relational experiences will shape the interpersonal dynamics at play and reflect wider socio-political perceptions. By listening to the dynamic processes emerging over time, I offer a therapeutic space for those complex experiences to be disentangled, felt, thought about, understood and perhaps replayed and reconfigured.

Learning disabled people have often experienced an a typical beginning. Sinason (1992: 146–7) notes how '(w)hen the wished-for baby does not appear it is hard for even the most loving, resourceful parent to feel deeply attached'. As illustrated in the following story, when a parent learns of his or her child's diagnosis of learning disability, that 'first mirror' does not always reflect 'beauty and joy' (1992: 147). Instead, the parental gaze is tinged with disappointment and grief.

The story that follows is one mother's account of her daughter's birth. The mother-to-be is on a trip to a botanical garden when she goes into labour. A small girl skipping by comes to represent the mother's idealised notion of the anticipated child. After the shock of an emergency caesarean, there is a sense that something isn't right. The parents are avoided by nursing staff who await the paediatrician's return after the bank holiday weekend. The parents begin to bond with the baby before they are confronted by the news that she is learning disabled. The news is delivered by a paediatrician who seems ill-equipped to hold the emotional impact of the news. A junior doctor is able to sit by the parents when their world is turned upside down by the shocking news. The baby is an unexpected guest and the parents too find themselves on the threshold of an unexpected and unknown world.

In the humid Palm House at Kew Gardens, a pregnant woman descended the spiral staircase. Her stomach tightened and she clutched the iron hand rail to pause. The contraction passed and she continued to spiral down, sensing the tailback of August bank holiday visitors stretching behind like a giant tendril.

She became absorbed in the sensorial world of the Palm House. Metal hoses hissed like giant anacondas and steaming droplets of water cascaded onto the leaves of banana trees and cocoa plants in the simulated, tropical atmosphere. A bulging droplet fell from a leaf as if in slow motion. The leaf rebounded with a shudder. She felt the shudder echo in her spine and put her hands protectively on her stomach, feeling the baby beneath the tightly stretched skin. A small child in a floral dress skipped by, calling to her father. The woman smiled, remembering her visits to Kew as a child. As she did so, she gazed into the crystal ball of her baby's future: a carefree child, skipping into adulthood and sailing into the next generation. It was an uncomplicated vision.

Exotic scents hung in the hot air that brushed against her skin as sounds intensified in volume. The anaconda hissed at intervals from above. Conversation slithered in and out of earshot ... 'look daddy ... did you see the ...' Her eyes followed the little girl with tousled ringlets, skipping back and forth as her parents wandered around the palm house. Her stomach tightened again.

Her partner turned to her.

'I think we should go,' she said.

In the maternity ward, they put her on a monitor. She saw the panic on the faces of the nurses.

'The heart's dipping,' she heard. 'Sign this form.' She held the pen over the paper and watched it scribble illegibly. The anaesthetist peered at her over his green face-mask and the world went black. Her husband waited anxiously in an adjacent room. The baby was lifted into the world and wrapped in a blanket. As the woman came to, her partner greeted her, holding in his arms the tiny being with silky blonde hair.

That night the woman lay awake on her back, unable to shift position due to the caesarean. Her arm was tucked around a small bundle of white blankets.

'Just hold her for a moment and I'll be back to put her in the nursery ...' said the nurse, 'she's rather small and getting cold.'

The nurse threw the woman a fleeting glance and raced out of the room. She didn't return.

The woman peered at the tiny baby, overwhelmed by the delicate softness and the delicious smell of new-born skin. The exquisite features and the thick mop of blonde hair held an unfamiliar wonder to the woman, who'd never seen anything quite so beautiful. The curtains were open and a full moon hung in a clear velvet-blue sky. She stroked the fine hair on the baby's skin with the back of her hand.

Her husband phoned around with the news. Hearts warmed. Glasses were raised in celebration. Knitting needles crafted pink matinee jackets. Congratulations filled carefully chosen cards. The news echoed through the trees. The anaconda hissed a warning into the air, which hung suspended, waiting to fall from the edge of a leaf. Mother and baby drifted into a blissful sleep.

'Don't tell me you've had this baby in your bed all night!' a nurse scolded, not long arrived on her Sunday morning shift.

The woman woke with a start. The bright sun shone through the window, making her blink. The baby was whisked into the nursery with talk of a bottle to top her up.

'Please don't give her a bottle,' said the woman.

The nurse ignored her, 'You get some rest now ... we'll bring the baby back later.'

The woman didn't want to rest, she wanted her baby back. She had a strange sense of being avoided by staff. They raced in and out of her room, avoiding eye contact. Her husband arrived.

'The baby is in the nursery; can you get her back?' said the woman.

After a while, her partner wheeled the baby back into the room. The nurses had said they needed to consult the paediatrician. It was a bank holiday weekend and medical staff were mostly away. The baby was small and slightly blue, they'd said.

Visitors came with cards, flowers and presents. A helium balloon on pink ribbon wavered in the heat that shimmered from the hospital radiators.

The bank holiday weekend was over. The paediatrician entered the room with a junior doctor and some anxious looking nurses.

'Well, how are we all?' said the paediatrician brightly.

The room was lined with professionals, looking anywhere but in the woman's eyes. The woman had made her way tentatively from the bed to a chair.

'May I take the baby?' asked the paediatrician, lifting the baby from the mother's arms. She held the baby at arm's length before placing her on her tweed lap. Unwrapping the blanket, she allowed the baby's arms to flop down either side of her knees. The paediatrician's natural-tan tights had a sheen, which caught the sun, causing a shaft of light to curve over her knee and follow the contour of her athletic calf muscle down to her black-patent court shoes.

'Have you noticed anything about your baby?' she asked, slowly shifting her attention from baby to mother.

The woman felt her chest tighten and her spine straighten. She shifted her glance from the paediatrician's professional smile to the baby. As she did so, the paediatrician began to bounce the baby's arms in her hands.

'Can you see she's a bit floppy?'

The woman wanted the earth to stop turning. She wanted to be back in bed with her arm round the baby, as the full moon shone through the window. The paediatrician put her fingers in the baby's palms. The baby didn't respond, but instead, moved her head to gaze towards the line of nurses, each standing upright, as straight-backed as Mary Poppins.

'... and it would be usual for the baby to grip,' she went on. The woman continued to stare, her blue eyes piercing the paediatrician's charm, defying the theft of her dream.

'... and have you noticed the shape of her eyes?' the paediatrician went on, 'the epicanthic folds, which are typical of a certain syndrome. Do you

see what I'm getting at?' She drew her finger-tips slowly together to indicate a thin, elliptical shape. The paediatrician was becoming unnerved by the woman's expressionless stare, which gave nothing away. The woman sat silent in her chair. The paediatrician held her precious baby on her lap like a faulty specimen.

'The baby obviously has Down's Syndrome ...' the paediatrician paused. '... you hadn't noticed? And I suspect there's a problem with her heart, as she is blue around the mouth. It's not uncommon ... there can be little doubt, but obviously we'll do tests ... um ... straight to the special care baby unit I think,' said the paediatrician, over the woman's head 'we'll get her to Great Ormond Street a.s.a.p. ... oh, and can someone get mum and dad a cup of tea?'

With that she smiled with a sympathetic tilt of the head, put the baby in the plastic hospital cot and swept out of the room. The anaconda hissed a billion pieces of shattered glass into the hospital air. The professionals clicked their heels and stepped up their choreographed routine, reflecting back the paediatrician's reassuring, professional smile. A nurse pushed the baby out and was followed by a procession of professionals, who jostled for a hasty exit.

Suddenly the room was empty, except for the woman and her husband. They stood staring at the open door. A shiny blue hospital floor led down an empty, silent corridor. They stood in a deathly silence. The paediatrician's words echoed in the woman's mind '... you hadn't noticed?' Why hadn't she noticed? They stared at each other in disbelief. Tears welled up in their eyes and in their confusion they quickly averted their gaze from each other. The flowers spilled out of the hospital vase and the helium balloon blushed a deeper shade of pink. A baby began to cry from an adjacent room. The sound was unbearable and cut through the air, shattering any small illusions that remained. The beautiful baby with the soft skin and the shock of blonde hair, who'd slumbered in her arms by the light of the full moon, hurtled out of sight, into oblivion. The young girl with the tousled hair, stopped skipping back and forth and turned to stone. Warmed hearts turned to ice. Celebratory glasses slid inconspicuously back into the cupboard. The scribbled words of congratulations turned to mournful lamentations. The knitting needles stopped in their tracts and the half-finished pink matinee jacket was put to one side in remembrance of what might have been. The room became a deep pit of grief and despair. There was no cup of tea for mum and dad.

The woman headed slowly for the door and her partner followed her into the lift. As the doors opened at the bottom they came face to face with their first visitors of the day. The woman's face was ashen. She looked at her friend, whose beaming smile crumpled, as the woman lifted her shoulders in despair 'Speak later?' she managed to say. Her friend kissed her on the cheek, whispering 'God bless' into her ear.

At the special care baby unit, the parents were given green gowns and were instructed to wash their hands. The room was even hotter than the ward.

Her baby lay in a transparent incubator and had a white knitted hat on her head. There was a tube in her nose, strapped to her face with plaster and she was wired up to a heart monitor. She lay on her back, with her head tilted to one side.

'The paediatrician would like to see you when you're ready,' said a nurse with a kindly smile.

They hovered at the office door. The paediatrician hadn't seen them coming and was on the telephone. She looked up.

'Oh, sorry to keep you waiting, do come in,' she said brightly.

'To be honest,' she said, 'you need to think very carefully about what you do. It's quite OK to leave the baby with us and there are always foster carers who can take on these sorts of children. You're both young. It might be best just to go home and start again. It looks like there's a serious heart problem as well, so I imagine the chances of survival aren't great. There's another one in the corner over there. He's not so poorly, but the parents already have one child and have decided that he would be too much.'

Feeling stunned, the couple went back to the baby and sat either side of the incubator. The junior doctor, who had accompanied the paediatrician when the news was delivered, approached them. She pulled up a chair and sat close by. She said nothing for a while. After a couple of minutes, she said quietly 'I don't think you got that cup of tea you were promised. Sorry about that.' The couple looked at her. The dad shook his head. 'Not to worry,' he said and they all looked back at the baby. Some more minutes passed and the doctor said 'It's a lot to take in.' She continued to sit with them, gently suggesting that she could offer further information when they felt ready to hear it.

The journey had begun. The small baby lying in the incubator had entered the world.

The loss of the imagined child

The initial shock at the loss of the imagined child sends a parent into a process of grieving in coming to terms with a child's learning disability, as a medical diagnosis and as an immediate lived experience (Al-Yagon, 2015; Barr and Millar, 2003; Harnett and Tierney 2009; Kenyon, 2013; Leff-Taner and Hilburn Walizer, 1992: Rolfe, 2013; Sinason, 2002; Strecker *et al.*, 2014). When a parent becomes aware of his or her child's disability, he or she needs to adjust from the idealised child constructed in his or her mind's eye.

The process of grieving this lost imagined child is complex and the parental adjustment is a non-linear process (Rolfe, 2013). Barr and Millar (2003: 189) cite 'shock, confusion, anger or disbelief' as common responses to the initial diagnosis. This response to the news begins a process of adjustment which can continue to be brought to the surface, for example, in milestones such as going to school, reaching puberty and entering adulthood. The capacity of the parents to manage that adjustment varies enormously (Neely-Barnes and Dia, 2008). It is interesting to note that in a recent empirical enquiry into the emotional and coping resources of parents of learning disabled children, the attachment patterns were found to be more influenced by the parents' own developmental histories, than by the stress of parenting a learning disabled child alone (Al-Yagon, 2015). The wider picture of the impact of the diagnosis on parent and child has many variables that reflect the particular circumstances of each respective family. However, caring for a learning disabled child brings with it increased challenges to the family environment, which has enormous potential to lead to increased levels of stress and health issues (Heiman, 2002).

Feelings of shame can lie beneath the experience of being a disappointment to the world as the idealised child is lost. For the learning disabled person, the world can be a confusing, hostile and unaccommodating environment. Research exploring the direct experience of learning disabled people, demonstrates that low self-esteem is a common feature of that experience along with feelings of shame and of being stigmatised (Dyson1996; Jahoda and Markova, 2004; Kenyon *et al.*, 2013). Profoundly and multiply disabled folk can become 'defined by their most prominent "deficits" rather than being seen as complex beings …' (Sheehy and Nind, 2005: 35). As oppressed and marginalised members of society, learning disabled people can be vulnerable to mental health problems. However, research into 'Things That Make People with a Learning Disability Happy and Satisfied with Their Lives' (Haigh *et al.*, 2013: 26) concludes that when they have access to the necessary provision and are supported to make decisions, learning disabled people can feel happy and satisfied with their lives. This right to participation is supported by the key principles of the Mental Capacity Act, which underpins good practice in supporting learning disabled people to make significant decisions in their lives (Ramasubramanian, 2011) within an enabling context.

A particular subjectivity

As with labels attributed to any category of people, the notion of learning disability brings with it culturally specific definitions (Neely-Barnes and Dia, 2008) and constructed beliefs, that carry barriers, oppressions, potentials and opportunities. The definition 'learning disability' describes a person only by his or her diminished capacity for cognitive thought. The body is absent from this definition and the individual is identified by what he or she is not. In her book *Unimaginable Bodies* Hickey-Moody (2009), notes that a diagnosis such as Down's syndrome, generally arises from medical discourses, which have evolved in the quest to repair and resolve. These discourses are based on an idea about how bodies and minds *should* function and serve as tools for fixing, rather than tools for thinking (Hicky-Moody, 2009). Such discourses carry powerful potential to suggest that particular physical features denote 'a specific kind of subjectivity' (2009: 13). Social identity and individual subjectivity becomes bound to medical knowledge and these medical discourses shape the world, rather than conceptualise human diversity. The imagined normal body holds enormous power, and this notion is embedded both in the cultural psyche and in the individual stories of learning disabled people and their families. As practitioners working with the body, it is crucial that we remain connected to our own relationship with embodied otherness, both comfortable and uncomfortable, familiar and unfamiliar, to build a mutually understood embodied language as central to the therapeutic relationship. Understanding the subjectivity of learning disabled people may lie primarily in our capacity for nonverbal ways of listening, experiencing and attuning through an embodied sensitivity.

Embodied awareness

The intricacies of the moving body are primary to the human experience. Stern (2010: 104) notes how the foetus in utero becomes increasingly responsive through movement as he or she develops a 'felt aliveness'. In the therapeutic process, the intersubjective language of the body can serve as an immediate source of communication and this emergent 'felt aliveness' (2010: 104) becomes a place where therapist and client can begin to converse and to listen and respond through the senses.

Our embodied awareness is particularly crucial with clients who may have limited speech (Corbett, 2009; Sinason, 2002). The ability to attune on an embodied level and to mirror the affective essence of the client's story opens opportunities for the therapist to experience and understand the transference and for the client to feel heard, seen and understood. Bridges can thus be built between the client and the immediate environment, between the therapeutic space and the outside world and between past experience and the current reality of the therapeutic relationship.

Corbett (2009), a psychotherapist, writes about the intensification of his own embodiment when working with a learning disabled client. He needed to remember his own aliveness with a brisk walk to 'remain fully alive in the face of severe deprivation, abuse or mindlessness' (2009: 58). Corbett notes the 'overwhelming tide of primitive emotions' (2009: 59) that can characterise some of our work with learning disabled clients. The implications of these dynamics can be echoed in the disability transference in therapeutic work with learning disabled clients, when the therapist can find herself 'working with lack, absence, and the birth of the baby who is longed for and not longed for' (2009: 55). Movement is ideally placed as a modality in this work due the primacy of movement as 'our most primitive and fundamental experience' (Stern, 2010: 19).

Working in the transference

Working in the transference is central to psychodynamic psychotherapy, as the therapist attends to the live, dynamic interplay of unconscious processes that arise in the immediate relationship. Internalised models of significant relational figures shape the dynamics of that relationship. The specificity of learning disability, as a lived experience, offers layers of complexity in this relational process. In the 'disability transference' (Corbett, 2009: 49) the therapist can find that she or he needs to provide an anchor that grounds the learning disabled client in a sense of his or her own embodied presence. Corbett (2009: 57) suggests that as therapists, we need to be prepared to hold the difficult feelings of 'hopelessness, dread, deadness and fear' that are potentially overwhelming for, and disavowed by, the client. One of our tasks as therapists is to bring these feelings to consciousness so that they can be experienced, felt and thought about, rather than defended against and acted out.

I remember working with Julie, who seemed only able to discover her feeling of aliveness in front of the mirror attached to the wall in our therapy space. It was as if Julie's 'dynamic forms of vitality' (Stern, 2016: 7) had been muted. Julie had been born into an atmosphere of loss. A teenage sibling had died just before her birth and at the same time, the father had left the family home. The already grieving mother was then confronted with the label of 'learning disability' when her baby was a few months old. Relationship was risky for Julie, who took comfort in her own reflection, unable to trust that another would be able to welcome her into a connection and to hold her range of intense feelings. I processed the strong counter-transference feelings of being unwelcome, useless and excluded. In defence of those feelings, I found myself becoming bored and extremely tired during sessions. Something in the embodied connectivity seemed dead. I found a way to make myself physically and psychologically present by bringing my awareness to my muscles, bones and joints to foster my own capacity to enter the session in a state of embodied awareness. I managed to open my awareness to Julie's unbearable projections, so that I could tolerate and contain them. As I became more conscious of how I was being impacted on a somatic level, I became better able to provide a welcoming space for Julie. A fleeting glance seemed to be the beginning of a process of building a connection which developed through a sigh, a shrug and a shared wriggle. I learned to experience whatever emerged as not only as *enough*, but also as intriguing. I was able to begin to disentangle the complex interpersonal fantasies and to facilitate a shared reality between us.

It is crucial, then, that the therapist has explored his or her own unconscious relationship with the notion of disability, in order that unprocessed personal and collective constructions of disability become conscious in the therapist's awareness. This awareness includes a fear of dependency, of imperfection, of being under-valued and of exclusion, fears that might otherwise become unhelpful unconscious projections. Working with learning disabled people requires that we have mourned our own idealised notion of the human condition, our own disappointed desire and our own yearning for a utopia in which illness, madness and imperfection are eliminated. It is then that we can facilitate the therapeutic process with an eye on new beginnings as I discovered in my work with Oliver.

Oliver was eight years old. He was diagnosed with a significant learning disability and attended a school for children with complex needs. Oliver lived with his mother and younger sister and had had no contact with his father since he left the family home when Oliver was three. Oliver had had a difficult beginning.

His mother was attentive and supportive and struggled to manage his volatile behaviour at home. In school, Oliver was resistant to adult direction and the teacher experienced him as destructive in the classroom, displaying physical aggression towards adults and children. I remember feeling apprehensive about working with Oliver and in supervision found myself acknowledging the feelings of dread as I wondered how I could open a welcoming psychic place for our work together.

Oliver's ability to express himself through his body became immediately apparent, despite his limited capacity to communicate through speech. DMP provided a nonverbal medium through which he could communicate issues that were potentially 'pre-verbal, unverbalised and unverbalisable'(Winnicott, 1971: 130). In the first session, Oliver avoided eye contact with me, ran straight to the play tunnel, dived inside and rolled from side to side. He shouted the word 'dark' from inside the tunnel. I sat nearby and wondered out loud if beginning our sessions together felt like being in a dark, perhaps frightening place. He became still and a finger poked out of the tunnel. Another followed and gradually a hand appeared and began to balance on its fingertips, hopping from side to side. The other hand appeared and a fight ensued. One hand lay defeated and limp on the floor while the other danced in victory. The fight resumed and the sequence repeated. Eventually the hands became locked in battle, both fell to the ground and were dragged back into the tunnel. The narratives enacted by his hands emerging from the tunnel became a repeated feature of sessions. With the hand perhaps representing a 'symbol of human agency and ownership' (Leader, 2016: 4), Oliver found a way to communicate his inner conflicts and struggles to locate himself in the world as a learning disabled child with little sense of his own agency. With his hands now disappeared back in the tunnel, I waited for what seemed like an age until Oliver slithered out of the tunnel. There was a look of apprehension on his face and I was taken aback by the intensity of the gaze that he fixed on me, projecting almost unbearable feelings of exposure. His serious expression turned into delight as he broke into peals of laughter. He grabbed the stretch cloth and handed one end to me, indicating that he wanted a game of tug o' war. I held tight to my end and he too clasped his end of the cloth firmly. Our eyes met again and he began to jump, enjoying the tension in the cloth. He then let it go and, as it fell to the floor, he ran forwards to pick it up and repeated the jumping. He repeated this sequence of clasping and letting go, keeping a close eye on my reaction.

These symbolic themes emerging in that first encounter held many of the rich and powerful symbols with which we worked in the ensuing months. The enclosed space of the tunnel became a place that Oliver explored the monsters of his imagination; those parts of himself that he wanted to keep hidden from me, perhaps through an unconscious fear that I would reject those 'monstrous' parts of him. In subsequent weeks, Oliver became a hungry monster thrashing around within the boundaries of the tunnel. The monster's voice was gruff and threatening, whilst Oliver's voice was weak and feeble as he shouted for help. Eventually

Oliver was eaten by the monster who lay still, full-up and snoring. I spoke quietly to the monster and looked in the end of the tunnel. The monster gave an angry roar to frighten me away. I wondered out loud why the monster was so angry and what he might need. Oliver then curled up and closed both ends of the tunnel in the cloths that he had requested that I hang over each end to enclose the space. On this particular occasion, Oliver began to rock the tunnel from side to side, keeping it very close to me. I held the tunnel as it rocked until he was ready to push himself out. His fear of his capacity for destruction seemed to be expressed by the hungry monster and it was towards the end of the session that Oliver crawled out of the monster's stomach, leaving the monster in the tunnel, for me to 'look after' until the following week. Outside of the tunnel, the theme of holding on and letting go developed, alongside games of appearing and disappearing. So too explorations of falling and being caught and games of hide and seek became a common feature. These games represented symbolic explorations of the rhythms of attachment and loss in a playing-out and replaying of the subtle dynamics of meeting each other in the intersubjective, potential space between us, providing an opportunity for some 'fine-tuning of (the) intersubjective field' (Stern, 2010: 138). Further into the therapeutic process, Oliver left the safety of the tunnel and began to explore whole body movements of rolling and sliding, feeling his body in contact with the ground. We developed a movement relationship that involved leaning, pushing, balancing and supporting. As I became increasingly able to attune to his movements, so he became able to 'listen' to my response and we established a mutually understood embodied language.

Conclusion

This chapter offers a point of curiosity about how a learning disabled person is welcomed into the world. I am linking this fundamental primary experience to the dynamic, unconscious process between the DMP practitioner and the learning disabled client. Working in transference harnesses the potential of the live enactment of early relationships in the immediate therapeutic relationship (Hernandez-Halton et al., 2000) and as such can offer a space for processing complex psychic material in relation to the lived experience of learning disability.

Beginning, like ending, is crucial to the therapeutic process and the facilitating environment can benefit clients best if it is enabling, empowering, welcoming and receptive to all that is there. The experience of entering the world for many learning disabled people brings with it those dynamics present in that initial diagnosis, in which the infant or child is met with disappointment and grief, rather than joy and expectation. This reflects a wider issue of inclusion in relation to the social, cultural and political participation of learning disabled people. As therapists, it's important to understand the dynamic process that is set up with a diagnosis in order to try to understand the complex nature of the disability transference. The diagnosis of learning disability is an opportunity to think about how to accommodate diversity rather than how to fix differences.

References

Al-Yagon, M. (2015) 'Fathers and mothers of children with learning disabilities.' *Learning Disability Quarterly*, 38(2): 112–128.

Anastasiou, D. and Kauffman, J. (2011) 'A social constructionist approach to disability: Implications for special education'. *Exceptional Children*, 77(3): 367–384.

Barr, O. and Millar, R. (2003) 'Parents of children with intellectual disabilities: Their expectations and experience of genetic counselling'. *Journal of Applied Research in Intellectual Disabilities*, 16: 189–204.

Corbett, A. (2009) 'Words as a second language: The psychotherapeutic challenge of severe intellectual disability'. Cottis, T. (ed.) *Intellectual Disability, Trauma and Psychotherapy*. London: Routledge.

Dyson, L. (1996) 'The experience of families with children with learning disabilities: Parental stress, family functioning and sibling self-concept'. *Journal of Learning Disabilities*, 29(3): 280–286.

Haigh, A., Lee, D., Shaw, C., Hawthorne, M., Chamberlain, S., Newman, D., Clarke, Z. and Beail, N. (2013) 'What things make people with a learning disability happy and satisfied with their lives: An inclusive research project'. *Journal of Applied Research in Intellectual Disabilities*, 26: 26–33.

Harnett, A. and Tierney, E. (2009) 'Convention of hope–communicating positive, realistic messages to families at the time of a child's diagnosis with disabilities'. *British Journal of Learning Disabilities*, 37: 257–264.

Heiman, T. (2002) 'Parents of children with disabilities: Resilience, coping, and future expectations'. *Journal of Developmental and Physical Disabilities*, 14(2): 159–171.

Hernandez-Halton, I., Hodges, S., Miller, L. and Simpson, D. (2000) 'A psychotherapy service for children, adolescents and adults with learning disabilities at the Tavistock Clinic, London'. *British Journal of Learning Disabilities*, 28: 120–124.

Hickey-Moody, A. (2009) *Unimaginable Bodies: Intellectual Disability, Performance and Becomings*. Rotterdam, Netherlands: Sense Publishers.

Johada, A. and Markova, I. (2004) 'Coping with social stigma: people with intellectual disabilities moving from institutions and family home'. *Journal of Intellectual Disability Research*, 48(8): 719–729.

Kenyon, E., Beall, N. and Jackson, T. (2013) 'Learning disability: Experience of diagnosis'. *British Journal of Learning Disabilities*, 42: 257–263.

Leader, D. (2016) *Hands*. London: Penguin Random House UK.

Leff-Taner, P. and Hilburn Walizer, E. (1992) 'The uncommon wisdom of parents at the moment of diagnosis'. *Family Systems Medicine*, 10(2): 147–168.

Neely-Barnes, S. and Dia, D. (2008) 'Families of Children with Disabilities: A Review of Literature and Recommendations for Interventions'. *Journal of Early and Intensive Behavior Intervention*, 5(3): 93–107.

Ramasubramanian, L., Ranasinghe, N. and Ellison, J. (2005) 'Evaluation of a structured assessment framework to enable adherence to the requirements of Mental Capacity Act 2005'. *British Journal of Learning Disabilities*, 39(4): 314–320.

Rolfe, L. (2013) 'Factors that impact on adjustment in parents of children with a learning disability and/or autism spectrum disorder'. Unpublished Doctorate in Clinical Psychology, The University of Edinburgh, June 2013.

Sheehy, K. and Nind, M. (2005) 'Emotional well-being for all: Mental health and people with profound and multiple learning disabilities'. *British Journal of Learning Disabilities*, 33: 34–38.

Sinason, V. (1992) *Mental Handicap and the Human Condition: New Approaches from the Tavistock*. London: Free Association Books.

Slorach, R. (2016) *A Very Capitalist Condition: A History and Politics of Disability*. London: Bookmarks Publications.

Stern, D. (2010) *Forms of Vitality*. Oxford, UK: Oxford University Press.

Strecker, S., Hazelwood, Z. and Shakespear-Finch, J. (2014) 'Postdiagnosis personal growth in an Australian population of parents raising children with developmental disability'. *Journal of Intellectual and Developmental Disability*, 39(1): 1–9.

Winnicott, D. W. (1971) *Playing and Reality*. London: Tavistock.

Chapter 2

A reflexive account of significant changes in learning disability values

A parent/practitioner story

Jackie Edwards

This chapter tells the story of how my experience as a parent led me to become a dance movement psychotherapist (DMP) and offers my understanding of the historical relationship between dance movement psychotherapy (DMP) and people with learning disabilities in the United Kingdom. Having raised two adult sons who experience communication difficulties, I am aware that there have been many different professionals working with them offering interventions and approaches that have been helpful or unhelpful. For example, both of my sons with a diagnosis of autism have benefited from individual DMP sessions. I discuss in this chapter my families' experience of DMP and how this has enabled us to develop communication skills and express ourselves emotionally.

I have three adult sons. Ceri is aged twenty-eight and has a diagnosis of dyslexia (a specific learning difficulty). Rhys is aged twenty-six and has a diagnosis of autism, severe learning disabilities and epilepsy. Rhys is a nonverbal communicator; therefore information is communicated to Rhys using a range of augmented approaches such as picture symbols and Makaton sign language in addition to spoken words. Rhys' preference is to communicate his needs through his movements, gestures and vocalisation, which are recognised and understood by those who know him well. James is twenty-five and has a diagnosis of Asperger syndrome.

Ceri and James are able to give their verbal and written consent. Rhys is unable to give verbal or written consent but is able to communicate through his actions, behaviour and movements. Rhys' perspective cannot be directly included; therefore, a parental view is offered with the understanding that Rhys is able to give assent. For example, when Rhys is not in agreement he will express this through his movements and vocalisations such as 'nah nah', which, depending on the context and associated gestures, may be understood as 'No'.

I include a brief discussion on the history and context of cultural and policy changes in the way adults with a learning disability are supported within the health and social care system in the United Kingdom. For example, the Department of Health White Paper 'Valuing People' (DOH, 2001) that was refreshed in 2009 meant that the large institutionalised residential health care model has been replaced with a social care 'supported living' and enabling model of care within the community. This has given adults with a learning disability the opportunity to choose where they live and move into their own homes (DOH, 2009). The education and employment opportunities for adults with a learning disability have also increased as a result of the priorities set out in 'Valuing Employment Now' (DOH, 2009).

An outline of the accepted psychological theories of autism will be discussed later in this chapter in addition to sensory integration and the sensory and motor differences, which can be experienced by individuals diagnosed with autism (Edwards, 2015; Erfer, 1995). How DMP can be a useful intervention (Hartshorn *et al.*, 2001; Scharoun *et al.*, 2014) will also be included, along with vignettes of how the knowledge and skills that I have learnt as a therapist and as a parent of two adult sons with autism interweave and nurture both my personal life and professional practice as DMP.

Parenting and special educational needs

I became a parent for the first time at the age of twenty-six. This was a very exciting time for me, and for my father, as my eldest son was the first grandchild for both mine and my husband's family. As my mother had died when I was seventeen, she was not able to offer me any advice or support on how to be a mother. I found this particularly difficult at the age of twenty-eight when my second son, Rhys, was born, six weeks prematurely and with a very low birth weight (two pounds, two ounces). He had to stay in intensive care for the first eight weeks of his life and needed to be kept warm when he was finally allowed to leave the hospital. His birth was very traumatic for him, for me and for all his close and extended family. By the age of twelve months, Rhys was still only the size of a three-month-old baby and he had a few words. When Rhys was aged two years, he finally mastered standing up and walking but had lost all his language skills and continued to be delayed generally in his development. My third son James was born around this time; he weighed a healthy nine pounds, which was a relief to everyone, including the health team who had been monitoring him closely for signs of retarded growth in the womb.

All three boys got on well and my eldest son Ceri always took the lead with any games or activities. My middle son Rhys found it difficult to keep up and preferred to spend his time exploring toys in his own way. He discovered Thomas the Tank Engine videos and Pingu, which he watched on fast forward and rewind for hours at a time, while the other two played more creatively.

As they grew old enough to play outside with other children from the neighbourhood, both Rhys and James, my youngest sons, found it difficult to socialise and integrate with the other children. Rhys would run up and down the side of the house using his peripheral vision and keeping his eyes on the wall as he ran. James began going into our neighbour's house while her son was in ours or returning to ours when Ceri and the other children went next door. Although everyone found this quite amusing, it was also becoming a concern that James was not speaking outside the house and did not want to join in with the other children.

Once it was time to begin playschool and nursery it became apparent that both Rhys and James had special educational needs. Rhys was diagnosed with autism at the age of two and James was initially thought to have 'learnt' behaviour from spending too much time with Rhys at home and not socialising. He was picked up by an educational psychologist at the age of five and given the diagnosis of an 'elect mute'. It was when he was aged nine that this was changed to Asperger syndrome (autism without a learning disability). This followed a difficult period the previous year, during which his mental health deteriorated and he was assessed by Child and Adolescent Mental Health Services (CAMHS).

My eldest son Ceri also found learning at school difficult; although very socially able, Ceri was unable to read or spell at the same level as his school friends. This was also thought to be as a result of having Rhys as a brother. It is only when Ceri was aged ten that he was finally diagnosed with severe dyslexia and mild attention deficit disorder (ADD).

CAMHS offered James a brief art therapy intervention of six weekly sessions and continued to monitor his progress until he reached the age of sixteen. James described these sessions as 'art without the stress', as James said that he found any demands placed on him when at school difficult and anxiety provoking. He said this was because he 'did not know what they wanted' him to do or say. I then realised that although Rhys had received music therapy from the age of five, I had not understood that any of the arts psychotherapies were anything more than playing with the art form, that is, art making or using a musical instrument. As a parent, it had not been explained to me how music therapy might help with communication difficulties or offer an alternative form of self-expression. I did not have the opportunity to meet the therapist at the time and although I was shown photos of Rhys playing kettle drums, I thought this was a 'nice' activity rather than psychotherapy.

How my children introduced me to DMP

Rhys

Rhys' development continued to be very different to that of a 'typically developing' child (a psychology term used for research that I do not privilege) and in order to meet his level of educational needs he was placed in a special unit within the local special educational needs day school, rather than have to be considered for an out of area residential school placement. This was something my husband and I agreed to as Rhys' level of autism was severe. At that time the school opened a new autism unit to accommodate Rhys' level of needs locally. It was extremely fortunate that they had the foresight to follow this through and were able to change their system and put the finances in place rather than exclude Rhys. This took place in 1997, the start of inclusive education, a significant change in the educational system in the United Kingdom, which saw similar structural changes within schools in subsequent years (Education Act 1996).

Changes in learning disability values   25

At the age of eleven, Rhys was still not speaking and his behaviour was receiving the description of 'challenging'. I began to attend parent–family carer groups to find out more about autism and learning disabilities generally. I could see that his adulthood was not too far away and yet I did not feel prepared for Rhys' future, once he could not go to school anymore. A local consultant psychiatrist, who had an interest in researching movement in relation to autism, suggested DMP might be a useful intervention for Rhys. On his recommendation, I contacted a DMP, who had been introduced to the parent–family carer group that I belonged to. This led to my enrolling on a summer school introduction to DMP course in 2002 when Rhys was aged twelve. Following this, Rhys' school was invited to send his class (of six nonverbal students with autism) to attend a taster session at Dance Voice, a local DMP charity service for people with learning disabilities. This amazing experience sparked off a journey of discovery for me that has continued ever since.

Rhys, his school teachers and his classmates had a great time during this taster session and it was obvious to those of us present that the session offered a special form of communicating and connecting, without words and without demands or unrealistic expectations. Following this significant experience, Rhys' class was invited to attend regular DMP sessions for the remainder of the academic year. Although I was not present during these sessions, I noticed that Rhys became animated and began communicating more effectively through his movements at home and we became more aware of how to 'see' his movement communications more clearly. Rhys began to blossom and I was interested in learning more about DMP.

I was therefore delighted when the consultant psychiatrist I mentioned offered to give regular movement sessions for Rhys, aged thirteen, as part of his own ongoing enquiry into autism and nonverbal communication. Although he had completed a year-long basic DMP training course, he was not practising as a registered DMP. I was able to witness these sessions and learnt new ways of understanding, listening to and communicating with my son.

Rhys is now twenty-six and continues to use movement as his main form of communicating. Interestingly, he does not show interest in using picture symbols, sign language or other forms of augmented communication approaches that have been taught to him over the years as another option.

James

When James was sixteen he wanted to leave school and attend the local college to study music technology. Although James is a gifted guitarist and very able musically, he was aware that he still found it difficult to speak and his movements were not like 'Mick Jagger' but more like 'Bill Wyman' from the Rolling Stones. James asked if DMP might also help him. He decided he did not want to go through CAMHS anymore as he preferred not to be associated with mental health difficulties. Instead he chose to use his DLA (Disability Living Allowance) benefit to pay for private DMP sessions. Although I did not ask him what he discussed in the sessions, or even how they went, James shared that although he did not really understand how DMP works, 'something clicked' during the ten months of weekly individual sessions and he felt more connected to himself and more able to take on the college course. James was able to complete an NVQ Level 3 qualification, which included a live public performance. He still thinks fondly of his therapist as someone who helped him without having to 'talk'. James is now working locally and is being accepted as a member of the team.

Ceri

Ceri, our eldest son, worked as a support worker while studying at university and was introduced to DMP through an adult with learning disabilities whom he was supporting to attend regular weekly sessions. Ceri could see the benefits of this way of working:

> *[A] good therapist can bring everyone together into one group, despite varying abilities and communication styles, so that the whole group can meet and interact with each other on an equal level without having to be able to speak or move well to be heard.*

> (Ceri, 2016)

Ceri and James and their introduction to DMP training

Ceri chose to enrol and complete an introduction to DMP course when he was twenty-one in 2009, which encouraged James to attend in 2011, aged twenty, as part of his own learning and self-development. They both found it very interesting and as a family we often communicate nonverbally through movement, which also makes us laugh as others give us a strange look, including their dad. Ceri found the course brought his attention to the importance of movement for his own mental well-being:

> *The course brought my awareness to the fact that I feel good when I move, and I don't move enough. Movement affects my moods quite significantly, for example when I don't move I start to feel low, and I now know how to regulate myself through movement. Whereas before the course, I wasn't aware that I could.*

> (Ceri, 2016)

James also found the course helpful and said that he did not move his body often, so it was new for him especially as this was a group of people he did not know before the course. James said that he liked an exercise where they were asked to make and wear a mask while moving together as a group. He said this was because he was able to hide who he really was. James struggled with the teaching styles between the tutors. For example, he found it confusing that some tutors let people talk while others encouraged more movement. James got quite confused when other students on the course fed back their interpretations and reflections from his movements. This could be related to his difficulty with understanding 'theory of mind' (Baron-Cohen *et al.*, 1985), a psychological theory which relates to social understanding.

The main psychological theories associated with autism as defined by DSM-I (APA, 2000) are 'Theory of Mind': an understanding that other people may have different thoughts and feelings to ourselves (Baron-Cohen *et al.*, 1985); 'Weak Central Coherence': a tendency to focus on fine detail and difficulty 'seeing' the whole (Attwood, 1998); and 'Executive Functioning': a difficulty with sequencing and planning an action (Attwood, 1998). Although these psychological theories are not limited to individuals with autism, it was thought that the weaknesses observed contribute to the social and communication difficulties associated with the symptomology of autism.

Diagnostic tools developed for children and adults with autism are based on the medical model as defined by the DSM-IV. However, autism has been revised under DSM-5 (APA, 2013), which amalgamated all the previously known autism spectrum sub-types into one category which recognises sensory integration differences. Autism is now considered to be a neurodevelopmental disorder with a neurobiological and sensory basis (Scriber, 2010). Although these theories were part of my learning as a parent attending a mix of professional and self-advocate training and awareness events, hearing self-advocates' lived experiences contributed to my decision to explore a less medical perspective for my sons through DMP as an intervention.

Becoming a Dance Movement Psychotherapist

It was only when Rhys turned eighteen and transferred from children to adult services that I understood how much I had been doing as his mother and primary carer. He was assessed by adult social services as needing 3:1 care before he could go out in the community. I then became aware of how much we, as a family and his school, had been 'holding' to keep him and those around him safe. Rhys quickly developed the label of challenging to services as a series of residential assessments took place as part of his transition plan. Eventually, a suitable placement was found 150 miles from our home within a specialist provision for young adults with autism and challenging behaviour. This placement went well for three years and Rhys had a person-centred plan (Ritchie *et al.*, 2003), which included us as a family. I was invited to help the new staff team understand how to communicate with Rhys through movement. After three years, our local authority arranged for Rhys to return to the local community that he had grown up in and offered him his own home with a 'supported living' package of care, near to our home (DOH, 2009). This has been very successful for Rhys, who no longer requires three-to-one support. Rhys' care staff have learnt how to interpret his nonverbal, movement-based communication. He is currently well supported, on a one-to-one basis at all times and on a two-to-one basis when out in the community, by care staff who have enabled Rhys to develop his ability to make choices and express himself as an adult.

It was in 2007, when Rhys was eighteen, that I decided to leave my career as a practising accountant to complete a DMP Master's training to become a registered DMP. During the course, I found myself wanting to learn about as many different client groups as I could, mental health in particular, although my original personal interest was in learning disabilities from a social and communication perspective. During my training, I realised how much I was benefiting from the opportunity to be educated as a DMP and the difference this was making to how I parented all three of my sons, not only Rhys. For example, I became more aware of how I was relating to them and their dad, especially when we needed to express emotions.

I trained locally, on a primarily humanistic course, although other theoretical approaches including psychodynamic and developmental theories were introduced as part of the programme. We learned about Bartenieff's fundamentals (Hackney, 2002), and other movement-based developmental stages, which helped me to become more aware of the significance of how my own sons' movement patterns as children aged zero to three years had all been very different.

- Ceri – crawled at five months and walked at nine months (possibly too soon?).
- Rhys – bottom shuffled until he was two, when he finally managed to walk.
- James – sat and did not crawl or reach for toys as much as a typically developing[1] child. He walked at thirteen months.

When he was eleven, James was offered the opportunity to complete a year-long Institute for Neuro-Physiological Psychology (NPP) intervention (Goddard, 1996) as part of his school day. This involved another opportunity to develop early movement patterns such as creeping and cross-lateral crawling. The basic rationale for this intervention was to develop primitive reflexes that were thought to be uninhibited and associated with his autism and dyspraxia symptomology. It is unclear how much this programme of ten minutes twice a week actually helped but, interestingly, a visit to the optician at the end of the year identified that James' eyesight had improved, which the optician said she was unable to explain. Therefore, she suggested the movement exercises may have supported his general development, including improvements in his eyesight, which meant he no longer needed to wear glasses. Noticing how my son's physiology was influenced by movement, I became aware of how much my own experiences of movement as a child were influenced by the opportunities that I was given based on the education, culture and social understanding of my parents and the community of people where I lived.

This wondering about my childhood and family context later fed into my DMP training, where learning about the work of Carl Rogers (1957) felt particularly relevant for my own family and also for people with a learning disability. The core conditions identified by Rogers (1975) include unconditional positive regard, congruence and empathic understanding.

I noticed how much these were present when engaging with a range of health practitioners who adopted a person-centred approach to how they worked with Rhys and us as a family. This contrasted with my experience as a parent within a competitive social parental environment at a time when the government introduced 'Standard Assessment Tasks' (SATs) tests for seven- and eleven-year-olds and schools became graded on the results of these tests by the introduction of league tables. Adult social care services were becoming more focused on choice and control and person-centred approaches (DOH 2001; 2009). This differed to my experience of the educational system, where such an approach was not yet being developed.

Through my reflective practice, I became more aware of the socio-political changes in values and understanding of the range of special educational needs that I had experienced as a child and now as a parent of a son with learning disabilities. Personal therapy gave me the opportunity to revisit my childhood: growing up with Irish Catholic parents in Wales; being taught in Welsh, when my parents could not speak Welsh; and being the only girl with three brothers. I realised that I was privileged to have been given the opportunity to attend ballet classes from the age of two to sixteen and piano and violin music lessons, although these would have been very expensive and my parents were not from an affluent background.

At the same time, I was aware as the third child of four that both of my older brothers found it difficult to settle into learning at school or adjust to being taught through the medium of the Welsh language. Even as a young child aged about seven, I noticed that my parents were struggling to know how to support my older brothers within the education system. When they became teenagers, my father began to stop attending their parents' evenings, preferring to encourage them to 'find a trade'.

As a parent myself, and realising that Ceri also struggled to learn how to read despite his intellectual and verbal abilities, it became clearer to me that dyslexia and autism were not understood when I was a child. I now wonder what information or support my brothers or parents were offered compared to what is currently available under the Department of Education 0–25 system (DfES, 2015). I am also aware that had Rhys been born before the 1980s, he would have been taken from us, a common practice in those days, either from birth or by the age of two and placed in an institution for 'mentally handicapped' children, the term used at that time (Edwards, 2013). Around the time that my children were attending local schools, there were many changes to the Education Act (1981; 1993; 1996). As a result, education practices have evolved and become more inclusive of all children, regardless of their ability, with a growing awareness of the need to maintain family connections (DfES, 2015).

During my training as a DMP, I found learning about attachment theories (Blau and Reicher, 1995) and the psychological stages of development of particular interest. I recognised how stressful it was for me when Rhys moved away from our family home at the age of eighteen. This led me to wonder what effect sending my eldest brother to Ireland to live for a year with my grandmother and aunt must have had on him and my whole family, when my second brother was born in 1960. Although this was culturally acceptable and common practice in Wales at that time, the stories my parents told as I grew up suggest that it was a traumatic experience: my brother was a one-year-old baby being sent to live far away from home, across the sea to another country, when the transport systems were not as advanced as they are today. I realised that my parents would not have been educated about the importance of secure attachment, or how these are formed during the early developmental stages of an infant.

Although understanding within health and education has improved greatly since then, practitioners continue to find it difficult to know how to differentiate between autism and attachment difficulties, therefore making it difficult for parents to receive the required support. This is explored by Moran (2010), who developed the 'Coventry grid' to give some guidance to practitioners working with children in this field. However, in my experience working within mental health services, this continues to be unclear. There is a need for practitioners to have more training and understanding of how autism, trauma and attachment behaviours may present or overlap in adults and children.

I consider myself very fortunate that Marie Ware, a pioneer of DMP in the United Kingdom (Dance Voice, 2016) and the first person who introduced me to DMP, was also known to many of the health and social care professionals working with Rhys up to the age of eighteen.

My experience of DMP within cultural, social and political changes in education, health and social care services

DMP in the South West was founded by Marie Ware. She piloted DMP in the local learning disability institutions in the 1970s, which included hospital settings as well as large communities and farms in quiet rural areas. Marie brought DMP into the local special educational needs schools and founded Dance Voice, a now well-established local centre for DMP, as a registered charity in 1989 (Dance Voice, 2016). Her work with adults and local health and social care professionals expanded by 2007 to include training at Master's level for students from Europe and the United Kingdom.

By the 1990s, many cultural and political changes led to the National Health Service and Community Care Act (1990), which changed how services were being commissioned. As a result many of the local hospital institutions in the South West closed. This impacted DMP, which in this particular area became a community-based intervention that adults now living in the new community group homes had the opportunity to continue accessing. Although a person-centred model was being introduced (DOH, 2001) in 2007 when the white paper was being 'refreshed', many support workers misinterpreted the guidance and sought to individualise everything; at the detriment, in some instances, of attending to the basic human need to socialise and the importance of being with familiar and close people.

Support workers did not always remember that individuals in their care may have had strong bonds or formed close relationships (as couples, for example); the new model of care, therefore, triggered significant distress as these individuals were being separated. It was thus all the more beneficial for them to be able to socialise and meet up for twice-weekly group DMP sessions with people they had lived and formed relationships with for many years. Unfortunately, some of the adults living in the large institutions found it very difficult to move into smaller group homes. For example, care staff planning people's care noticed this and as a result commissioners were also alerted to this problem. Subsequently, several autism-specific commissioning documents were developed as understanding of the needs of people with autism increased (DOH, 2014).

With greater social awareness of the needs of people with autism and learning disabilities, services began to adapt to more specific needs. As a consequence, DMP continues to adjust to the changing education, health and social care structures as they develop, such as those set up by the Department of Health (2001, 2014). This includes funding for local authority-commissioned DMP and enabling service users to have increased choice and control, through offering personal budgets, as part of the values introduced in 2001. For example, DMP may be viewed as a health intervention and offered through a CAMHS or NHS referral; it may also be offered as a social or educational intervention and a referral made as part of a person-centred social care plan. There is scope with the introduction of the 0–25 Education, Health and Social Care plans (DfES, 2015) for DMP to become recognised as an intervention that supports health, social care and educational needs of individuals.

Some adults with autism and behaviour that challenge services continue to be supported under the Mental Health Act (1989) in hospital settings or in the community within a specialist provision for people with autism. Specific guidance and legislation is being developed to support the development of more inclusive services for this group, included as part of 'Transforming Care' agenda and the Autism Strategy (Department of Health, 2014).

Rhys may have been considered difficult to reach, had we, as his family, not been introduced to movement as a form of communication when he was eleven. Introducing Rhys' social care support staff to this form of communication enabled Rhys to demonstrate that he is more aware of the world around him, and of other people, than might at first be apparent. It has become possible to gain a better sense of his emotional needs and a clearer insight into how Rhys expresses his emotions (such as level of anxiety) by his vocalisations, jumping and flapping his hands. Rhys has significant sensory differences: hypersensitivity in some areas, such as to touch, sound, and smell; hyposensitivity to other senses, also known as low registration, such as when he needs to open his bowels or feels pain.

By understanding sensory issues in autism (Edwards, 2015; Erfer, 1995) and other psychological theories related to autism, it is becoming clearer to me that DMP can be a helpful intervention for this group of children and adults. Integrating the exploration of hyper- or hyposensitivity is integral to the work of DMPs working with children and adults with autism (Erfer, 1995; Leventhal, 1981). DMPs have given an account of how they are able to make adjustments to attune, based on each child's experience of sensory and motor perceptions (Devereaux, 2012; Erfer, 1995; Leventhal, 1981; Tortora, 2006). As an example, during my own study (Edwards, 2015), I found that by turning the lights down, avoiding sudden unpredictable movement, being aware of not giving too much eye contact and allowing the group processing time for verbal and nonverbal communication, the four adults with Asperger syndrome I was working with at the time became more aware of each other's needs as well as their own emotional and mental states. Their feedback from the study included the following quotation: 'Find a way to unwrap autism – it becomes layers on layers' (Edwards, 2015).

Conclusion

Experiencing DMP as an intervention, both Rhys and James have found their way through a difficult experience of learning how to understand their own needs and how to communicate with those around them, through school, college and now as adults living in their local community. Rhys and James have maintained their mental well-being, and are more able to express their emotional needs, despite periods when they were younger, when this was a challenge for them and for us as a family. Ceri has learned how to support his brothers and others with autism and/ or learning disabilities and the importance of using and understanding movement as a form of communication.

It is unclear how much spoken language Rhys understands. He is unable to speak but his movements are clear and expressive. When he needs to be alone to process information, he will wrap himself up and roll himself into a small space away from others, but when he is happy, he jumps, smiles and interacts through his movements. It has been particularly beneficial for Rhys' staff to be given guidance and training on how to communicate with him through movements. DMP input in his life and specifically the introduction of movement-based communication has directly influenced the level of paid support that Rhys now needs (i.e. from three-to-one to two-to-one in the community). I would therefore argue that from my personal experience as a parent, DMP has enabled a significant saving in the staff provision for my son, who might be labelled 'hard to reach, with behaviour that challenges services'.

As part of my ongoing learning, I am now a PhD candidate focusing on DMP and autism. The aim of my study is to research how other DMPs are working with children with autism and what the value of this way of working is for the parents and carers of the children they are working with. My research will contribute to the body of studies that highlight the role DMP can play in supporting individuals with a diagnosis of autism and their families. My study will build on the work of DMPs such as Tortora (2006), who works with families to support the child and their parent to develop their relationship, and international studies (Devereaux, 2012; Koch *et al.*, 2015). The constructive use of nonverbal

Changes in learning disability values 33

communication, creative dance and movement explorations may not have always been thought possible in the past. Fortunately, the studies mentioned above are establishing that DMP is an intervention that enables children and adults with autism to develop relationships with the therapist and the environment in which they live.

My experience as a parent and practising therapist is that DMP is a holistic approach that has enabled my sons and me to attune to each other and the world around us more openly and effectively. DMP has many layers: movement communication, person-centred principles of acceptance, becoming aware of behaviour patterns, thoughts, perceptions and beliefs held and the importance of secure attachments. It has enabled us all as a family to be more aware of ourselves and each other, so that we are able to make connections in a way that is not possible through words alone.

Note

1   A term used in psychology research for comparison studies, although not one I necessarily choose to use.

References

American Psychiatric Association (2000) *Diagnostic and Statistical Manual of Mental Disorders. DSM-1V-TR.* Washington, DC: American Psychiatric Association.

American Psychiatric Association (2013) *Diagnostic and Statistical Manual of Mental Disorders. DSM-5.* Arlington, VA: American Psychiatric Association.

Attwood, T. (1998) *Asperger Syndrome – A Guide for Parents and Professionals.* London: Jessica Kingsley.

Baron-Cohen, S., Leslie, A.M. and Frith, U. (1985) 'Does the autistic child have a "theory of mind"?', *Cognition*, 21: 37–46. MRC Cognitive Development Unit, London No. 5, October 2002.

Blau, B. and Reicher, D. (1995) 'Early intervention with children at risk of attachment disorders'. Levy, F. J. (ed.) *Dance and Other Expressive Art Therapies – When Words Are Not Enough.* London: Routledge.

Department for Education and Skills and Department of Health. (2015) *Implementing a New 0–25 Special Needs System LA's and Partners: What You Need to Do and By When.* London: Crown copyright, Department for Education and Skills and Department of Health.

Department of Health (2001) *Valuing People: A New Strategy for Learning Disabilities for the 21st Century.* London: HM Government, Department of Health.

Department of Health (2007) *Services for People with Learning Disability and Challenging Behaviour or Mental Health: Mansell Report 2* (Revised Edition 2007). London: Crown Copyright, Department of Health.

Department of Health (2009) *Valuing People Now – A New Three Year Strategy for People with Learning Disabilities.* London: HM Government, Department of Health.

Department of Health (2014) *Think Autism, Fulfilling and Rewarding Lives, the Strategy for Adults with Autism in England: An Update.* London: HM Government, Social Care,

Local Government and Care Partnership Directorate, Department of Health (an update to the 2010 Strategy).

Devereaux, C. (2012) 'Moving into relationship: Dance/movement therapy with children with autism'. Gallo-Lopez, L. and Rubin, L. (eds.) *Play-Based Interventions for Children and Adolescents with Autism Spectrum Disorders*. New York: Routledge.

Education Act (1981) Office of public sector information, crown copyright. London: HMSO.

Education Act (1993) Office of public sector information, crown copyright. London: HMSO.

Education Act (1996) Office of public sector information, crown copyright. London: HMSO.

Edwards, J. (2013) 'History and context of learning disability: A parent's perspective'.Broussine, E. and Scarboroughm, K. (eds.) (2012) *Supporting People with Learning Disabilities in Health and Social Care*. London: Sage publications.

Edwards, J. (2015) 'Exploring sensory sensitivities and relationships during group dance movement psychotherapy for adults with autism'. *Body, Movement and Dance in Psychotherapy*, 10(1): 5–20.

Erfer, T. (1995). 'Treating children with autism in a public school system'. Levy, F. J. (ed.) *Dance and Other Expressive Art Therapies*. London: Routledge.

Goddard, S. (1996) *A Teacher's Window into the Child's Mind and Papers from the Institute for Neuro-Physiological Psychology*. Eugene, OR: Fern Ridge Press.

Hackney, P. (2002) *Making Connections: Total Body Integration Through Bartenieff Fundamentals*. London: Routledge (first published by Overseas Publishers Association, 1998).

Hartshorn, K., Olds, L., Field, T., Delage, J., Cullen, C. and Escalona, A. (2001) 'Creative movement therapy benefits children with autism'. *Early Child Development and Care*, 166: 1–5.

Koch, S.C., Mehl, L., Sobanski, E., Sieber, M. and Fuchs, T. (2015) 'Fixing the mirrors: A feasibility study of the effects of dance movement therapy on young adults with autism spectrum disorder'. *Autism: The International Journal of Research and Practice*, 19(3): 338–350.

Leventhal, M. (1981) 'An overview of dance therapy for the special child'. Workshop presented at Laban/Bartenieff Institute of Movement Studies. New York.

Levy, F., J. (1995) (ed.) *Dance and Other Expressive Art Therapies*. London: Routledge.

Moran, H. (2010) 'Clinical observations of the differences between children on the autistic spectrum and those with attachment problems'. *Good Autism Practice*, 11(2): 44–57.

Ritchie, P., Sanderson, H., Kilbane, J. and Routledge, M. (2003) *People, Plans, and Practicalities – Achieving Change through Person Centred Planning*. Edinburgh, Scotland: SHS Ltd.

Rogers, C. R. (1957) 'The necessary and sufficient conditions of therapeutic personality change'. *Journey of Consulting Psychology*, 21: 95–103.

Scharoun, S. M., Reinders, N. J., Bryden, P. J. and Fletcher, P. C. (2014) 'Dance/Movement Therapy as an intervention for children with autism spectrum disorders'. *American Journal of Dance Movement Therapy*, 36: 209–228.

Tortora, S. (2006) *The Dancing Dialogue: Using the Communicative Power of Movement with Young Children*. Baltimore, MD: Paul H. Brookes Publishing Co.

Online resources

Dance Voice website (2016). Available at www.dancevoice.org.uk/about-us/history/ (Accessed 31/01/16).

Schriber, L. (2010) 'Autism: A neurological and sensory based perspective. Stone, JH. and Blouin, M. (eds) *International Encyclopedia of Rehabilitation*. Available at http://cirrie. buffalo.edu/encyclopedia/en/article/285/ (Accessed: 02/01/2016).

Chapter 3

DMP assessments for children and young people with learning disabilities and special needs

Fiona Hoo

Introduction

> *I am walking down a corridor in a school and suddenly a teacher stops me because she needs to tell me about a pupil in her class. She is concerned about this pupil because he has become very withdrawn recently and has had angry outbursts at staff members. She is really struggling to keep him engaged during lessons when he starts behaving aggressively towards others and so has resorted to sending him out of the class. The teacher thinks that this pupil needs therapy and she asks if I am able to take on some therapeutic work with him.*

This information provided by the teacher is useful because she has described his behaviour and its impact on staff and other pupils. However, I need a way of understanding and learning more about his needs and other relevant contextual information in order to determine what kind of support and treatment might best suit him. For this, I would need to do an assessment.

This chapter focuses on the process of assessment in dance movement psychotherapy (DMP) within a special needs education setting for children and young people with learning disabilities and autism. The aims, function and process of assessment are discussed.

Later in the chapter, I present a framework for DMP assessment to help organise the information gathered, drawing on current DMP, counselling and psychotherapy assessment models.

An integrative approach to Dance Movement Psychotherapy

My approach to DMP is integrative; it is informed by psychodynamic, ecosystemic and social constructionist theoretical perspectives. The co-creation of meaning and mutual influence in the therapeutic relationship form the core of my work. This way of working promotes a phenomenological inquiry and curiosity towards human experiences and discourses (Burr, 2004) and invites me to constantly challenge my beliefs and assumptions about my practice.

Assessing children and young people 37

I also believe that the process of the body and the psyche are interdependent and reflective of the body–mind connection (Berrol, 1992; Dosamantes-Beaudry, 1997). My career-long task remains one of learning how to integrate an embodied practice and multidisciplinary theoretical perspectives in an ever-changing world.

For my work in special education needs settings, this integrative approach has been very helpful both in therapy and assessments as it allows me to have a fuller understanding of the children I work with in the context of their education, social and cultural milieu. It also keeps me mindful of the biases and assumptions which I carry both into and outside of the therapy session.

The context of DMP in learning disability and special education needs and disability settings

Whilst the difference between the terms 'learning disability' (LD) and 'learning difficulty' is still a subject of debate internationally, it is widely accepted in the United Kingdom that 'learning disability' refers to individuals who find it harder to learn, understand and communicate, whilst 'learning difficulty' refers to individuals who have specific problems with learning due to either medical, emotional or language complications (Emerson and Heslop, 2010). The former includes the presence of an impaired intelligence and social functioning and has its origins in early life. The latter includes individuals with 'specific learning difficulties', such as dyslexia, who do not have impaired intelligence. The special education needs and disability (SEND) classifications of moderate, severe and profound learning difficulties all refer to varying severities of generalised learning difficulty and disability (DfE, 2015). As such, an individual with an LD could have impairments that include intellectual disability, learning difficulties and autism (DfE, 2015; Schneider, 2014).

Some literature suggests that there are always emotional issues that accompany serious impairments and that those on the autistic spectrum struggle with issues of anxiety and depression (Paxton and Estay, 2007; Ruberman, 2002). Although there are cases of individuals who experience secondary emotional disabilities as part of the trauma of their original impairment, the propensity to attribute the emotional difficulties experienced by this client population to their disability rather than to their emotional state or needs is common (Hollins and Sinason, 2000; Sinason, 1986). In my experience, it is reasonable to surmise that children and young people with learning disabilities can experience emotional and behavioural problems despite their disability (Arthur, 2003). There is a growing body of research on the emotional development of people with learning disabilities that shows that they experience emotional difficulties and can benefit from psychological interventions (2003).

There is a long history of DMP work with children and young people with special education needs, including learning disabilities and autism (Bannerman-Haig, 2006; Erfer, 1995; Duggan, 1995; Leventhal, 1980; Levy, 1992). The various approaches to working with this client group are reflective of the variety and range of presentations among individuals. There is a broad spectrum of differences among clients' physical abilities, cognitive function, verbal capacities and sensory processing. DMP with this client group has employed movement interventions that focus on developing body image, sensorimotor and perceptual motor development, coordination and socialisation (Duggan, 1995; Erfer, 1995; Martin, 2014; Scharoun *et al.*, 2014). DMP research shows that embodied interventions in DMP can help children with autism increase their capacity for social connectedness and are an effective treatment (Devereaux, 2012).

Many people with learning disabilities struggle to communicate verbally due to factors such as underdeveloped language and communication skills, lack of cognitive capacity for reflection, or difficulty in making connections between emotions and behaviour (Upton, 2009). Given that nonverbal and gestural communication precedes language development (Cochet and Byrne, 2016; Iverson and Goldin-Meadow, 2005), DMP offers the possibility to establish pathways to communication at a pre-verbal level. This is accomplished both through self-expressive movement and with the benefit of a therapist's movement interventions (Boris, 2001; Payne, 1992). The dance between therapist and child may be seen as the unspoken dialogue through which they communicate and build their relationship. For such clients, DMP as treatment offers a holistic approach based on the body-mind connection, integration and expression that transcend their limitations from disability.

Paying attention to and allowing unified expression between the body and the mind allows the space for 'internal and internalised relationships, whether on a biochemical, neurological, muscular or emotional level, [to] get constellated and acted out in [the] external relationship' (Soth, 2006: 130). Hence the ability to include nonverbal aspects of communication are integral to working with this client group, especially where they have difficulties communicating verbally or rely on nonverbal means of communication.

When working with children who have little or no words, attending to the unspoken dialogue between us enriches the communication and allows me to pick up subtle emotions and responses that I might otherwise miss. When I observe their use of nonverbal communication, I can see how they relate to others and to their environment, which is especially useful during the early stages of the therapeutic work and assessment.

The aims of assessment and the case for an ecosystemic approach

Remember the case example at the beginning of the chapter? This is a common example of how referral is made to me when working in a school. Informal conversations along corridors with teachers and other professionals working with the children are quick ways of highlighting a concern about a child and provide essential information about them. I have also been approached by parents in some schools and have listened to their worries about their child as they accompany their children to and from school. In schools where a referral system exists, formal referrals can be made through the school's referral protocol.

Whenever a referral has been made, informal or otherwise, I conduct an assessment at the start of therapy. As the therapy progresses, it may be necessary to conduct re-assessments to ensure that the treatment offered is still suitable. Throughout the duration of therapy there are opportunities for clinical audits to ascertain validity and measure progress, and review procedures at the end of therapy enable me to evaluate the treatment.

What sort of information needs to be gathered about the child and how should it be organised? Where might this information be found or who can offer it? In the following sections, I consider the aims of the assessment, referrer biases, therapist assumptions and biases, and therapist adaptations needed for working with these children.

The main aim of an assessment is to gather information about the client's needs, presenting issue/s and background information, in order to formulate what the client might need support with and to determine suitability of treatment. This information enables the therapist to hypothesise what might be happening for the client and to recommend a suitable form and length of treatment. It is worth acknowledging that in undertaking a DMP assessment, I must allow for the possibility that DMP might not be the best treatment for the client referred.

Bayne *et al.* (1994) outline six main objectives of assessment which are applicable irrespective of theoretical orientations. I find these suit DMP assessments for the children I work with:

1   To understand the nature of the client's presenting problem and related issues.
2   To identify factors associated with presenting problem and the client's experience or behaviour.
3   To determine the client expectations of treatment and desired outcomes.
4   To collect baseline information for subsequent evaluations of progress in treatment.
5   To facilitate some level of client's self-awareness by sharing the therapist's perspective of the presenting problem.
6   To suggest a treatment plan based on the therapist's hypothesis of what might be happening for the client.

In my practice, I also add a seventh aim:

7   To identify the client's personal strengths and unique competencies that would help create change.

It might take some weeks to achieve these aims in practice and sometimes I manage to achieve most but not all of them. However, I find this format useful for thinking about a child when they are referred to me, and to keep a clear focus on the child throughout the assessment process.

With the development of family therapy paradigms since the late 1960s (Hair *et al.*, 1996), the assessment process for children and young people has been enriched as it offers the understanding of the interconnections between the child's struggles and the wider context (Rustin and Quagliata, 1994). In general, there is need for a more holistic and comprehensive treatment approach that takes into account social and emotional problems in children and adolescents within a broader framework of barriers to learning (Adelman and Taylor, 1998; Kourkoutas *et al.*, 2010). Hence the argument for an ecosystemic way of working, which allows the therapist to form a fuller picture of the client (French and Klein, 2012; Kourkoutas *et al.*, 2010).

The essence of an ecosystemic approach (Kourkoutas *et al.*, 2010) is:

- an understanding that emotional–behavioural struggles cannot be attributed only to the individual but also from the interaction between people;
- seeing behaviour patterns as non-linear; positive change to one part of the system can cause change in the whole system; intervention strategies must include the client and the people around them; and
- individual treatment is integrated into a family-systemic perspective.

An ecosystemic approach allows me to be flexible, go beyond the limits of traditional therapeutic work with the client and 'physically enter the world of the client' (Hair *et al.*, 1996: 294). I am able to take on roles and interventions anywhere within the ecosystem of the client, so that an imbalance within the system can be addressed (1996). This way of working helps me to think holistically about the therapeutic work and allows me to make important links between what is happening in therapy and the child's environment.

The therapy service in UK schools exists within a complex system of education and well-being, which is designed to support the key principles of the 'Every Child Matters Policy' (2003). The five key principles of the government initiative are to support all children in being healthy; staying safe; enjoying and achieving; making a positive contribution; and achieving economic well-being. This policy covers all children up to the age of nineteen, or twenty-four for those with disabilities. As such, addressing emotional or social needs of pupils is part of a wider approach of supporting learning in most school environments (French and Klein, 2012; Karkou, 2010).

Regarding taking on roles within the system, it might be necessary for me to make links with other professional agencies working with the child and their families. This could include the class teacher, learning support assistants, home-school liaison officer, special education needs coordinator (SenCo), the team around the child (TAC), and multi-agency work (MAW).

I have also experienced that the culture and priorities of each school will influence the emphasis placed on learning and emotional well-being (French and Klein, 2012). As a result, how therapy is viewed and the degree to which it is welcome, accepted and supported will depend on the school culture. Therefore, therapists working in schools should be aware of the school's perspective of therapy and be prepared to adopt an approach to assessments that best fits the setting (French and Klein, 2012; Regev *et al.*, 2015).

The process of assessment

The word assessment means to 'evaluate or estimate the nature, ability or quality of something (OED, 2016). The root of the word assessment is from the Latin '*assidere*', which means to 'sit by' (2016). These basic definitions may be useful to remember when conducting an assessment as it suggests both the need for a level of objectivity and an empathic stance of the assessor (Gilroy, 2012; Palmer and McMahon, 1997). Assessment is part of the therapeutic process and a well-informed assessment provides the foundation for the subsequent clinical treatment (Gilroy, 2012; Rustin and Quagliata, 2004).

While it is possible to have one session or interview with a client to gather enough information for the assessment, several sessions with a client may also prove useful as it allows the anxiety of 'the encounter with what is not known [which] is at the heart of an assessment' to settle (Rustin and Quagliata, 2004: 4), and hence the more unconscious relationship dynamics to surface. In assessment and/or therapy sessions, clients bring with them their history of learnt patterns of relating to others and their life experience. These patterns, also called transferences, are enacted in the relationship with the therapist. Identifying and understanding these relationship dynamics provides essential information about the client, which is useful for treatment at a later stage (French and Klein, 2012). I have found this to be true in my own practice: conducting assessments that last several sessions, plus interviews with the children's families and professionals working with them, offers more reliable observations and results.

In summary, so far we have established that the assessment process usually starts with a referral from someone who knows the child personally or professionally. This could be a teacher, the special education needs coordinator, parent, other professionals such as the TAC, MAW or other therapists working with the child. The assessment then usually entails observations of the child and meetings and dialogues with the child and their parents/guardians and the various professionals who work with them. They could be formal, informal or a mixture of both. Many DMPs have become skilled at informally assessing clients through observation and conversation with the people around them (Karkou and Sanderson, 2001). This is especially true for those who work in environments that have no formal referral process and require a contextualised way of working.

While information from the referral source can be invaluable in helping me understand more about the individual, the information could be influenced by the referrer's agenda (Geldard and Geldard, 2012). As therapist, I remain sensitive to the anxieties and projections, both conscious and unconscious, which may be present in the referral. For example, a teacher referring a child may be primarily concerned about their disruptive behaviour and have less focus on the child's emotional struggles. Or a parent may view their child as a 'problem child' and expect the therapist to 'fix' the child's behaviour. It is a challenging task to receive such information in a way that furthers my understanding of clients without forming biases about the client. However, given the integrative nature of my approach, I am interested in gaining an all-rounded perspective of the child from different sources and give high value to the intersubjectivity of the assessment process. So, the referrer's perspective of the child becomes one side of the story in my assessment.

This may inevitably bring to the forefront and challenge my omnipotent fantasies, self-esteem, and the assumptions and beliefs that could influence the outcome of the assessment. For example, a child might remind me of someone I have strong feelings for; this could sway my perception of them. These thoughts and feelings arising in a therapist during an assessment or therapy are known as countertransference and occur generally as an unconscious process in the background of the work. Rustin and Quagliata (2004) mention that feelings and thoughts which have their origins in the therapist's own personal world need to be bracketed as they are not helpful to the assessment process. However, it is not always easy to be in touch with my unconscious feelings and thoughts in the moment and be able to put them aside. The need for strong supervision and reflective practice is vital in supporting this aspect of my work.

An active self-awareness of our potential bias as therapists is necessary but not sufficient to the assessment process. In my experience, reflexivity in practice needs to be complemented (or supplemented) by reflective practice (Schon, 1983); this includes the use of supervision during the process of assessment. Being reflexive provides me with an opportunity to think dynamically about the interactions between me as the therapist, my client and the context of our work together. The opportunity to discuss the work in supervision forms a double-loop learning or second-order reflection and is essential to the quality of the assessment I conduct (Bager-Charleson and Van Rijn, 2011; Rustin and Quagliata, 2004). Through supervision and reflective practice, it is possible to become more attentive to levels of self-awareness, identify personal biases and to recognise blind spots as well as parallel processes that are enacted within the work. This part of the process is helpful to me and my client in that I am able to formulate a treatment that is best suited for the client and ensures a better client–therapist match.

An assessment meeting is in essence a therapeutic encounter; so, building a therapeutic relationship during the assessment phase, which incorporates empathy and trust, is essential at this stage in the work (Palmer and MacMahon, 1997). As part of the therapeutic relationship, my countertransference during an assessment can provide valuable information. The feelings and thoughts that get evoked during the work in relation to the child give insight about what they are trying to elicit in me, which in turn sheds light on the child's inner world. For example, I might feel particularly motherly with one child and more like a big sister to another.

There are many moments when words become secondary and nonverbal communication evokes strong emotions and somatic effects in the countertransference.

As Orbach (2003) points out, there is no such thing as a body on its own but only bodies in relationship with each other. It therefore is no surprise that somatic countertransference is likely in the work. Somatic countertransference is experienced as bodily sensations that I might feel in the countertransference (Bloom, 2006; Orbach and Carroll, 2006). However, strong countertransference responses are not particular to DMP practice only. Rhode (2004), a child psychotherapist, observes that a therapist conducting an assessment or therapy with children who struggle with verbal communication may experience powerful emotions in the countertransference. In recounting his work with a man with severe intellectual disability, Corbett (2009), an art therapist working with adults with learning disabilities, also described experiencing powerful emotions in the countertransference.

Using movement observation to inform the assessment

There are several DMP assessment tools available for different populations and settings. The DMP assessments as described by Cruz (2006), Dayanim *et al.* (2006) and Powell (2008) are movement observation-based and address psychopathology, developmental movement, body image and neurotrauma. Meekums (2002) offers a more generic assessment structure for working with adults that includes the therapist's explanation of DMP, client's personal history, risk assessment and client's movement profile. Research suggests that assessment procedures based on movement analysis are not being used despite the fact that many DMPs may have been trained in movement observation (Karkou and Sanderson, 2001). The research explains that existing movement observation procedures use a lot of jargon that make it difficult to convey assessment results to professionals outside of DMP (2001). Some methods also require the use of video recording, which in itself raises ethical concerns about confidentiality and impact on the client–therapist relationship.

I believe that movement observation is an essential component to include in a DMP assessment despite any difficulties encountered. The observations of a child's movement and body as a mediator for the relationship between the self and external environment are unique to DMP. Part of the DMP clinical experience includes having to translate what is observed in movement and embodiment of the child to colleagues outside of DMP because it adds value to the overall understanding of the child.

In my practice, when using DMP-specific models of assessment, I have found that using elements of Laban Movement Analysis (LMA) (Newlove and Dalby, 2004) and of Tortora's (2006) work yields assessment information that is sensitive and respectful to the context and presentation of the child. I share more about how I have integrated both these frameworks within my assessments later in the chapter.

DMP is particularly interested in the qualitative aspect of movement as related to the mover's emotions and mental states. LMA effort theory, offers a framework that enables me to interpret, describe and notate the wide spectrum of qualitative body movement. The efforts of space, weight, time and flow correspond to the associated qualities of attention, intention, decision and control respectively (Bloom, 2006). LMA discusses the effect of feelings on movement and notes that *how* a movement is executed is more related to feeling than the form of the movement (Newlove and Dalby, 2004). By observing the use of a person's efforts, I am observing their inner attitude towards the effort elements and consequently an impression of the associated psychological quality. For example, observing that 'a child is putting marbles into a jar' is just a description of his action but does not tell us *how* he is doing it. By applying the lens of LMA effort theory, I may note that he is using the qualities of 'direct space' and 'bound flow' (Newlove and Dalby, 2004) whilst performing this action. A shorthand way of recognising that he is *carefully* putting marbles into the jar, demonstrating a focused attention and precision control. Then I might further note that he has good fine motor skills and good attention span. It is possible to see from this example how using movement observation helps me to infer his mental state and capacities in a succinct form.

Tortora (2006) designed the 'Ways of Seeing' approach, within which she gives a list of nonverbal movement criteria used in an education setting as a guide for classroom observations. This list of nonverbal movement criteria is not specifically described for use with children with learning disabilities. However, its focus on the nonverbal communicative aspects of the use of the body and communicative style and education setting makes it applicable to this client group. Her model addresses nonverbal communication and movement from a socio-emotional, embodied experience and cognitive focus. This model of observation is divided into three categories: the child's use of space during specific activities; the child's body level awareness; and changes in nonverbal style during different classroom activities (Tortora, 2006).

I wish to note the usefulness of continual observations through informal contact. Whilst I may formally set up observations of the child in certain periods and environment, for example during dance class or snack time, it is possible to also glean important information during informal contact. The passing by of the child in the corridor or the shout across the playground to a peer is as valuable an observation as sitting in the classroom and listening to the teacher.

Therapist adaptations when working with children and young people with learning disabilities and autism

There is a wide range of physical and cognitive functionality, which I encounter when working with children with learning disabilities. The variation in the capacity and ability for verbal communication, cognitive ability and physical and sensorimotor functions are just some of the factors to consider in the assessment. The most effective assessment with this client group can be made when I adapt to the clients' presenting needs. Hurley *et al.* (1998) recommend a number of adaptations for psychotherapists working with intellectual and developmental disabilities, which is also useful in schools settings. These adaptations integrate well into the ecosystemic approach and enhance the assessment experience for both me and the client. Some elements are more applicable in the case of assessments lasting a few sessions but I find it generally a very applicable model, which may be helpful in assessments.

Some of the adaptations that Hurley *et al.* (1998) suggest therapists use are:

- Simplified language and sentences when communicating with client.
- Using shorter length sessions to accommodate differences is attention span.
- Adapting activities and interventions to include nonverbal ones, such as using movement and drawing.
- Integrating the client's developmental and cognitive level into activities and interventions, for example, using visual guides.
- Involving caregivers to help with change, if necessary. For example, rehearsals at home with help of staff or family to achieve independence with the expression of feelings.

The role of ethics and confidentiality in the assessment process

According to the Children Act 1989, Section 17 (10), all disabled children are classified as 'Children in Need'. This covers all children and young persons under eighteen years of age with physical disabilities, sensory disabilities, learning disabilities or emotional and behavioural disabilities. The legal and safeguarding implications for all professionals working with these children requires robust ethical guidelines.

As a DMP, I adhere to the code of ethics and professional practice as set out by the Association for Dance Movement Psychotherapy UK (ADMP UK, 2013) for relevant principles, standards and guidelines when conducting an assessment.

A DMP assessment framework for use with children and young people with learning disabilities and special needs

My search for a more comprehensive and inclusive assessment framework when working with this client group is ongoing. Having considered the aims, function and processes of assessment, I seek to apply the concepts discussed towards a DMP assessment framework consistent with an integrative approach.

I have designed an assessment form that seeks to organise relevant information needed for a DMP assessment for working with children and young people with learning disabilities, including those on the autistic spectrum. Below is a case example, followed by a completed assessment form related to this example.

Case Example

(The child described in this case example is a fictitious person made up of composite cases.)

Recall John from the beginning of the chapter. He is fourteen years old and has autism and dyslexia. John's teacher stops me in the corridor and shares with me her concerns about him. She says that he has lost the sparkle in his eyes and has become withdrawn recently. She finds it very difficult to keep him engaged in class. He stares out at the window and sits very still for long periods of time. When staff approach him, he lashes out in anger. He shouts and flails his arms about violently. Sometimes he headbutts them. No one can get close to him. Until two weeks ago, the concerned teacher was able to help him calm down by offering him his favourite cuddly toy. But now he seems inconsolable and nothing makes him feel better or less angry. The frequency of John's anger outbursts has escalated to three times a week and she has resorted to sending him to the class quiet room, or de-escalation room, because he is too disruptive and the other pupils are becoming afraid of him. She asks if I would be able to see John for therapy.

I follow up this informal referral with further information gathering on John's case by speaking to the SenCo and his parents. The SenCo tells me that John's grandmother died a month ago and that he was very close to her up until the day she died. She also says that it was his mother's mother who passed away and that his mother has appeared quite depressed since the loss.

I arrange for an interview with John's mother. She arrives very late for our meeting and is a little untidy in her appearance. She has tousled hair and is wearing what appears to be her pyjamas. She says that she is feeling depressed because she is grieving for her mother. She finds it such a struggle to look after John, whose behaviour has become very difficult and challenging at home since his grandmother died. I find out from his mother that John used to spend all his holidays with his grandmother and that they were very close. She knows he must be feeling sad too, but does not know how to comfort him. He will not let her get close to him. He is not sleeping well, waking up in the middle of the night and banging the wall with his bare hands. She thinks he does this out of frustration and grief.

Next, I arrange to observe and meet John in his class during a literacy lesson. When I arrive in his classroom, John is sitting at the edge of the class group and faces away from the teacher. He is looking out the window, silent and still. A teaching assistant encourages him to pay attention to what his teacher is saying. There is no response from him. She tries again and gently touches his elbow in the process. All of sudden John turns and shouts at her to go away and thrashes his arms about and pushes her away. She is taken aback and falls off her chair due to the suddenness of his response and the forcefulness of his push. John stands up and continues to shout; he seems very angry. He stares at the teaching assistant angrily and rushes towards her in an attempt to headbutt her. Fortunately, she gets

Assessing children and young people 47

Table 3.1 Framework for DMP assessment: example case study

DMP Assessment: Learning Disabilities and Autism (under eighteen years of age)

Name of child: *John*   Setting: *SEND secondary school*

Date of birth/Age: *Fourteen years old*   Date: *9 September 2016*

1   **Presenting Issue/Referral**: *Class teacher reports poor engagement and challenging behaviour in class in the last few weeks (e.g. headbutting).*

2   **Personal History**: (e.g. significant life events, socio-demographic, personal strengths and unique competencies) *John comes from a single-parent family and lives with his mother. No siblings. His maternal grandmother has passed away in the last month. He had a close relationship with her and spent all his holidays with her. He can communicate verbally and used to be able to self-soothe using his favourite cuddle toy.*

3   **Therapeutic History**: *None reported.*

4   **Client Expectations and Aims for Therapy**: *To set up further observations and meetings with John to confirm this.*

5   **Health Issues and Medication**: (e.g. diagnoses: allergy, asthma, epilepsy, physical disability, etc.) *Autism and dyslexia.*

6   **Information from Significant People in Client's Environment**: (e.g. parents/ carers, teachers, other professionals) *Class teacher notes that John has become withdrawn and emotionally unsettled, often angry. Usually he can self-soothe using his favourite cuddle toy but this has not been useful to him lately.*
     Mother reports challenging behaviour at home. He is not sleeping well, some occasions of 'banging the wall with his hands' when he wakes up in the middle of the night. She thinks that he does this out of frustration and grief.
     SenCo and mother both confirm John's loss of his maternal grandmother in the last month. SenCo observed that his mother seemed 'quite depressed since the loss'.

7   **Nonverbal/Movement Observation**: (Any preferred method of movement observational assessment may added to and/or used here, e.g. LMA Effort Theory) *John was sitting still and staring out the window during literacy lesson. He did not seem to be paying attention to what the class teacher was saying. He came across as very passive in LMA Efforts except for flow as he seemed to be deep in feeling. He thrashed his arms and pushed away his teaching assistant when she tried to engage his attention. His use of sudden time when he reacted to her suggests he did not want to be disturbed. His use of strong weight in pushing her away may have indicated how much he did not want to be disturbed. Then he tried to headbutt his teaching assistant and scratch her arms. He was very focused on her as indicated by his use of the direct space. He needed two other members of staff to escort him to safety in the quiet room. He banged his fists on the walls of the quiet room. His use of strong weight to perform that action got lighter as he became tired. Then he slumped into the corner and stared at the floor. He seemed calmer. Perhaps the corner provided a contained space and a sense of being supported as he gave his weight passively to the walls. He offered me a fleeting eye contact as I approached the door of the quiet room.*

Tortora's (522006: 385–387) nonverbal cues to look for in an educational setting for children:

7.1   **Use of Space During Specific Activities**: *John does not use the whole classroom. His use of space is small and confined to where he is sitting unless he gets agitated. He appeared calmer when he was sitting in the corner of the quiet room. I wonder if the small corner space and leaning passively into the walls has a calming and containing effect on him.*

(continued)

48   Fiona Hoo

Table 3.1 Continued

> 7.2 **Body Level Awareness**: *John offered me some eye contact when I was at the door of the quiet room, this suggests an awareness of me. When he pushed away his teaching assistant and attempted to headbutt her, his body movements were coordinated. I did not observe any mobility problems.*
>
> 7.3 **Nonverbal Style During Different Classroom Activities**: (e.g. individual work, free play, snack time) *John was quiet and did not talk during lesson. He was not paying attention to class activity and seemed absorbed in his own feelings. I have not yet observed in other activities.*
>
> 8   **Recommendations for Treatment**: (e.g. treatment plan, referral to other services) *Based on observations and reports from significant adults, John's current behaviour and emotional responses appear to stem from his grief about the loss of his maternal grandmother. Further observations and a few assessment sessions might reveal other emotional needs. Pending further observations/assessment, he could benefit from regular DMP sessions to address his grief from his loss.*

up in time and manages to avoid his headbutt. However, John is not giving up. He tries to scratch her arms. Two members of staff come to separate John from his teaching assistant and assist him to the quiet room. While in the quiet room, he bangs his fists strongly on the wall. This behaviour goes on for several minutes until it slowly fades as John gradually becomes tired and stops. He then slumps into a corner of the quiet room and stares at the floor, not moving at all. I move closer to the door of the quiet room from the edge of the classroom. John notices me and glances at me and then resumes his position.

This completed framework for DMP assessment provides me with a focused outline of the needs of the client and clarity of reasons for the referral. I am then able to consider the most suitable manner of working with the child.

Conclusion

Conducting an assessment is a complex process and often is the start of a therapeutic relationship. It is a time for preparation for therapy and possibly a significant process in itself containing therapeutic potential (Rustin and Quagliata, 1994).

I have shared my way of working in this context and discussed the aims and process of assessment. Whilst doing so, I have highlighted the usefulness of including movement observations in the assessment, being mindful of therapist's adaptions that can be made, and offered a framework for DMP assessment. The experience of writing and researching this topic has helped me to appreciate the complexities of the assessment process and given me a chance to be more at ease when communicating with other professionals about my work.

Clients come to me, as a therapist, with various complexities and abilities for insight and articulation of their inner world. It is my role to offer them a service that is in their best interest. A robust assessment process sets up a good foundation for the therapeutic work that follows.

References

Adelman, H. S. and Taylor, L. (1998) 'Reframing mental health in schools and expanding school reform'. *Educational Psychologist*, 33(4): 135–152.

Arthur, A. R. (2003) The emotional lives of people with learning disability. *British Journal of Learning Disabilities*, 31: 25–30.

Bager-Charleson, S. and Van Rijn, B. (2011) *Understanding Assessment in Counselling and Psychotherapy*. Devon, UK: Learning Matters Ltd.

Bannerman-Haig, S. (2006) 'Stretching, tensing and kicking: Aspects of infantile movement in dance movement therapy with children and adolescents in special education'. Payne, H. (ed.) *Dance Movement Therapy: Theory, Research and Practice*. London: Routledge.

Bayne, R., Horton, I., Merry, T. and Noyes, E. (1994) *The Counsellors' Handbook*. London: Chapman & Hall.

Berrol, C. (1992) 'The neurophysiologic basis of the body-mind connection in dance/movement therapy'. *American Journal of Dance Therapy*, 14(1): 19–29.

Bloom, K. (2006) *The Embodied Self: Movement and Psychoanalysis*. London: Karnac.

Boris, R. (2001) 'The root of dance therapy: A consideration of movement, dancing, and verbalization vis-à-vis dance/movement therapy'. *Psychoanalytic Inquiry*, 21(3): 356–377.

Burr, V. (2004) *Social Constructionism*. (Second Edition) Hove, UK: Routledge.

Chief Secretary to the Treasury (2003) *Every Child Matters*. Norwich, UK: The Stationery Office (Cm 5860).

Children Act (1989) London: HMSO.

Cochet, H. and Byrne, R. W. (2016) 'Communication in the second and third year of life: Relationships between nonverbal social skills and language'. *Infant Behaviour & Development*, 44: 189–198.

Corbett, A. (2009) 'Words as a second language: the psychotherapeutic challenge of severe intellectual disability'. Cottis, T. (ed.) *Intellectual Disability, Trauma and Psychotherapy*. Hove, UK: Routledge.

Cruz, R. F. (2006) 'Assessment in dance/movement therapy'. Brooke, S. (ed.) *Creative Arts Therapies Manual*. Springfield, IL: Thomas Books.

Dayanim, S., Goodwill, S. and Lewis, C. (2006) 'The moving story effort assessment as a means for the movement assessment of preadolescent children'. *America Journal of Dance Therapy*, 28(2): 87–106.

Department for Education. (2015) *Special Education Needs and Disability Code of Practice: 0–25 Years*. Crown copyright.

Devereaux, C. (2012) 'Moving into relationships: Dance/movement therapy with children with autism'. Gallo-Lopez, L. and Rubin, L. C. (eds.) *Play-Based Interventions for Children and Adolescents with Autism Spectrum Disorders*. New York: Routledge.

Dosamantes-Beaudry, I. (1997) 'Reconfiguring identity'. *The Arts in Psychotherapy*, 24: 51–57.

Duggan, D. (1995) 'The "4s": A dance therapy program for learning disabled'. Levy, F. J., Fried, J. P. and Leventhal, F. (eds.) *Dance and Other Expressive Art Therapies: When Words Are Not Enough*. London: Routledge.

Emerson, E. and Heslop, P. (2010) *A Working Definition of Learning Disability*. Lancaster, UK: IHAL, supported by the Department of Health.

Erfer, T. (1995) 'Treating children with autism in public schools'. Levy, F. J., Fried, J. P. and Leventhal, F. (eds.) *Dance and Other Expressive Art Therapies: When Words Are Not Enough*. London: Routledge.

Geldard, K. and Geldard, D. (2012) *Counselling Children: A Practical Introduction* (Third Edition). London: Sage Publications.

Gilroy, A. (2012) 'What's best for whom? – Exploring the evidence base for assessment in art therapy'. Gilroy, A., Tipple, R. and Brown, C. (eds.) *Assessment in Art Therapy*. London: Routledge.

French, L. and Klein, R. (eds.) (2012) *Therapeutic Practice in Schools*. London: Routledge.

Hair, H., Fine, M. and Ryan, B. (1996) 'Expanding the context of family therapy'. *The American Journal of Family Therapy*, 24(4): 291–304.

Hollins, S. and Sinason, V. (2000) 'Psychotherapy, learning difficulties and trauma: New perspectives'. *British Journal of Psychiatry*, 176: 32–26.

Hurley, A. D., Tomasulo, D. J. and Pfadt, A. G. (1998) 'Individual and group psychotherapy approaches for persons with mental retardation and developmental disabilities'. *Journal of Developmental and Physical Disabilities*, 10(4): 365–386.

Iverson, J. M. and Goldin-Meadow, S. (2005) 'Gesture paves the way for language development'. *Psychological Science*, 16: 367–371.

Karkou, V. (ed.) (2010) *Arts Therapies in Schools*. London: Jessica Kingsley.

Karkou, V. and Sanderson, P. (2001) 'Report: theories and assessment procedures used by dance/movement therapists in the UK'. *The Arts in Psychotherapy*, 28: 197–204.

Kourkoutas, E., Plexousakis, S. and Georgiadi, M. (2010) 'An ecosystemic intervention in the context of a special needs education setting'. *Procedia Social and Behavioural Sciences*, 2: 4773–4779.

Leventhal, M. B. (ed.) (1980) *Movement and Growth: Dance Therapy for the Special Child*. New York: New York University.

Levy, F. J. (1992) *Dance Movement Therapy: A Healing Art* (Revised Edition). Reston, VA: American Alliance for Health, Recreation and Dance.

Newlove, J. and Dalby J. (2004) *Laban for All*. London: Routledge.

Martin, M. (2014) 'Moving on the spectrum: Dance/movement therapy as a potential early intervention tool for children with Autism Spectrum Disorders'. *The Arts in Psychotherapy*, 41: 545–553.

Meekums, B. (2002) *Dance Movement Therapy*. London: Sage Publications.

Orbach, S. (2003) There is no such thing as a body. *British Journal of Psychotherapy*, 20(1): 326.

Orbach, S. and Carroll, R. (2006) 'Contemporary approaches to the body in psychotherapy: two psychotherpaists in dialogue'. Corrigall, J., Payne, H. and Wilkinson, H. (eds.) *About a Body: Working with the Embodied Mind in Psychotherapy*. New York: Routledge.

Oxford English Dictionary. (2016) Oxford, UK: Oxford University Press.

Palmer, S. and McMahon, G. (eds.) (1997) *Client Assessment*. London: Sage Publications.

Paxton, K. and Estay, I.A. (2007) *Counselling People on the Autism Spectrum – A Practical Manual*. London: Jessica Kingsley.

Payne, H. (1992) 'Shut in, shut out: Dance movement therapy with children and adolescents'. Payne, H. (ed.) *Dance Movement Therapy: Theory and Practice*. London: Routledge.

Regev, D., Green-Orlovich, A. and Snir, S. (2015) Art therapy in schools – The therapist's perspective. *The Arts in Psychotherapy*, 45: 47–55.

Rhode, M. (2004) 'Assessing children with communication disorders'. Rustin, M. and Quagliata, E. (eds.) *Assessment in Child Psychotherapy*. London: Karnac.

Ruberman, L. (2002) 'Psychotherapy with children with pervasive developmental Disorders'. *American Journal of Psychotherapy*, 56: 262–273.

Rustin, M. and Quagliata, E. (eds.) (2004) *Assessment in Child Psychotherapy*. London: Karnac.

Scharoun, S. M., Reinders, N. J., Bryden, P. J. and Fletcher, P. C. (2014) 'Dance/movement therapy as an intervention for children with Autism Spectrum Disorders'. *American Journal of Dance Therapy*, 36: 209–228.

Schneider, B. H. (2014) *Child Psychopathology: From Infancy to Adolescence*. Cambridge, UK: Cambridge University Press.

Schon, D. A. (1983) *The Reflective Practitioner: How Professionals Think in Action.* New York: Basic Books.

Sinason, V. (1986) 'Secondary mental handicap and its relationship to trauma'. *Psychoanalytic Psychotherapy*, 2: 131–154.

Soth, M. (2006) 'What therapeutic hope for a subjective mind in an objectified body?' Corrigall, J., Payne, H. and Wilkinson, H. (eds.) *About a Body: Working with the Embodied Mind in Psychotherapy*. New York: Routledge.

Tortora, S. (2006) *The Dancing Dialogue: Using the Communicative Power of Movement with Young Children.* Baltimore, MD: Paul H. Brookes Publishing Co.

Upton, J. (2009) 'When words are not enough: Creative therapeutic approaches'. Cottis, T. (ed.) *Intellectual Disability, Trauma and Psychotherapy*. Hove, UK: Routledge.

Online resources

Association for Dance Movement Psychotherapy UK (2013) *Code of Ethics and Professional Practice*. Available at www.admt.org.uk/wp-content/uploads/Code-of-Ethics-and-Professional-Practice-PDF.pdf.

Powell, M.A. (2008) *Assessment in dance/movement therapy practice: A state of the field survey.* Philadelphia, PA: Drexel University [Online]. Available at dspace.library. drexel.edu/bitstream/1860/2944/1/Powell.pdf (Accessed 27/02/16).

Chapter 4

Dance Movement Psychotherapy as part of a holistic intervention team in a SEND school

Jeni Wilson

Introduction

This chapter looks at my developing role as a dance movement psychotherapist (DMP) within a Special Educational Needs and Disabilities (SEND) School. In 2006, I was employed at the school as a teaching assistant. This role entailed me working one-to-one with a pupil with a physical disability. I then progressed through the school to become a special support assistant, where I prepared and differentiated work for small groups of pupils so that they could access lessons that they were struggling with. When I finished my DMP Master's I was promoted to associate teacher, a role in which I have developed, specialising in DMP. The following quote from my Master's paper demonstrates my progressive thinking at the time:

> I am more aware of who I am becoming, I am able to communicate clear boundaries with the pupils and staff as to who I am becoming and what my 'Role' will exactly be within the school. This will hopefully diffuse any confusion or mis-conception of what DMP is and how it can be facilitated within special educational systems.
>
> (Wilson, 2011: 65)

Five years on, I now work from a safe therapeutic space as part of a successful holistic intervention team. The two main lessons I have learnt through this journey of establishing DMP within the school is that communication is key, and that making one's self heard is not something to be afraid of. I now know my role, and the staff that I work with know this too, as well as understanding the purpose of DMP in this setting.

DMP is important to the pupil's educational journey, as it gives them the time and space they need to move, explore and express their thoughts and feelings. Infants, primary, Years Seven and Eight now have DMP as part of their curriculum. Years Nine to Eleven can continue their DMP journey via referral if needed. DMP supports the children and contains them, giving them the opportunity to feel safe and to enjoy their education.

Over the years working as a DMP and associate teacher within education, I have increased my knowledge of the importance of safeguarding pupils that are participating in DMP sessions. Although at times it may feel that there could be conflict between two ethical frameworks, one as a DMP, the other as an associate teacher, it is possible to make them work alongside each other. The child's safety is by far more important in some cases than DMP–pupil session confidentiality. So, there are times when session confidentiality is overridden to protect the child. In this instance, I communicate with the pastoral care manager, who then speaks to the necessary professionals or parents in regards to the well-being of the child.

The role of associate teacher is created for members of staff who are not teacher trained but have skills that pupils would benefit from as part of their school day. In my case, being a qualified DMP, my role in the school has developed through my instigation of DMP sessions and through constructive discussions with my line manager and other professional members of staff over time. Through this collaborative dialogue, the benefits of DMP have become more apparent, and as a consequence my role as DMP has increased.

During my first year practising as a DMP we had a visit from The Office for Standards in Education, Children's Services and Skills (Ofsted, 2011). Although DMP was not on their agenda, an inspector still asked if he could look at how the space was used and how the sessions were run. Ofsted is in place to look at and assess the care of children and young people within education. Therefore, as a DMP working within an educational environment, I need to be aware of Ofsted expectations.

Although DMP is not part of a curriculum area, through discussions between the head teacher, the teaching staff and the holistic intervention team, it has become recognised as a valuable addition to the pupils' timetable, with aims and objectives that can helpfully run in conjunction with subjects such as English/ Language, personal social development, physical education, music and drama.

At the time of that Ofsted visit, there was also a behaviour support counsellor at the school, who delivered support to pupils within the secondary school department. The DMP and behaviour support counsellor roles then ran quite separately from one another within the school. However, both roles delivered sessions that had a similar purpose: to help support children within education through holistic interventions. The Ofsted inspection prompted some anxiety about evidence in support of both these services. What if Ofsted were to ask about how DMP and behaviour support are monitored, supported and recorded? We spent some time discussing how we could support each other and drafted a proposal for the head teacher to coordinate a team of professionals delivering holistic interventions. Our intention was to take a child-centred approach through a shared discussion on exactly what intervention a child would need on referral, followed by half-termly meetings to discuss the progress of the pupil.

Setting

The school discussed in this chapter is in the south of England and is a SEND school. Therefore, there are pupils with moderate learning difficulties (MLD) and additional special needs. These include autistic spectrum condition (ASC), specific learning difficulties, speech and language difficulties, attention deficit hyperactivity disorder (ADHD), physical disabilities, complex medical difficulties, and sensory impairments. The age group ranges from five to sixteen years.

I use the term ASC instead of autistic spectrum disorder (ASD) because I believe that the word 'disorder' could be perceived to highlight differences as not being 'normal', whereas the word 'condition' is a word that can be used to describe differences in a positive or negative way. Simon Baron-Cohen *et al.* (2009: 500) write:

> We favour the use of the term autism-spectrum condition rather than autistic spectrum disorder as it is less stigmatizing, and it reflects that these individuals have not only disabilities that require a medical diagnosis, but also areas of cognitive strength.

I have chosen to use the word 'difficulties' rather than 'disabilities' when referring to pupils, as in my experience, they have a difficulty in learning new/complex information or skills but have the ability to develop and learn; it just may take them longer. According to the 'Learning Disability Department of Health Policy and Practice' documents in *Valuing People* (2001), if the word 'disabilities' is used it indicates that a disability is linked to an overall cognitive impairment with lasting effects on development. This suggests, therefore, that there is a possibility that the pupils would be unable to develop the ability to learn new/complex information or skills.

The terminology I use in this chapter is in accordance with that of the SEND school concerned here, and by the government with regards to the recent change from special educational needs (SEN) to SEND (April 2015).

Teacher/therapist

DMP theorists such as Walli Meier (1997) and her ideas about working as a DMP in education, Suzi Tortora's 'Ways of Seeing Approach' (2006), and Marcia Leventhal's 'Five Part Session™' (1987) are all huge influences on my work as a DMP within this SEND school.

When I started working as a DMP within the school, it was important to find my authority in this role. Looking closely at the roles of teacher and therapists, I was particularly inspired by Walli Meier (1997) and her ideas around teachers and therapists working together and appreciating each other's role to help children within special education to develop to their full potential. Wengrower (2001) describes the roles of therapists and teachers as different cultures, and that the eventual communication between the two roles is seen as 'intercultural dialogue' (Wengrower, 2001: 114). This description helps us understand the journey of the DMP entering the world of education. Working within a school can at times feel like one is speaking in a foreign tongue. However, both teacher and/or therapist serve the same objective: for the child/pupil to develop to the best of their abilities. So, having an 'intercultural dialogue' (2001: 114) will help to fully meet the child/pupil's needs. In fact, I compare my role as a DMP to that of a translator between pupil and teacher; an intermediary person who forms the dialogues needed to communicate pupils' emotions and bring them to teachers' awareness.

It is well known that unfortunately teachers lack time to build relationships with pupils and, consequently, opportunities to address some of the challenges in the pupils' emotional, social, cognitive, communicative and physical needs that may be affecting their learning. This gap is where I envisioned the value of holistic interventions. Now, five years on from starting my dual role, various holistic interventions are offered within my workplace, such as DMP, behaviour support, play therapy, rebound therapy,[1] listening to music (recorded or live), talk time, soft play room and interactive sensory room.

Pring (1976, cited in Smith-Autard, 2002) states that a teacher is seen to be someone with great knowledge from whom the pupil can learn through copying and letting themselves be told by the teacher what to do and how to do something. Therefore, a teacher shares their thoughts, what they know and what they have learnt with their pupil through experience. Although this reference is from an educationalist in the 1970s, this statement still rings true. This could also be said of the role of the therapist: one difference being that a therapist is more non-directive in their approach and would not necessarily tell the pupil/child exactly what to do, but would offer a thought process of 'what if'. For example, 'what if you were to try and do something this way? How would that make you feel? Would that help? Would that work?' Rather than, 'this is how you are going to do this. This will be the outcome; this is how it works'. It could be said that education is about the end result, whereas therapy is about the process over time. Wengrower's table on the 'emphasis on general and relative differences – comparison and contrast' between teacher and therapist's roles, helpfully states that 'the teacher teaches, makes demands, gives exams; the pupil is tested, completes for achievement' (Wengrower, 2001: 111).

Meier (1997) agrees with Pring (1976) that a teacher's task is to develop the ability to learn and gain knowledge, skills and concepts. In her table for 'Differential Techniques and Converging Processes' of the teacher and the therapist (Meier, 1997: 10), Meier shows that a teacher follows the national curriculum, taking a directive approach in class situations, which is seen to be a very open space.

There is an expectation for teachers to fulfil the guidelines of the national curriculum and Ofsted. This restricts the teacher's time in meeting the non-educational needs of pupils. A document for schools called Special Educational Needs Coordinator (SENCO) states that in regards to special education:

> Teachers and assistants must be prepared to try different approaches, review, and change where necessary ... The child himself/herself is essential if a consistent, holistic and successful approach is to be achieved.
>
> (East and Evans, 2006: 5)

Comparing Meier (1997) to East and Evans (2006), one can see that within nine years the approach of a teacher/teaching assistant has developed and changed. The approach to teaching has shifted from being teacher centred to being child centred; teachers are required to adapt to better children's educational development. The literature suggests that teachers and assistants who work within special education are being guided to take a more holistic and open approach to teaching, which is seen by the school to be beneficial for the pupils. In my experience, the teacher's child-centred approach is currently developing, and teaching is becoming more therapeutic and holistic. This stance in fact correlates more with Meier's definition of a therapist, whom she describes as someone who attends and accompanies a journey. Meier writes that a therapist uses non-directive interventions in one-to-one or small group situations, in (mostly) private spaces (Meier 1997).

Tortora (2006) describes the role of the therapist as somebody who is receptive to cues from their clients and therefore does not hold on to 'preconceived notions based on the therapist's knowledge' (Tortora, 2006: 227). As mentioned previously Meier (1997) writes about the importance of teamwork between teacher and therapist and of both having an awareness of the other's aims. This is supported by Wengrower (2001: 112), who says that 'there is no doubt that the need for change and flexibility is vital to both sides, and would benefit their mutual encounter'.

Meier (1997) and Wengrower (2001) stress the importance of both roles. They believe that one role should not be seen as more useful to a child than the other, but that both teacher and therapist need to work alongside each other and communicate with one another.

I have spoken a lot about teachers adapting and having a more holistic approach, but this is only good practice if the therapist can do the same in regards to adapting their role to meet educational expectations and standards.

Working within the educational system, certain aims and objectives need to be met. The governing body of the school is responsible for monitoring the quality of education provided in all curriculum areas, on a regular basis.

To maintain a rigorous and ethical practice, I adhere to the Association for Dance Movement Psychotherapy UK (ADMP UK) Code of Ethics (2013), to the ethical principles and Code of Professional Conduct of the UK Council for Psychotherapy (2009), to the ethical principles stated by The British Association for Counselling and Psychotherapy (revised in 2010), to the policies of the school, for example, those concerning pastoral care, intimate care, special educational needs and to the professional standards stated in my DMP/associate teacher job description.

How DMP works in this school

Working full time within special education with a dual role of associate teacher and DMP can be challenging and rewarding. From my perspective, the rewards far outweigh the challenges. My role as a DMP enables a varied timetable, giving me the opportunity to work with individuals, small groups and full class groups (of twelve maximum). This timetable allows the DMP journey with pupils to flow throughout their whole experience of education from infants right up to Year Eleven.

In my experience, the needs of the pupils have become more and more complex over the years. This being said, the school environment has also gradually become more sensitive and responsive to such complex needs. This has made me aware of the need for my emerging role and how beneficial it has been for pupils to access DMP sessions. I have the opportunity to witness the pupils throughout the whole school day in structured lessons, free play and social situations and therapeutically. Having a wider view of the pupil's needs and abilities helps my therapeutic approach and gives me the ability to be able to work at a deeper level with the pupils.

Creating a confidential and consistent space was a significant challenge in the establishment of DMP in the school. It was extremely fortunate that a room was allocated that was an appropriate size; the unfortunate part was that it could be accessed via three doors. I spent a lot of time trying to highlight the importance of sessions not being interrupted by staff or other pupils who would try to use the space as a cut through or escape route. The school aims to create a trusting and safe environment where the pupils are valued and respected, seen and happy. As the year progressed, it became more apparent, due to the frequent session interruptions, that the space was no longer a confidential and consistent space for DMP sessions and that a new room was needed. Following successful discussions with the head teacher, a more confidential and uninterrupted space for the following academic year was allocated.

Because of the ever-changing needs and abilities of pupils, my next challenge was to adapt sessions to meet the variety of abilities and needs for each individual or group. Nonverbal structures were put in place using symbols, lighting, music and placement of cushions in the DMP space when appropriate. Now, a clear session structure influenced by Marcia Leventhal's 'Five part session™' (1987) is in place. This session structure is built up of circle time, warm up, movement and play, cool down and independent reflection. A typical infant, children with ASC, and Primary DMP session will follow this structure, which I view as a directive tool that helps to lift any anxiety that pupils have about what is expected of them within a session. This structure allows them to feel safe and able to move freely and in a non-directive way in the space.

These ASC infant DMP sessions are very sensory based, with exploration of movement and play within the DMP space. These sessions are heavily influenced by Suzi Tortora's 'Ways of Seeing' approach, where my experiential knowing is always guided by detailed observations. The latter is carried out, as mentioned earlier, during those times when I can observe the pupil's behaviour throughout a whole school day. These observations inform my ways of attuning to and mirroring the pupil's nonverbal actions and nurturing the development of a dancing dialogue (Tortora, 2006). Tortora's 'Ways of Seeing' programme was developed over a twenty-year period. It is based on the nonverbal observational principles of Laban Movement Analysis (LMA) (Davies, 2006),[2] the discipline of Authentic Movement (Pallaro, 1999),[3] DMP practice and early childhood developmental principles (Tortora, 2010). This approach, which focuses on the nonverbal dialogue, is ideal when working with children with special needs and disabilities who find it hard, if not impossible, to share their feelings with words.

During DMP sessions, I encourage movement through play as much as possible because many of the pupils do not know how to play or have been given the impression that it is no longer acceptable for them to play. I have found that once a child is playing they can communicate their needs or emotions with ease; a lot of the time this evolves unconsciously. I am then able to bring this into the conscious, by acknowledging the feelings expressed or bringing awareness to what a child is sharing within the session through creative movement expression and voicing what I experience.

The structure of the DMP sessions delivered to secondary school pupils vary greatly depending on their needs and abilities. Some of these pupils will access a session that has the same structure as that of primary school pupils; others will have a needs-suitable theme for the sessions from the start, which they either bring to my awareness within the sessions themselves or that I am made aware of through their referral. The latter structure is used with pupils who are able to communicate their thoughts and feelings and use dance and movement to explore their emotions quite freely.

Holistic intervention documents

Over the past five years, I have developed my role and the way that I log sessions. This enables me to keep pupil–therapist confidentiality whilst considering the importance of child protection and Ofsted. I have developed various documents to communicate the aims and objectives of sessions, as well as evidence pupils' DMP journey. I share four main documents:

- Holistic Intervention Referral Form (Table 4.1), which is filled in by teachers or tutors.
- Weekly DMP log (Table 4.2), which is filled in at the end of each session.
- Holistic Intervention Referral Review Form (Table 4.3), which is completed by the holistic intervention team every half term.
- DMP Journey Form (Table 4.4), which I complete after a pupil has been discharged or at the end of the academic year.

The Holistic Intervention Referral Form (Table 4.1) is constructed so that our referral system is child centred. Referrals are made either as an outcome from the pupil's annual review, where it has been discussed that the pupil needs extra support for recent behavioural and/or emotional changes due to a change at home, in their health and/or at school; or pupils are referred directly through the pupil's tutor who has noticed a change in the pupil's behaviour.

Table 4.1 Holistic intervention referral form

Holistic Intervention Referral Form	
Student Name:	Student Class:
Date of Birth:	Date of Referral:
Current concerns and presenting issues:	
Pupil History:	
Which style of intervention do you think would suit the pupil?	
Dance Movement Psychotherapy Behavioural Support Other	
Any other information:	
Is the pupil accessing any other forms of therapy? If so please explain.	
Lessons available that student can be released from for sessions: (Please list 3 options)	
Signed	

From previous years, I became very aware that at times I was taking on referrals where DMP was not the most effective or appropriate intervention needed for the pupil and what they actually needed was to see the behaviour support counsellor. So, with the new holistic intervention team in place and the new referral process in action we can communicate with each other and staff more effectively and really work out what is needed for the pupil.

The weekly DMP log (Table 4.2) shows the development of pupils within a DMP session. This document uses a colour-coded system inspired by a monitoring software called 'classroom monitor' (2013), which is used throughout the school to track pupils' academic progress. The colour coding used shows whether pupils are 'Engaging in' (green), 'Accessing' (orange) or 'Not accessing' (white) different aims/objectives of a DMP session. It is presented in the form of a table,

60 Jeni Wilson

Table 4.2 Weekly DMP log

DATE									
To participate in circle time									
Share movement ideas in the warm-up									
Move/play independently									
Move/play with another pupil									
Move/play with an adult									
To communicate verbally									
To communicate using sound									
To communicate using movement									
Initiate movement/play									
Take part in relaxation									
Was able to say how they are feeling									
Was able to say one thing they like doing									
Was able to explore imagery through movement									
Was able to express feelings through movement									
Colour Coding									
Green = Engaging in									
Orange = Accessing									
White = Not accessing									

which gives a clear picture of a pupil's journey each term, and gives me the ability to view how beneficial a pupil's DMP sessions are. It is a document that directly informs and supports my communication with the appropriate staff members and with parents. This document shows whether the pupil/pupils need to be accessing an alternative holistic intervention or whether they have reached the end of their DMP journey and can be discharged.

As you can see from Table 4.2, I have chosen fourteen aims of a DMP session, which can give staff members, parents or other educational and therapeutic professionals an insight into what may be explored and/or discussed in a DMP session without breaking pupil–therapist confidentiality.

In addition to using this system, I also use a more in-depth way of logging sessions which only I have access to. These sheets have written observations and details of sessions for reflection in holistic intervention meetings and supervision. This additional form follows four simple headings to help me log sessions:

- Young person's feelings and energy before the session.
- Themes during the session, interventions made.
- Young person's feelings and energy after the session.
- Any other comments.

Holistic intervention in a SEND school 61

Table 4.3 Holistic intervention referral review form

Holistic Intervention Referral Review Form
Student's Name: Class:
Date of Referral: Date of Review:
Staff/Carers Present:
Intervention Style Suggested:
Staff/therapist:
Sessions:
Start Date:
Starting Point:
Any Other Information:
Date to Be Reviewed:

Every half term the team meets to review the pupil's referral and to discuss whether progress is being made or whether any other underlying issues have become apparent. This review is a perfect time to discuss the length of the intervention and communicate with the team as to whether the sessions need to come to a close or whether the pupil needs a different intervention or more interventions. If needed, when a pupil is seen to be in crisis for example, the team can call a review earlier; this is where further interventions will be discussed, and when Child and Adolescent Mental Health Services (CAMHS) may need to be involved. This is the only point where, as the DMP, I would share information that a pupil has disclosed in a session. With pupils being so vulnerable, child protection takes priority in these cases. At the start of the DMP journey with pupils, I make it very clear as to whom I share information with and the reasons why. At the point of disclosure,

62 Jeni Wilson

Table 4.4 DMP journey form

DMP Journey		
Student name:	Date:	Colour Code
• to gain the confidence to participate in a DMP session		
• to share movement ideas with the group/ DMP		
• to share how they feel with the group/DMP		
• to explore feelings/emotions through movement		
• to explore imagery through movement		
• to communicate with the group/DMP		
• relaxation		
• play		
• to be able to initiate play in the DMP session		
• to become more aware of their own body		
• to be able to reflect on their DMP journey		
Further comments:		

Colour Coding	
Green = Engaging in session	GRN
Yellow = Accessing/attending	YLW
Blue = Not Accessing/attending	BLU
DIS = Discharged	DIS

I again make the pupil aware that I will be taking that information to the holistic intervention team to discuss how we can support them further.

The review form (Table 4.3, page 61) looks at the intervention suggested and the area that has been the focus. It looks at the starting point of the sessions and how that is developing.

Adhering to the necessary policies and principles, I have created a system which helps me monitor DMP sessions and enables me to share this information with educational professionals and parents to show the quality of DMP sessions without disclosing session information and without breaking pupil–therapist confidentiality. This is what I call the pupil's 'DMP Journey' (see Table 4.4). In this form, I collate information from my weekly log form. I return to this form at the end of each academic year to evidence pupils' progress in DMP. A copy of this form goes into the pupil's DMP file; another is given to their tutor, who then puts it into a pupil's school file; and a copy is sent home to parents. This document uses the same colour coding as the session log (Table 4.2).

It is beneficial to have these documents in place as they share with the staff, Ofsted and parents the purpose, progress and benefits of the role of DMP within this SEND school without breaking sessions' confidentiality. Having spent the last four years creating and developing my role within this SEND school, I now have everything I feel I need in place to deliver DMP sessions in a rigorous manner.

Having a child-centred approach is something that the school is working towards. Annual reviews with pupils and parents/carers at the school now follow a holistic approach. This is part of the new SEND code of practice that was put in place as part of the Education and Health Care Plan (EHCP) in accordance with The Children and Families Act (2014). This approach became law and was put in practice from September 2014. It aims to focus on the child's needs and hopes for the future and includes parents in the decisions made for the child's development as a whole, in regards to home, education, future goals, socially, mentally, emotionally, spiritually and physically. This push towards a holistic approach within education in general has made DMP more accessible for pupils. In the school discussed here, holistic interventions have become integral to the school and are now part of the annual review process.

Conclusion

As I have grown in confidence about the value of DMP in education, I have also been fortunate to find myself in a school and at a time when holistic interventions and a child-centred approach are being valued and implemented.

The holistic intervention team now in place within the school means that I can continue to work professionally and efficiently within my workplace with the dual role of associate tutor and DMP. This team consists of the pastoral care manager, a dance movement psychotherapist and a behavioural support counsellor. Holistic intervention referral forms, review forms, DMP session logs and DMP journey forms have been devised to relate to the expectations of the various protocols and standards of practice that govern the school. In this way, sessions are logged to meet Ofsted standards while maintaining session confidentiality. Having these documents in place offers me the professional means to hold the pupil sensitively at times when situations may be very complex to manage or navigate. They have also helped to support the integration of my interventions within the school, the rights of the pupil and inform the communication I need to have about DMP with my colleagues within the school, as well as outside with parents and carers and where communication with other professionals is needed. I now have a confidential and consistent room in which sessions take place. DMP has grown so much within my workplace and is now part of the timetable for Infants, Primary and Years Seven and Eight. At some point within their education, pupils will access DMP whether it is only for a term or for their whole time at the school. Special education is forever changing and developing to acknowledge and meet pupils' needs and abilities, which I hope in future will allow teachers to have time to address the non-educational needs of pupils too. None of these things would have been possible if I had sat in silence; as I sought to make the children's emotional needs integral to their education journey within the school, I found my voice and place as a practitioner within the educational system. I hope that the information I have shared here enables the integration of DMP within other schools.

Notes

1   Rebound therapy was founded in 1972 in the UK by Eddy Anderson. It uses trampolines to promote movement in a therapeutic way for people with a wide variety of difficulties and needs (2014).
2   Laban Movement Analysis is a theoretical and experiential system for the observation, description, prescription, performance and interpretation of movement created by Rudolph Laban (Davies, 2006).
3   Authentic Movement is an exploration of the unconscious through movement and inner listening in the presence of a witness (Pallaro, 1999).

References

British Association for Counselling and Psychotherapy (BACP) (2001) *Ethical Framework for Good Practice in Counselling and Psychotherapy.* Rugby, UK: BACP.
Davies, E. (2006) *Beyond Dance.* London: Routledge. First published 2001.
East, V. and Evans, L. (2006) *At a Glance: A Practical Guide to Children's Special Needs.* New York: Continuum International Publishing Group.
Leventhal, M. (1987) 'The ancient healing art of dance'. *Keynote Speech, First Annual Dance Therapy Conference*, Melbourne, Australia. Original manuscript, Roehampton University.
Meier, W. (1997) 'The teacher and the therapist'. *e-motion*, IX(1): 9–10. ADMP UK.
Pallaro, P. (ed.) (1999) *Authentic Movement.* London: Jessica Kingsley.
Smith-Autard, J. M. (2002) *The Art of Dance in Education.* London: A & C Black.
Tortora, S. (2006) *The Dancing Dialogue: Using the Communicative Power of Movement with Young Children.* Baltimore, MD: Paul H. Brooks Publishing Co.
Tortora, S. (2010) *From the Dance Studio to the Classroom: Translating the Clinical Dance Movement Psychotherapy Experience into a School Context. Arts Therapies in Schools: Research and Practice.* London: Jessica Kingsley.
Wengrower, H. (2001) 'Arts therapies in educational settings: An intercultural encounter'. *The Arts in Psychotherapy*, 28(2): 109–115.
Wilson, J. (2011) *Making Myself Heard. A Heuristic Inquiry into My Embodied Journey, Exploring the Therapist and the Teacher.* Original manuscript, Roehampton University.

Online resources

ADMP (2013) *Code of Practice.* Available at http://admp.org.uk/dance-movement-psychotherapy/code-of-professional-practice/ (Accessed 14/01/16).
Baron-Cohen, S., Scott, F. J., Allison, C., Williams, J., Bolton P., Mathews, F. E. and Brayne, C. (2009) 'Prevalence of autism-spectrum conditions: UK school based population study'. *The British Journal of Psychiatry*, 194: 500–509. Available at www.autismresearchcentre.com (Accessed 01/02/15).
Classroom Monitor (2013) *Classroom Monitor.* Available at www.classroommonitor.co.uk (Accessed 29/09/16).

GOV.UK (2001) 'Valuing People: A New Strategy for Learning Disability for the 21st Century'. *Valuing People.* Available at www.gov.uk (Accessed 01/02/15).

GOV.UK (2011) *Ofsted.* Available at www.ofsted.gov.uk/publications/110001 (Accessed 01/02/15).

GOV.UK (2015) *SEND Code of Practice.* Available at www.gov.uk/government/publications/send-code-of-practice-0-to-25 (Accessed 15/05/15).

Rebound Therapy.org (2014) *What Is Rebound Therapy?.* Available at www.reboundtherapy.org (Accessed 29/09/16).

UK Council for Psychotherapy (UKCP) (2009) *Ethical Principles and Code of Professional Conduct.* Available at members' area www.psychotherapy.org.uk (Accessed 01/02/15).

West Sussex County Council (2015) *SEND Local Offer.* Available at wsx-local-offer-alpha.herokupp.com/localoffer@westsussex.gov.uk (Accessed 01/10/15).

Chapter 5

Using video to increase sensitivity and attunement with caregivers of children with a disability

A Dance Movement Psychotherapy perspective

Bethan Manford

Introduction

This chapter provides an overview of the use of video as a method for thinking about and understanding disability within various contexts. Caregivers of children and young people with neurodevelopmental, learning or physical disabilities are the heart of this work. I shed some light on how dance movement psychotherapists can work in supervision or consultation using video to support colleagues' learning. I found that looking back at visual data brings valuable insight in terms of witnessing and analysing what is expressed beyond words. Video provides a method for thinking about how nonverbal communication (through gesture, movement and the body as a whole) supports various aspects of a young person's development. Filming in a range of settings led me to discover video interaction guidance (VIG) (Jarvis and Polderman, 2011; Velderman, 2011). VIG is an evidence-based method that has furthered my understanding of how to effectively use video and principles of attunement to help families in their goals and relationships. Attunement is a key area for enhancing interactions and relationships (Bowlby, 1982; Jarvis and Polderman, 2011), which Kennedy *et al.* (2011: 290) define as 'a harmonious and responsive relationship where both partners share positive emotions within a communicative dance'.

I have used video as a method of intervention with child–caregiver dyads where the focus was built around collaboratively chosen goals. The use of video images enabled caregivers to reflect, mentalise (as defined later in the chapter) and build attuned interactions within the dyad. Video work has been part of parenting programmes within Child and Adolescent Mental Health Services (CAMHS) for learning disabled (LD) children and family services. Here, group members would be encouraged to reflect and provide feedback on the child–caregiver footage shared. The aim of the group feedback was to develop peer support based on what group members witnessed and experienced.

I have also worked with video within a special needs school environment for self-reflection in order to further understand the children and the group processes. This opportunity aided my role in supporting staff to think about choices they made when working closely with the children.

Reflective practice through psychotherapy and psychology posts that I have held has supported my thinking about psychodynamic theory, attachment and attunement. Since moving into the field of learning disability and neurodevelopmental disorders, I have adopted an approach which integrates the above theoretical frameworks together with systemic theory. I feel that there are greater benefits to the referred young person when different narratives about the life of the child are pieced together. At times, clients are referred to as 'symptom bearers' (Horigian *et al.*, 2004: 254), as they may carry and externalise difficulties within their relationships or communities which are not being voiced or coped with well. Systemic thinking creates a significant shift from the individual to the interpersonal (Hedges, 2005); collectively thinking with families or other professionals enables systemic strengths and difficulties to be captured.

Special education needs school

I introduced dance movement psychotherapy (DMP) to a specialist school setting for children with a diagnosis of autism spectrum disorder (ASD) and a moderate to profound learning disability. According to 'Future in Mind' (DoH, 2015), services catering for children with these difficulties ought to provide interventions that support both physical and mental health needs (Rossiter *et al.*, 2015). DMP is an intervention that integrates body–mind approaches and therefore meets this outcome specification.

I provided training to help staff understand how this form of therapy could support children with ASD and I was fortunate to facilitate a group with a staff team who had a good understanding of autism and of the children's preference for predictability to reduce their anxieties (Shields and Stevens, 2008). They, therefore, maintained group boundaries but were flexible to support some changes in the use of video, music and props, tailoring the session to the children's needs and group dynamics. Staff were shown how to follow the child's lead, how to wait and observe nonverbal communication, to consider ways of mirroring and of joining in with the children's movements, attuning to the qualities or rhythms they shared (Berrol, 2006). This is a very important component of the work because within a systemic approach one needs to educate, communicate and consult with the systems around the child or young person (Johnstone and Dallos, 2006). I believe that part of my role includes developing a shared ownership of knowledge and broadening of thinking in and between those who surround the child or young person. In this way, there is an emphasis on enriching and thickening the understanding and narratives of the important people in the child or young person's life. This also helps me to gather information from families or supporting professionals, which in turn informs or changes hypotheses or formulations around the case.

Research shows that imitating actions of children with ASD can improve vocalisation, gaze and creative play (Dawson and Galpert, 1990), alongside increasing children's own emotional awareness (Jonsson *et al.*, 2001; Trevarthan and Aitken, 2001).

As group sessions came to a close, the adults present were asked to share observations about the children so that each child was verbally noticed and acknowledged. This collective witnessing in itself was nourishing because information was highlighted that I otherwise may have missed. My choice to pursue exploration with video was prompted by my curiosity to learn more about how DMP helped children with ASD; I wanted to see moments of connection and exploration and to look back and reflect on what had occurred within sessions in greater detail.

Staff member case study

When facilitating a group with children who have disabilities alongside their assigned supporting adults (often one adult per child), I found that I needed to be mindful of all group members. I noticed that one supporting adult (whom I will call Freda) was less intuitive and attuned to the children in the group; Freda was less able to follow the children's nonverbal communication. I offered guidance to her in sessions through instructions and modelling to help her discern how the children led play; yet she seemed to struggle in allowing the children to make their own choices of ways to engage in the therapy. Tortora (2006) describes how care-givers of children with social interaction and communication difficulties can be intrusive in play. I noticed that a boy (whom I will call Pedro) was becoming upset and anxious, running away from Freda to the group periphery. I thought about this in supervision and whilst analysing videos before sharing selected video clips with Freda. She talked about Pedro fleeing from her and how anxious he was. We noticed that when adults slowly and sensitively drew closer to Pedro without presenting demands, this furthered his communication and social abilities. Freda told me that it was personally difficult for her when the children showed signs of wanting to disconnect because it raised sensitive memories of her relationship with her mother. Freda recognised the links between the feelings evoked in her when the children pursued movement in isolation. We thought about how children with ASD relate to others and how this can leave caregivers with strong feelings, which can often be held in the body (Forsyth and Sked, 2011). DMP can support an embodied awareness and understanding of underlying thoughts and feelings (Bloom, 2006). Tuning into and thinking about one's own bodily sensations can inform one's understanding of a client. Interpreting whether our felt experiences are our own or those belonging to a client can help us to make sense of interpersonal nonverbal communication and behaviours. Freda recognised the impact that her early relationship with her own mother can have on her ability to cope with her interactions with the children. Freda's example illustrates how video is effective for reflective practice, where caregivers can consider their own communication style and self-understanding and develop more attuned interactions (Kennedy et al., 2015).

Opportunities for reflection for adults supporting children with disabilities in special schools are scarce, particularly when children have complex needs. The

DMP group provided staff with a space to explore beliefs and hypotheses about the needs of children they worked with. Video functions as a retrospective analytic tool (Kennedy *et al.*, 2015). I found that strengths could be highlighted to those who worked closely with the children and often experienced interactions as stressful. A video recording would capture moments of joint attention, embodied engagement in relationships, sensitive mirroring or shared use of creative props. Images of footage showing moments of connection and successful interactions were shown to the children as the therapy ended and their responses were witnessed and received by the adults. Video narrated the children's experiences and watching them provided a channel for the children to process their experiences (Tortora, 2006). Some children were curious, looking on intermittently whilst smiling or calling out their own name. Moments of significant interaction could be reviewed and relived by the group, acknowledging the children's unique contributions (Tortora, 2006).

Learning disability CAMHS

Children referred for support in this setting have moderate to profound learning disabilities and other difficulties (genetic, neurodevelopmental[1] or medical conditions). Often children experience delays in various areas of development (health, social, psychological and/or educational) and have physical, cognitive or communication impairments. Caregivers tend to seek support in their journey of accepting and understanding their child. Often changes can be made and improvements are observed when caregivers learn to understand nonverbal behaviour as communication. We also see further understanding of their child's inner world, when caregivers are attuned to their own ways of communicating nonverbally (gesturing, signing, listening and mirroring the sounds their child makes).

Within parenting groups

Video was incorporated within a parenting group program for children with a learning disability whose developmental age was between three and eight years (this was a group for children without autism, as there were other evidence-based programs tailored for this condition). Mid-program, following a play and praise training, we organised a filming session where caregivers were asked to play with their child. The videos were analysed by my colleague (a clinical psychologist) and me in order to find suitable clips where caregivers could gain insight into their parenting interactions and style. We would look for moments of shared enjoyment, joint attention or affection in the interactions. During analysis, we noticed that different movement qualities and personality traits were initiated depending on whom the child played with (e.g. mum or dad). This highlighted the significance that different relationships and interactions can have on the presentation of a child or young person.

When the videos were watched in the group, caregivers were asked to think together about the strengths of their parenting interactions. Images from the video were also used as stills to think about particular moments that highlighted shared enjoyment or where caregivers were connecting with their children with attentiveness. We found the use of child–caregiver images to be a powerful form of feedback due to the communicative strength of visual stills and video, particularly when English was not the first language for caregivers. As Cross and Kennedy (2011) explain, visual processing of emotions comes prior to our cognitive response. Therefore, when caregivers see themselves responding to a child positively, a strong emotional connection and a 'neurological response to experiencing and seeing attunement' (2011: 64) comes forth.

Caregivers demonstrated new perspectives about ways to further the play of their children. For example, one mother observed that she was asking many questions to her boy in an effort to teach him rather than playing. One father noticed that he had steered his son away from objects that he was interested in, rather than accepting, joining and expanding his child's play. Caregivers reflected on their own responses and some shared experiences of not being able to find ways to play with their child and of not understanding some of their needs (e.g. sensory seeking or avoidance behaviours, difficulties in emotional regulation, or lack of skills for interactive play). Feedback was provided about encouraging aspects of their interactions and communication alongside difficulties. A number of caregivers became more focused on how their actions could be maintaining difficulties that their child presented with. This prompted my curiosity about how video could be used to positively support caregivers of children with disabilities, and my interest in working individually with child–caregiver cases.

Complexities and progress: A case story

I use video with families for targeted work. For example, I provided long-term support for a parent and her three-year-old daughter (whom I will call Amanda) for feeding problems related to Amanda's development and disability. Amanda was born prematurely, had global developmental delay, a hearing impairment and speech and language difficulties. She required enteral[2] feeding and experienced significant delay in her feeding skills. Amanda's mother (whom I will call Jemima) experienced significant stress and trauma as a consequence, which brought tension and strong emotions to her relationship with her daughter. Herman (1997) describes how trauma can dominate and take over initially healthy family relationships. Research shows that distress and trauma can result in child–caregiver interactions becoming less sensitive (Velderman, 2011). Noticeably sensitive parental responsiveness is key in secure attachment formation (Celebi, 2014) and feeding (Didehbani and Kelly, 2011).

A primary and instinctual need for a mother is to feed her child (Douglas, 2000); however, barriers due to Amanda's developmental journey led Jemima to force feed her daughter. In turn, Amanda refused food from her mother.

Caregivers of children with disabilities 71

This can be extremely traumatising for infants and caregivers, further complicating the feeding process: 'Continued rejection of food can be experienced as rejection by the parent and feelings of desperation, frustration and depression can build up' (Douglas, 2000: 45). Amanda tried to regulate her own bodily functions and communicate her needs to her mother; however, her nonverbal cues were misread. Jemima did not understand the meaning of Amanda turning her body away at meal times or walking out of the room. Various interventions were offered to improve Jemima's understanding of her child's developmental abilities and difficulties. These included individual sessions to formulate and devise strategies in line with evidence-based parenting approaches. Jemima was referred to adult psychological services and the assessment highlighted how mum was experiencing severe anxiety and depression. When talking to Jemima, it became apparent that some of her core beliefs were quite concrete (Blisset *et al.*, 2005) and difficult to reframe. She would tell me that her child 'does not eat'. I observed that Amanda was able to eat selective foods in small portions; she was in fact overweight. Practical approaches including messy play and cooking sessions were tried in order to increase her exposure to a variety of foods. Jemima was shown when to praise Amanda on the occasions when food was explored through her senses, when she smelt, touched or licked different types of food. School observations and liaison with other multidisciplinary professionals offered holistic support to the family. However, the most significant changes were made when video was introduced as a way of thinking about what Jemima saw in their interactions at mealtimes.

DMP works on the premise that body posture and movement reflect emotional and psychological processes. During an early video of a mealtime, I noticed that Jemima sat near to Amanda but her body was turned away from her. Jemima's facial expressions showed sadness, frustration and despair when Amanda would only eat a few spoonsful of food. Her body formed a narrowing, contracted and hollowing shape (Kestenberg Amighi *et al.*, 1999).[3] Jemima's body attitude was sunken and collapsed (Barteneiff and Lewis, 1980).[4] Accompanying this physical embodiment, she used negative words and sentences, which created further distance and brought negative emotions to mealtimes. I distinctly recall leaving the family home embodying these feelings, as if I was carrying the burden and lack of hope for change. When I showed the video to my supervisor, she highlighted a number of strengths that Amanda was showing regarding her feeding (e.g. touching and playing with food and putting new foods to her mouth). However, I felt that Jemima's communications with me, her everyday experiences and general mental state overshadowed any progress that Amanda made.

Stress and anxiety can suppress appetite and the physiological feeling of hunger (Berlin *et al.*, 2009; Mitchell *et al.*, 2013). There may be a lot of tension at mealtimes, particularly when a parent is keen for their child to eat. Factors relating to Jemima's relationship to Amanda appeared to be maintaining the feeding problems. There was also a lack of space to think about Amanda's emotions and experience. Intrusiveness and control became part of everyday mealtime interactions and there was an absence of satisfaction and fun. Video stills were shown to Jemima to support her in developing attunement with her daughter. Jemima noticed that she was sitting at a distance from Amanda, often looking away from her. We thought together about the importance of family meal times, where Amanda could learn from her mother through social modelling. Development and progression through the 'steps to eating hierarchy' (Toomey and Sundseth Ross, 2011) takes place when children watch their caregiver touching, interacting with, smelling or chewing their own food. Evidence about the function of mirror neurons supports this advice. As research suggests, simply observing the actions of another provides the viewer with the same brain activation and feeling. Wolf *et al.* (2001) refer to the mirror neuron system as the biological correlate of intersubjectivity. Research also evidences the neurological response to seeing and experiencing attunement: 'Through the mirror neuron system for action and the viscera motor centres for affect, the same neurons are activated in the observer as the actor' (Forsyth and Sked, 2011: 146). Holding this in mind, I was concerned about the emotional strain on Amanda and her mother due to the fact that when chronic and persistent feeding concerns present, child–caregiver dyads experience distress numerous times in a day. I observed that pleasure within their relationship was minimal and many other positive aspects of their relationship were absent. I therefore anticipated that it would take time to facilitate significant progress.

I recall feeling positively astounded when a video towards the end of our work (around thirteen months) showed connectedness between Jemima and Amanda, who sat in closer proximity, facing each other. Jemima was encouraging Amanda to eat using positive verbal and nonverbal communication and shorter sentences. She also accompanied her speech with gestures when communicating with her daughter. She said 'mummy's turn', then 'Amanda's turn', and used visually clear signals like a thumbs up when Amanda did something that she wanted to encourage. This led to independent eating and self-feeding, which in the past was rarely observed. Not only that, but Jemima was attuned to Amanda, enjoying her company. She watched her with merriment, waited for her communication and followed her lead in a dance of reciprocity (Jarvis and Polderman, 2011). There was a beautiful moment when Jemima mirrored Amanda, who was moving her head, tilting it side to side playfully whilst chewing. Amanda smiled in response, and looked at me as if to share this connection. I had never seen them interacting this way before.

When looking back at the final video with Jemima, she noticed that they were turning towards each other, making good eye contact and smiling at each other. Jemima shared that Amanda looked happy and said that things were much better and that her daughter was now eating more. Amanda seemed more at ease with Jemima and would turn towards her seeking interaction. She seemed less anxious in her body and more contained at mealtime and around Jemima; consequently, there was a greater sense of reciprocity and behaviour that she welcomed. As the Solihull Approach (2008) explains, first there needs to be containment of emotions and attunement from caregivers providing the infant with the experience of feeling understood. Only then can there be reciprocity, intersubjectivity and meaningful communication. Herman (1997) describes this change as occurring with the support of a healing relationship. Using video reflectively supported Jemima in increasing her attuned sensitivity (Music, 2011). This brought to life the bond between her and her daughter (Tortora, 2006). Jemima developed better understanding of her daughter's facial expressions and body language and I witnessed greater symbiosis and synchrony in the movements between mother and daughter. Sharing tension flow rhythms[5] (Sossin, 1999) evidences greater trust in the child–caregiver relationship. More comfort, parental empathy and adjustment took the place of conflict in Jemima's interaction with Amanda. Jemima was now able to imitate her daughter's nonverbal communication and further attune to her emotions. As Shai and Belsky (2011) explain, when caregivers have an embodied relational perspective of their child, this supports communication and attunement within the child–caregiver interactions. They describe this as parental embodied mentalizing (PEM),[6] which provides caregivers with opportunities to observe whole body movements of their child and to hypothesise about their mental state.

This leads me to 'Video Interactive Guidance' (VIG), an approach that incorporates mentalization and improves child–caregiver relationships.

Video Interaction Guidance

VIG is a relationship-based intervention that promotes attunement, empathy and well-being (Kennedy *et al.*, 2011). VIG has built on the work of Trevarthen (2001), who researched the subtle turn-taking interactions between caregivers and infants. Beebe and Stern (2013) also had a significant influence in thinking about attachment and attunement between caregivers and infants using video. VIG aims to 'rekindle communication within important relationships' by sensitively focusing on strengths and principles of attunement (Kennedy *et al.*, 2011: 13).

As a way of measuring outcomes and collaboratively deciding upon what change the family wish to make, a 'helping question' is created. VIG is a solution-focused approach where new narratives can be developed and difficulties can be received[7] (Celebi, 2014). VIG asks families to define a specific area where they wish to see change. The value of the intervention is then measured by clients rating between 1 ('not met') and 10 ('achieved'), at the beginning and at the end of an intervention (AVIGuk, 2013). Holding the helping question in mind, video of the child–caregiver interaction is then recorded. As the practitioner, one is looking for 'better than usual moments' (Kennedy *et al.*, 2011: 22), highlighting what one wants to see more often between the child and caregiver. The videos are micro-analysed (reviewed to find successful moments of caregiver-sensitive responses and child-led initiatives). The aim of the intervention is to promote successful communication: the heart of attuned interactions. A shared review[8] then takes place and the selected video clips or stills are explored in conversation with the client (in my work, this has been with the caregivers of young people with a moderate to profound disability). These reflective sessions are structured around thinking and looking for attuned interactions in the relationships between infant and caregiver. As a supportive parallel, shared reviews are also filmed and later viewed during VIG supervision,[9] when both child–caregiver and caregiver–practitioner footage is reviewed and analysed (Silhanova and Sancho, 2011).

VIG is informed by social constructionism, which posits that meaning is co-constructed through the framework of the interpersonal relationship (Kennedy *et al.*, 2011). Reliving vital moments in VIG parallels systemic appreciative inquiry (Hedges, 2005) in terms of how progress is thought about with clients. Change occurs partly through analysis of discourse and language that is used by caregivers (Cross and Kennedy, 2011). Reflective dialogue is drawn from both looking at the selected attuned images and the process of caregivers connecting with intuitive emotional responses. Practitioners may help caregivers to deepen their thinking by encouraging them to receive the initiatives of the other before responding, or by redirecting the attention back to the image or video chosen. According to Cross and Kennedy (2011), intersubjectivity and mediated learning are then actualised; care-giver attitudinal changes are identified and caregiver stress significantly reduces whilst self-confidence in parenting increases (Fukkink *et al.*, 2008).

I have found that collaborative video analysis and reflection leads to change in how parents think about their children. In the face of specific concerns and systemic difficulties, hope and strengths-based approaches such as VIG reinforce attachments (Cross and Kennedy, 2011). Often caregivers formulate their helping questions as if the problem belongs to the child. As Winnicott (1960: 587) said, 'there is no such thing as an infant'; with an infant comes a caregiver upon whom the infant depends. The child–caregiver relationship shapes how the infant responds and relates to the world. With space for reflection, caregivers can begin to see how self–other relational processes contribute to the child's presenting problem (Beebe and Lachmann, 2003). Looking at selected material together, caregivers seeking support begin to think more about themselves in relation to their child. For caregivers, re-witnessing interactions between themselves and their child increases their sense of responsibility regarding their emotional expression and coping. I have found that supporting caregivers to recognise and reflect upon positive interactions brings change in the helping question score and child–caregiver relationships.

VIG helps caregivers to develop observation skills and recognise reasons for successful interactions (James, 2011). One mother recently expressed that her child did not become as distressed when she (the mother) used a softer tone of voice and was more patient with him. Caregivers are supported to consider what they think might be going through their child's mind and also their own. Through exploration of internal representations of mental states and potential assumptions about mentalized thoughts, caregivers were able to consider the impact of self on other (Fonagy *et al.*, 2007). Initially caregivers shared a concrete or rational thought such as 'my mum is feeding me' or 'she likes the game'. However, with practice and support with using more reflective thinking, caregivers accessed more poignant thoughts about what their child may be thinking, like 'mummy loves me' (a quote from a parent whose child presented with behavioural challenges) or 'my daughter does not like it when someone leads her play' (a quote from a mother who was not providing space for her child to initiate interaction).

The role of the practitioner is to ask open questions that evoke thinking processes and psychological mind-mindedness (where the child's mind is held in the caregiver's mind). I find that asking questions about what the caregiver imagines that their child is thinking during reviews of visual images enables caregivers to learn how to mentalize interactively (Fonagy and Target, 1997; Fonagy *et al.*, 2007). This process can support caregivers in developing understanding about how their children think and feel, despite their difficulties with learning, social interaction, communication and flexibility of thinking. This may be particularly important with children who have autism, as research indicates that inferring what others may be thinking or feeling (Baron-Cohen, 2008) can be limited. Caregivers therefore often need to anticipate what their child may need or be experiencing. Communication difficulties can mean that children struggle to express what they want, especially when feeling emotional or stressed. Using visuals and maintaining structure and familiarity to support predictability can therefore be very helpful. However, caregivers also need to think about how their child may be feeling and thinking to reinforce their holistic well-being (James *et al.*, 2012). VIG supports caregivers of children with autism to adopt a culture of curiosity, to think about the intentions and behaviours of their child whilst considering their own thoughts, beliefs and ideas that shape their interactions (Gibson, 2014).

Research has also shown that VIG can increase initiatives in children with ASD (Forsyth and Sked, 2011). As caregivers become more aware of the difficulties and abilities of their child, more attuned responses are stimulated, which increases opportunities for social interaction. By using analysed video of 'better than usual moments', caregivers can focus on the connection and shared attention in their relationship, positively reinforcing principles of attuned interactions. VIG facilitates learning about antecedents for emotions and behaviours for children, alongside providing substance for development of effective methods to support emotional self-regulation (Loman, 1995). As an example, following VIG intervention, caregivers shared that they now appreciate a wider variety of channels that their child uses to communicate with them. VIG reinforces caregivers' positive feelings about parenting.

As an accredited training and evidence-based practice in itself, VIG lends itself particularly well to the areas of child and family work, reflective practice (Kennedy *et al.*, 2015), staff support, training and learning about specific conditions such as ASD. DMP specifically focuses on intersubjectivity, nonverbal communication and emotional reciprocity, which are particularly significant in learning disabilities (Karkou, 2010). VIG is therefore a compatible approach with DMP as both approaches are attentive to transference[10] and countertransference[11] processes. In both DMP and VIG, empathy and attunement to the caregiver's mental state, modelled by the therapist, contributes to the caregiver's ability to attune to their child (Kennedy *et al.*, 2015).

I have used VIG to think with caregivers about specific concerns, including feeding, anxiety and attachment in parenting a child or young person with a disability. Moving forwards, I have combined DMP and VIG principles to microanalyse nonverbal communication and understand interpersonal dynamics within our family therapy clinic. I also potentially have the opportunity to provide VIG for children and families in the trauma and attachment pathway and with premature babies and their families.

Recent economic, social and political pressures in psychology and psychotherapy public services, has led me to see how an approach like VIG could be of great benefit. Research shows effective results after six sessions (three filming sessions and three shared reviews) and documents that additional sessions do not show statistically significant improvements in outcomes generally. Without denying the value of long-term work, VIG is proving a very beneficial method for producing positive outcomes; its success over such a short course of sessions could also prove economically useful in times of austerity (Kennedy *et al.*, 2015).

VIG has a broad application, and research evidence is being gathered to date across a range of areas, including educational and clinical psychology, children services, community care and the criminal justice system; specific learning disabilities research into VIG include parenting sensitivity and child attachment security (Celebi, 2014; Fukkink *et al.*, 2008); interventions with children diagnosed with ASD (Landor *et al.*, 2014; Loughran, 2010) and deaf or hard of hearing children (Lam-Cassettari *et al.*, 2015), parenting in the area of neglect and child maltreatment (Cyr *et al.*, 2015); and premature babies (Hoffenkamp *et al.*, 2015) and trauma (de Zulueta, 2015). VIG is specifically recommended in the National Institute for Health and Care Excellence (NICE) guidelines (2012) for the development of attachment and attunement in child–caregiver relationships and is recommended by the National Society for the Prevention of Cruelty to Children (NSPCC) for children who have experienced neglect (Whalley and Williams, 2015).

In summary

As a DMP, I find the use of video recordings a very exciting way of working. In my journey to date, I have found that video can be used effectively within sessions for individual work and parenting groups.

Integrating video recordings into the various clinical contexts described in this chapter, I am able to work in a psychotherapeutic way, observing and looking back with caregivers at visual data. Video recordings enable me to explore, together with caregivers, how they are relating, communicating, containing and connecting with their children. I have the opportunity to observe the movements that children and families make individually and in relation to each other. Detailed analysis can be undertaken, frame by frame, thereby supporting caregivers to reflect on moments prior to attuned interactions. Such insight into the dynamic of their relationship with their child enables a deeper and broader appreciation of what is possible for them to nurture in future interactions. The use of video supports me to witness how the body and movement can highlight strengths-narratives within child–caregiver interactions (Gibson, 2014).

Using video complements the work that I facilitate as a dance movement psychotherapist. It is a tool that enables me to zoom into the intersubjectivity in relationships and adds layers in support of my thinking about attachment and trauma.

Notes

1 ASD is a neurodevelopmental disorder and is not classified as a learning disability. Children can have ASD and not have a diagnosis of a learning disability.
2 Enteral is a term used here for when food is passed through the intestine through an artificial opening. Amanda was fed via a nasogastric tube.
3 Kestenberg Movement Analysis is the comprehensive system for identifying psychological, developmental, emotional, cognitive and global health or imbalance through movement observation, notation and interpretation.
4 Bartenieff Fundamentals are a set of principles for corrective body movement exercises, based on concepts and principles of kinesthetic functioning.
5 Periodic alternations in muscle tension create discernable patterns called tension flow rhythms. Attuning to or sharing the same tension flow rhythms creates the foundation for empathy and communication (Kestenberg *et al.*, 1999).
6 PEM is parental capacity to conceive and understand an infant's mental state from the infant's kinaesthetic expressions.
7 Verbal and nonverbal communication is received prior to the practitioner responding. This supports the client being actively engaged in their own journey.
8 A specific session where a caregiver and practitioner look back on micro-moments of video footage, reflecting on what is seen, felt and thought. The practitioner is following a manualised guide to ensure successful attuned interaction occurs between themselves and the caregiver whilst discussing the child–caregiver interaction.
9 A specialist and therapeutic competence-based supervision provided for the VIG practitioner. VIG is a video-evidenced method of training through supervision and accreditation.
10 Transference is a phenomenon whereby unconscious feelings are redirected in the present from one person to another yet relate to feelings experienced in childhood relationships.
11 Countertransference is where complex feelings are evoked in the psychotherapist by a client.

References

Baron-Cohen, S. (2008) 'Theories of the autistic mind'. *The Psychologist*, 21(2): 112–116.
Bartenieff, I. and Lewis, D. (1980) *Body Movement: Coping with the Environment.* New York: Gordon and Breach Science.
Beebe, B. and Lachmann, F. (2003) 'The relational turn in psychoanalysis: A dyadic systems view from infant research'. *Contemporary Psychoanalysis*, 39(3): 379–409.
Beebe, B. and Steele, M. (2013) 'How does microanalysis of mother-infant communication inform maternal sensitivity and infant attachment?' *Attachment and Human Development*, 15(5–6): 583–602.
Beebe, B. and Stern, D. (1977) 'Engagement-disengagement and early object experiences'. Freedman, M. and Grand, S. (eds.) *Communicative Structures and Psychic Structures.* New York: Plenum Press.

Berlin, K. S., Davies, W. H., Lobato, D. J. and Silverman, A. H. (2009) 'A biopsychosocial model of normative and problematic paediatric feeding'. *Children's Health Care*, 38: 263–282.

Berrol, C. (2006) 'Neuroscience meets dance/movement therapy: Mirror neurons, the therapeutic process and empathy'. *The Arts in Psychotherapy*, 33(4): 302–315.

Blisset, J., Meyer, C., Farrow, C., Bryant-Waugh, R. and Nicholls, D. (2005) 'Maternal core beliefs and children's feeding problems'. *International Journal of Eating Disorders*, 37: 127–134.

Bloom, K. (2006) *The Embodied Self: Movement and Psychoanalysis*. London: Karnac.

Bowlby, J. (1982) 'Attachment & loss'. *Vol. 1: Attachment* (Second Edition). London: Hogarth Press.

Celebi, M. (2014) 'How video interaction guidance can promote attuned parenting'. *Journal of Health Visiting*, 2(2): 2–7.

Cross, J. and Kennedy, H. (2011) 'How and why does VIG work?' Kennedy, H., Landor, M. and Todd, L. (eds.) *Video Interactive Guidance: A Relationship-Based Intervention to Promote Attunement, Empathy and Wellbeing*. London: Jessica Kingsley.

Dawson, G. and Galpert, L. (1990) 'Mothers' use of imitative play for facilitating social responsiveness and toy play in young autistic children'. *Development and Psychopathology*, 2: 151–162.

Didehbani, N. and Kelly, K. (2011) 'Role of parental stress on paediatric feeding disorders'. *Children's Health Care*, 40: 85–100.

Douglas, J. (2000) 'Behavioural approaches to the assessment and management of feeding problems in young children'. Southall, A. and Martin, C. (eds.) *Feeding Problems in Children: A Practical Guide*. Oxon: Radcliffe.

Fonagy, P. and Target, M. (1997) 'Attachment and reflective function: Their role in self-organisation'. *Development and Psychopathology*, 9: 679–700.

Fonagy, P., Gergely, G. and Target, M. (2007) 'The parent-infant dyad and the construction of the subjective self'. *Journal of Child Psychology and Psychiatry*, 48(3/4): 288–328.

Forsyth, P. and Sked, H. (2011) 'VIG when working with children and adults on the autistic continuum'. Kennedy, H., Landor, M. and Todd, L. (eds.) *Video Interactive Guidance: A Relationship-Based Intervention to Promote Attunement, Empathy and Wellbeing*. London: Jessica Kingsley.

Fukkink, R. G. (2008) 'Video feedback in the widescreen: A meta-analysis of family programs'. *Clinical Psychology Review*, 28(6): 904–916.

Gibson, K. A. (2014) 'Appreciating the world of autism through the lens of video interaction guidance: an exploration of a parent's perceptions, experiences and emerging narratives on autism'. *Disability and Society*, 29(4)568–582.

Hedges, F. (2005) *An Introduction to Systemic Therapy with Individuals: A Social Constructionist Approach*. Basingstoke UK: Palgrave Macmillan.

Herman, J. (1997) *Trauma and Recovery: The Aftermath of Violence-From Domestic Abuse to Political Terror*. New York: Basic Books.

Hoffenkamp, H. N., Tooten, A., Hall, R. A. S., Braeken, J., Eliens, M., Vingerhoets, A. J. J. M., and van Bakel, H. J. A. (2015) 'Effectiveness of hospital based video interaction guidance on parental interactive behaviour, bonding, and stress after preterm birth: A randomised controlled trial'. *Journal of Consulting and Clinical Psychology*, 83(2): 419–429.

Horigian, V., Robbins, M. and Szapocznik, J. (2004) 'Brief Strategic Family Therapy'. *Brief Strategic and Systemic Therapy: European Review, 1, 251* 271.

James, D. (2011) 'VIG in the context of childhood hearing impairment: A tool for family-centred practice'. Kennedy, H., Landor, M. & Todd, L. (eds.) *Video Interactive Guidance: A Relationship-Based Intervention to Promote Attunement, Empathy and Wellbeing*. London: Jessica Kingsley.

James, D. M., Hall, A., Phillipson, J., McCrossan, G. and Falck, C. (2012) 'Creating a person-centred culture within a North East Autism Society: Preliminary findings'. *British Journal of Learning Disabilities*, 41: 296–303.

Jarvis, J. and Polderman, N. (2011) 'VIG and attachment: Theory, practice and research'. Kennedy, H., Landor, M. and Todd, L. (eds.) *Video Interactive Guidance: A Relationship-Based Intervention to Promote Attunement, Empathy and Wellbeing*. London: Jessica Kingsley.

Johnstone, L. and Dallos, R. (2006) *Formulation in Psychology and Psychotherapy: Making Sense of People's Problems*. London: Routledge.

Jonsson, C., Clinton, D., Fachmann, M., Mazzaglia, G., Novak, S. and Sorhus, K. (2001) 'How do mothers signal shared feeling states to their infants? An investigation of affect attunement and imitation during the first year of life'. *Scandinavian Journal of Psychology*, 42(4): 377–381.

Karkou, V. (2010) *Arts Therapies in Schools: Research and Practice*. London: Jessica Kingsley.

Kennedy, H., Landor, M. and Todd, L. (2011) *Video Interactive Guidance: A Relationship-Based Intervention to Promote Attunement, Empathy and Wellbeing*. London: Jessica Kingsley.

Kennedy, H., Landor, M. and Todd, L. (2015) *Video Enhanced Reflective Practice: Professional Development Through Attuned Interactions*. London: Jessica Kingsley.

Kestenberg Amighi, J., Loman, S., Lewis, P. and Sossin, K. M. (eds.) (1999) *The Meaning of Movement: Developmental and Clinical Perspectives of the Kestenberg Movement Profile*. London: Brunner-Routledge.

Lam-Cassettari, C., Wadnerkar-Kamble, M. B. and James, D. M. (2015) 'Enhancing parent-child communication and parental self-esteem with a video-feedback intervention: Outcomes with prelingual deaf and hard-of-hearing children'. *Journal of Deaf Studies and Deaf Education*, 20(3): 266–274.

Loman, S. (1995) The case of Warren: A KMP approach to autism. Levy, F. (ed.) *Dance and Other Expressive Art Therapies: When Words Are Not Enough*. London: Routledge.

Mitchell, G. L., Farrow, C., Haycraft, E. and Meyer, C. (2013) 'Parental influence on children's eating behaviour and characteristics of successful parent-focused interventions'. *Appetite*, 60: 85–94.

Music, G. (2011) *Nurturing Natures: Attachment and Children's Emotional, Sociocultural and Brain Development*. Hove, UK: Psychology Press.

Rossiter, R., Armstrong, H., Legg, G. and Woodrow, J. (2015) 'Delivering psychological services for children and young people with learning disabilities and their families'. Faulconbridge, J., Law, D. and Laffan, A. (eds.) *The Child and Family Clinical Psychology Review*. Leicester: The British Psychological Society.

Shai, D. and Belsky, J. (2011) 'When Words Just Won't Do: Introducing Parental Embodied Mentalizing'. *Child Developmental Perspectives*, 5(3): 173–180.

Shields, J. and Stevens, J. (2008) *NAS EarlyBird Programme; Parent Book*. London: The National Autistic Society.

Silhanova, K. and Sancho, M. (2011) Kennedy, H., Landor, M. and Todd, L. (eds.) *Video Interactive Guidance: A Relationship-Based Intervention to Promote Attunement, Empathy and Wellbeing*. London: Jessica Kingsley, 43–57.

Solihull Approach. (2008) *The Solihull Approach Resource Pack—The First Five Years: A Resource Pack for Care Professionals Who Work with School-Aged Children, Young People and Parents.* Cambridge, UK: Jill Rogers Associates Ltd.

Sossin, M. (1999) 'The KMP and infant-parent psychotherapy'. Kestenberg Amighi, J., Loman, S., Lewis, P. and Sossin, K. M. (eds.) *The Meaning of Movement: Developmental and Clinical Perspectives of the Kestenberg Movement Profile.* London: Brunner-Routledge.

Stern, D. (1971) 'A micro-analysis of mother-infant interaction. Behavior regulating social contact between a mother and her 3 1/2-month-old twin'. *Journal of the American Academy of Child Psychiatry,* 10(3): 501–517.

Toomey, K. A. and Sundseth Ross, E. (2011) 'SOS approach to feeding'. *American Speech-Language Association,* 82–87.

Tortora, S. (2006) *The Dancing Dialogue: Using the Communicative Power of Movement with Young Children.* Baltimore, MD: Paul H. Brooks Publishing Co.

Trevarthen, C. (1977) 'Descriptive analysis of infant communication behaviour'. Schaffer, H. R. (ed.) *Studies of Mother-Infant Interaction: The Loch Lomond Symposium.* London: Academic Press.

Trevarthen, C. and Aitken, K. J. (2001) 'Infant intersubjectivity: Research, theory and clinical application'. *Journal of Child Psychology and Psychiatry,* 42(1) 3–48.

Velderman, M. K. (2011) 'VIG as a method to promote sensitive parent-child interaction'. Kennedy, H., Landor, M. and Todd, L. (eds.) *Video Interactive Guidance: A Relationship-Based Intervention to Promote Attunement, Empathy and Wellbeing.* London: Jessica Kingsley.

Winnicott, D. W. (1960) 'The theory of the parent-infant relationship'. *International Journal of Psychoanalysis.* 41: 585–595.

Wolf, N., Gales, M., Shane, E. and Shane, M. (2001) 'The developmental trajectory from amodal perception to empathy and communication: The role of mirror neutrons in this process'. *Psychoanalytic Inquiry,* 21: 94–112.

Online resources

AVIGuk (2013) 'Belfast simple record of initial and final outcome'. VIG evaluation form. Available at www.videointeractionguidance.net (Accessed 09/06/15).

De Zulueta, F. (2015) 'From pain to violence and how to break the cycle'. *TEDxEastEnd.* Available at www.youtube.com (Accessed 13/03/16).

Department of Health (2015) Future in Mind: Promoting, Protecting and Improving our Children and Young People's Mental Health and Wellbeing. Available at www.gov.uk/government (Accessed 16/01/16).

National Institute for Health and Care Excellence (NICE) (2012) *Social and Emotional Wellbeing: Early Years.* Available at www.nice.org.uk (Accessed 12/09/15).

Whalley, P. and Williams, M. (2015) 'Child neglect and Video Interaction Guidance. An evaluation of an NSPCC service offered to parents where initial concerns of neglect have been noted', 6–7. Available at www.nspcc.org.uk (Accessed 17/05/16).

Chapter 6

On becoming a Monkey

Sue Curtis

> It is said a great Zen teacher asked an initiate
> to sit by a stream until he heard all the water
> had to teach. After days of bending his mind
> around the scene, a small monkey happened
> by, and, in one seeming bound of joy, splashed
> about in the stream. The initiate wept and
> returned to his teacher, who scolded him lovingly,
> 'The Monkey heard. You just listened.'
> > 'The Monkey and the River' (in *The Book of*
> > *Awakening* by Mark Nepo, 2000: 211)

During my training as a dance movement psychotherapist (DMP) and the initial year after I graduated, like the studious initiate, I bent my mind and body around many clinical scenes. I reflected, moved, processed, read, and discussed, yet I wonder if I ever truly 'got wet'! Did I ever really allow the emotional waters of clients' material to teach me?

In some aspects of my work it was easier to 'bound' into the water, to be like the Monkey, for example, witnessing clients discover their creativity, leadership skills, make friendships and dance and move without fear of being judged. At these times the water was warm and inviting but very soon I would be challenged to submerge myself in what felt like deep, rough waters and the fear of drowning. How do we as therapists, at these times, take the risk to 'make the leap' and hear all the water has to offer? How do we create space for the unimaginable? How do we become like the Monkey?

In my second year of practice as a DMP, ten of my clients died. I was working in a residential school for children and young people with profound and complex needs and whilst some had potentially life-shortening conditions, the school had never had more than two students pass away in any one year. It was profoundly shocking and the impact of loss and grief within the school community resonated to its core. It did, however, prompt a school-wide training on loss and bereavement and I was fortunate to be part of the team receiving training (from Winston's Wish, a charity for bereaved children) and thinking together with other key staff on policies and practice. That year of what seemed like never-ending losses, sadness and supportive training changed my practice, but more importantly changed me, from therein and I am eternally grateful for all I learnt and for being nudged from the river bank to become like the Monkey!

During the following year, the bereavement team spoke openly and honestly together, sharing our vulnerabilities and debating many points. Many issues arose for consideration:

How and who inform staff and students when a student passes away? What space is given for the community to both mourn and celebrate the life of one of its members? What creative means could we use to facilitate understanding, especially with nonverbal students? What understanding and experience do staff have of death and how might this influence how we facilitate students in their feelings and experience of losing a peer? How do we support each other as a staff team? Who attends the funeral? What support can we offer to families?

What became clearer was the level of comfort individual staff had in feeling and talking about the pain of loss. For example, a huge issue arose when the family of one deceased student wanted him to lay in rest in the school hall and start the funeral procession from there. The mother tearfully said 'this school was his other home and we don't want him to lie in some strange funeral parlour, but lay in rest amongst those who cared and loved him!' Strong opinions and ethical considerations were debated vehemently; again the question of 'understanding' was raised and some staff felt it might encourage 'voyeurism'. But despite all the difficulties and debate, one thing was never in question – we had lost a valued and loved member of our community and they would be honoured and remembered. Eventually the team decided that what was paramount was the honouring of his parents' wishes in gratitude for the 'home' their son had been such a vital part of. He was reverently laid to rest in the central hall of the school and pupils were given the choice to visit him there if they wished.

When faced with the news of the death of a client, it is vital that as therapists we are informed as soon as possible in order to support each other and our clients. An issue debated at the residential school was when and how we wanted to be informed and who we wanted to inform us. Each staff member identified a colleague whom they felt they wanted to have break the news and whether or not they wanted to hear by phone or wait until they were at work in the case of an overnight or weekend death. In the event that any member of staff might not be reached, a picture of a flower was placed at every entrance to the school. Thus anyone who hadn't heard would immediately know a child had passed away and could seek out their colleague for details.

In relation to the pupils, it was interesting to note between us that not all staff thought that a pupil's keyworker was necessarily the best person to talk with a child. Initially we settled on the teacher telling them in class during the day or possibly the care manager if the news broke during the evening. As classes were small, on average six to eight pupils, there was a sense that the intimate, more family-based class setting was the best. However, when it came to the third death within one class, the teacher was so overwhelmed with losing half her class that special effort was made to bring in another known member of staff to support and assist her.

As a school, we recognised that at any point a staff member may need a moment out of the class to themselves and this should not be judged as being either unprofessional or as a sign of not coping, but seen as a normal response to grief and loss. Likewise, pupils could also take time out and the school made part of its grounds into a quiet, sensory area where staff and pupils alike could find some peaceful, uninterrupted space.

In contrast, years later, I worked in a day school and two students passed away within weeks of each other. The staff had never had any students pass away before and were deeply impacted by the loss. However, I was shocked to find nobody had informed me and had I not overheard a chance conversation I would have gone into my group unaware. What was even more shocking was that a decision was made not even to tell most of the school, as 'they wouldn't really understand anyway and those that could might get upset'! When I tentatively approached the head about the impact on staff and students, he said, 'I don't touch death with a barge pole[!] … Any staff that can't cope shouldn't be in the job.' Within a week the students' photographs were taken down and their names erased from the register. There was no space for staff or students to grieve. A trainee DMP, on placement with me at the time, burst into tears at the way things were handled. As a mother herself, she said, 'I would be devastated if the life of my child seemingly meant so little.'

In this instance, not only were the staff unsupported, but they were actually frightened of showing any emotion for fear of losing their jobs. Thus it became difficult to come together as a school community and a vital opportunity for modelling ways of working with and through grief was stifled and lost and replaced with a culture of denial.

Dyregrov (2008: 22) says that the most common immediate reactions of grief in children are 'shock and disbelief, dismay and protest, apathy and being stunned, and continuation of usual activities'. Perhaps the continuation of usual activities contributes to why Mallon (1998: 8) believes that grief is one of the great unacknowledged hurts that children face and that the impact of loss is too often denied; he cites adults saying, 'Oh look, Jenny is playing. See she's over it now. It didn't really affect her.' In working with children with complex needs and limited communication this can be particularly prevalent, and many times I have heard staff say 'they don't really notice' when discussing the responses of children to the death of a classmate.

Grey (2010: 9) states:

> [F]or professionals working in this area, it can be difficult to access our own thoughts and feelings. We can be left to carry some of the grief and loss of an individual or family. The unconscious processes that are involved not only can be powerful but may also offer a route into understanding.

It is vital that schools support pupils' needs and Holland (2016: 11) notes that for this to be achieved there must be 'a combination of power, awareness and commitment of senior staff'. Believing schools are a potential block of support, he states:

'[P]lanning is a key part of the bereavement response, and having a system in place before any loss will ensure that things can be considered at a time of calm. If a plan is not in place, the response will be ad-hoc and have to be re-thought each time' (2016: 19). He provides an extensive audit in chapter 2 (2016: 33–49) that can help identify what is in place and the strengths and gaps, as well as highlight areas for training. As Chadwick (2011: 10) encourages, 'with informed, wise staff the school can become the secure, nurturing environment the bereaved child needs and at the same time provide a golden opportunity to add to pupils' understanding'.

In working with vulnerable children, Goldman (2014) believes that unresolved grief leads to an inability to learn and results in overwhelming and powerful feelings that get trapped. She states:

> As long as we deny any issue of grief or loss, at-risk young people emerge in a lonely environment. By our acknowledgement of their losses, children will feel we are affirming their reality. One of our primary challenges is to recognize the breadth and scope of the issues involving and relating to grief and to emphasize the interrelationship between unresolved grief, emotional challenges, educational success, and responsible adulthood.
>
> (Goldman, 2014: xiv)

Since Kübler-Ross (1980) defined her well-known stages of death – denial and isolation, anger, bargaining, depression and acceptance – many writers have theorised about grief and bereavement (Webb, 2011; Doka, 1995; Dyregrov, 2008; Fox, 1985; Goldman, 2013; Holland, 2016; Judd, 2014; Mallon, 1998; Nash, 2011; Thompson and Neimeyer, 2014; Turner, 2006; Worden, 2009). Others have also thought about loss specifically in relation to clients with learning difficulties (Blackman, 2003; Cottis, 2008; Grey, 2010).

Fox (1985) proposes a model defining four tasks that face bereaved children – to understand, grieve, commemorate and move on. Worden (1991) also outlines a four-task model of grief: to accept the reality of the loss, to work through the pain of the grief, to adjust to the environment without the deceased, and to emotionally relocate the deceased and move on with life.

Blackman (2003) suggests that Worden's model may be popular with grief workers due to its focus on 'work to be done' and offer apparent clarity over a process that is not clear at all. She also purports that phase models of grief that suggest there will be an end point or resolution to the work of grief is contestable and that mourning is an ongoing process and the time-scale unique to the individual.

Grey (2010) considers the following important when assessing suitability for therapeutic work with clients with learning difficulties: readiness, consent, contraindications (medication change), spoken and receptive language, language of client and ability to sustain a therapeutic relationship. Blackman (2003) also outlines considerations for the therapist working with a learning disabled client: communication – from concrete to symbolic, knowledge, confidentiality and suggestibility.

As helpful as these models are, when it came to working in the sensory, nonverbal world with pupils with profound and complex needs, I found myself feeling deskilled and often at a loss as to how to support them within DMP sessions. Like the Monkey, I needed to make the leap into the bodily felt experience of loss. As Webb (2002: 3) poses, 'if adults cannot confront and make peace with their own fears about the end of life, how can they possibly consider the reality of death in the lives of children?'

Six years ago I was diagnosed with a rare cancer that left me physically disabled. During the worst time of treatment and the ravaging tumour's height, I lost the use of my legs and half my hands. Night times found me in a new landscape as, unable to sleep, I discovered the three to five a.m. 'environmental rituals' that had usually passed me peacefully by. The bird's early dawn chorus, the first morning aeroplane overhead, my neighbour returning from a night-shift at work, the various lights that went on and off; they came to be markers that I relied upon to see me through the darkness. I could never distinguish one bird call from another, but I came to know the emerging song. The sounds flowed over me, surrounded me, comforted me by their presence and I found myself wondering about what would happen if any of them disappeared. What if I disappeared?

Sunderland (2003) writes beautifully in *The Day the Sea Went Out and Never Came Back* about a sand dragon named Eric who experiences the terrible sadness and loss of the sea never returning. In those dark nights of my own illness, my body's decline, disability and subsequent road to partial recovery, I had to discover and experience my own grief and ways of coping.

I remember when my hands were numb and I couldn't gauge touch properly with my fingers. The incredible experience of loss of everyday actions, like running my fingers through my hair, being able to write or grasp objects successfully or fully sense the texture and shape of things, and not being able to use parts of my body for comfort. My body simply grieved for what had previously been known and felt, for something familiar that was no longer part of my landscape.

However, the experience also took me into a deeper reflection of years of clinical work and I found myself contemplating the sensory world of clients who had lost the sound, touch, smell and feel of a classmate. Those whose landscapes had been changed forever and yet, potentially, denied a space to notice and respond in the presence of another.

How do we then find creative and appropriate ways of helping children and young people through the painful experience of loss and, as DMPs, be open to words, movement, sensations and feelings as part of the process?

The film *Children of a Lesser God* (1986) portrays a love affair between Sarah, who is profoundly deaf, and James, a speech therapist. Sarah knows her body intimately, often swimming naked in a pool, floating and sensing the water. As they begin their relationship she tells him she knows what 'waves' sound like by portraying beautifully the movement of a wave crashing against her body and subsiding. However, later when she asks him to show her in movement what his beloved Bach music sounds like, he is at a loss. He cannot find in his body a way to communicate it to her.

Sarah remonstrates to James that he wants her to be a 'speaking person', saying 'let me be me! You want me to be a deaf person so that you can change me into a hearing person'. She tells him of how throughout her life people 'could never be bothered to learn my language. I was always expected to speak. Well I don't speak! ... Until you let me be an "I" the way you are, you can never come inside my silence and know me'. After a dramatic scene where she attempts to speak and screams she feels like a 'freak!!', she leaves him.

In the ensuing weeks, he attempts to understand her silent world, immersing himself, naked, in the swimming pool. Underwater he floats, feels, touches his skin gently, expands his arms and closes his eyes to imagine her world. He literally makes the leap!

Can we come inside the world of clients with profound learning difficulties without trying to fix or change them and learn their language of grief? Can we be brave enough to 'make the leap' into the simple yet often excruciatingly painful sense of 'gone'?

In highlighting the tasks of counselling in bereavement and loss Grey (2010: 91) denotes that

> the importance of naming feelings and identifying what happens and what initiates an emotional reaction is very important in enabling people with learning difficulties to make sense of their loss. Often pictures and illustrations can inform this process if words are not the best mode of communication.

In my work in both mainstream and special schools, I was always seeking out images of relationships, feelings and so on, that I hoped would provide a starting point for children and young people that for a variety of reasons found words difficult to access. However, it is the children themselves who have helped me most in this. For example:

George raced into the newly decorated therapy room, in lightning speed scanned the fifteen animal pictures and forty-plus feeling faces on the wall, jumped onto the table and announced 'You've forgotten one'. 'What one have I forgotten?' I asked. 'Heartbroken,' he whispered, 'that's how I felt when my Nan died'. The next day 'heartbroken' was duly added to my collection!

In the bereavement team at the residential school we talked together about having a box of props that we could use when supporting pupils including a family of puppets, treasure/memory boxes, photographs, things that could be filled and emptied, put together and taken apart and so on. It was an ever-expanding resource and the value of it embodied the conversations of staff who together puzzled over what particular objects might be meaningful for pupils with a variety of sensory needs. It also aided us as a team to remember that 'talking' about loss was not always necessary and that sometimes pupils just needed to play out scenarios and/or encounter materials.

In response to an intern who asks how to get a teen to talk about their feelings, Edgette (2012: 1) responds "'Don't worry about getting her to talk about her feelings," I say to Jean. "If you're doing anything close to what Hannah needs you to do, you won't have to. She'll show you what her feelings are.'" These words were particularly pertinent for my DMP work with one teenager.

Fourteen-year-old Josh has a degenerative illness. Alongside the experience of his own deteriorating physical function and daily pain, both his parents died within a short time of each other, one of whom dropped dead beside him. His elder brother could not take care of him and so he was placed in a residential school. The enormity of his losses – parents, home and family – weighed heavily on me as I read his case file. He had apparently received bereavement counselling but never wanted to speak in the sessions. He was referred to me in the hope that a more nonverbal setting would help him.

In our first meeting, Josh drove his electric wheelchair all around the room, surveying the feeling faces, asking questions about the soft play props and then came to settle by a sink in the room. Unable to turn on the taps himself he asked me to run the water and silently he watched it run away. Periodically he would ask for the plug to be put in and then, with great pain, reach a finger under its chain and release the water down the plughole. He would gaze in silence as the sink became empty. This became the main theme and activity for weeks to come – sitting together watching the water disappear.

One day he asked for some washing up liquid to be put into the water and for me to make bubbles with my hand. He became fascinated by when they would pop and more curious still when he managed to pull the plug out and see how long he could hold onto any on his hand before they burst. Slowly he started to talk:

> *Josh – 'Where does the water go?'*
> *Me – 'Where do you think it goes?'*
> *Josh – 'It goes away.'*
>
> pause
>
> *Josh – 'Where do the bubbles go? … They're gone, aren't they?'*
> *Me – 'Yes, they are gone.'*
> *Josh – 'They're gone forever, aren't they?'*
> *Me – 'Yes, those ones are gone forever.'*
> *Josh – 'We can make more bubbles, can't we?'*
> *Me – 'Yes we can but they will be different bubbles.'*
> *Josh – 'Cos the other ones are gone forever.'*

In the following weeks, Josh interspersed his time with the bubbles with another activity. He would ask me to stack up the soft play rolls and squares into towers and then turn up the speed of his wheelchair so that he could drive into them and watch them topple to the ground. This gave him much delight and amusement, yet I was struck by the force (given his fragility) with which he ploughed into them.

88   Sue Curtis

Sometimes he would swear at them and call them stupid; other times he drove in silence. One week I commented that he seemed angry with them and he looked away and mumbled quietly 'Yes'.

This pattern of exploring destructive crashing and painful emptiness imprinted deeply within me and eventually we could reflect together that in the therapy what was important for me to understand was that 'anger' and things that are 'gone forever' went together. It was the closest Josh had ever come to speaking about his unbearable losses.

Sometimes the playing out and moving with loss has even less words and can involve sensory exploration of a movement metaphor. In my work with children with profound and complex needs, so often I had watched them (post the loss of a peer) wandering and searching as if seeking familiar touch, rhythms, sounds and smells, desperately trying to locate themselves again in a changed landscape.

Grace has experienced the loss of two classmates within a few months of each other. At best she has a vocabulary of eight to ten words, but in recent weeks she has said very little. Her seizures have become more frequent and she sleeps a lot. Her usual sunny disposition has seemed dimmed by the sadness of her bereavement. In the DMP room she sits shakily resting upon one arm. As the group checks in I notice her scanning the mats, preoccupied with the space where the four large mats meet. Slowly she reaches out her hand and starts to claw at the join, then with supreme effort lifts a corner and looks underneath. She repeats this and I am captured by the poignancy of the moment: it is as if she is searching for something lost. The rest of the group watch her and I lie next to her and peek under the mat as she lifts another. 'Not there,' I say quietly and as she looks at me she slowly drops her head. I am consumed by sadness and the overwhelming sense of feeling bereft. It was hard to hold back the tears!

Endrizzi *et al.* (2014: 75) state that health care professionals need to take care of themselves in order to take care of patients and that to be effective in their career requires them to combine 'technical expertise with high levels of empathy, personal well-being and connectedness with others'. Furthermore, they continue, 'a health-professional needs to be able to console and continue to assist without breaking down'.

However, I think there are times when the balance between assisting and being part of a grieving community may be helpful in modelling responses to children. Whenever a pupil died at the residential school the whole community would come together to commemorate their life. It was known as a 'Memory Time' and great care was taken to include the whole community in its planning. Staff were invited to contribute, songs, stories, artwork or any other offering they felt they wanted. Advance notice was given and the parents of the deceased child were invited and generally always attended.

At Roberta's 'Memory Time' celebration students and staff file quietly into the hall. A large display of a giant pair of hands is before us and in turn everyone plants a sticker to decorate the nails. Roberta loved having her nails done and as the colours fill the hands her colourful spirit fills the room. Her favourite music is playing and for twenty minutes wheelchairs and standing frames are jostled into place amid bursts of groans, laughter and random words that fill the air.

As I sit and take in the scene, I notice a support worker, Milly, squeezing through the row of seats towards me. She whispers in my ear 'Louie wants to give you a hug' and points to where fourteen-year-old Louie's wheelchair is. I catch his eye as he is craning forward in his chair, shoulder straps preventing him from falling out. I make my way to him and he flings out his arm, hooks it around my neck (nearly choking me!) and pulls my head to his. Milly says, 'He thought you looked sad.'

The following month

During the 'Memory Time' of another child, I spoke personally to the community about my time with her. Half way through I began to cry, signalled for people to bear with me and then resumed my recollections. We have just exited the hall and Janelle drives her wheelchair towards me, muttering 'Sue sad – crying'. 'You saw me crying,' I say, 'I felt very sad thinking about her and miss her.' 'Me too,' echoes Janelle, 'it's sad.'

Grey (2010: 76) states that 'questions and assumptions may be made about "what happens next" in terms of where people "go" after death … it is best to work with their beliefs rather than try to impose your own'.

Adewale was twelve-years-old when he died. His 'Memory Time' was a lively, African extravaganza! His parents beamed with joy, danced along in their seat as his favourite songs bellowed out and wept openly when staff recalled their loving memories of him. Afterwards, we all gathered for food and drink and his parents circulated the room, carrying a small photo album, inviting staff to look through. I watched as some people froze in awkward confusion whilst others appeared moved and touched their heart. When they came to me I opened the pages to see images of Adewale on his deathbed, adorned in a beautiful Nigerian print robe, a kufi cap and looking like a Prince. They had simply wanted to show how peaceful Adewale was at his moment of passing and include staff in their experience.

In her work with bereaved parents, Callahan (2011: 192) found that 'embodying the bereaved parents' movements and experiences while attuning to their body tensions and sensations, allowed for a deeper understanding of what these parents experienced which, in turn, enabled this author to look at life with new knowledge and appreciation'.

Sensing Adewale's parents' joy, sharing that precious moment, was something I deeply appreciated and has stayed with me to this day.

Very often when a child died the family would invite staff and pupils to the funeral. There was never a question about the practicalities of transport and so on, but there was always debate about appropriateness.

In the tiny chapel, Janie's small coffin stands before us. Take That's 'A Million Love Songs' echoes through the room as the first teenager in her wheelchair motors up to the coffin to lay a single white rose on its lid. One by one six others on walking frames, splints and crutches are helped to lay their roses alongside. The poignancy and sadness of the moment is suddenly pierced by the agonising scream of Janie's mother 'JANIEEEEEEEE, JANIEEEEEEEEEE – NOOOOOOOO!' and she collapses onto the arm of her husband, sobbing uncontrollably as the coffin silently disappears behind a curtain.

I am reminded of the staff conversation the week before, the debate about who should attend the funeral, which pupils would understand and the concern that maybe some would 'disrupt' the service with their repetitive questions or shouting out. I ponder the irony that our pupils were the quietest there!

Three days later ...

Joel lies on his stomach in the therapy room, watching me intently as I position myself between the other group members and place the leaflet of songs, stories and photographs from Janie's funeral in the centre of the floor. He pulls on his arms, dragging his limp body behind him, making his way to the paper and with all his strength pushes up on his elbow to look at its contents. He cannot read and has no words but glances quickly from the paper to my eyes, as if pleading for me to reveal its story. I ask if he wants me to read it and he lurches upwards and he lets out a huge grunt. Slowly, I read all the words, sensing both his and other students' tiny movements, sounds and responses. When I get to the end his gaze intensifies and I have the feeling this has not satisfied his curiosity or questions. The room is heavy with sadness and the silence is palpable. His eyes are piercing mine and I ask if he wants to know more. He exhales another sound and I go on to tell him more about the funeral, who was there, what happened and so on, and also how I felt. His piercing gaze remains and his brow has furrowed with worry. I ask if he has a specific question. He exhales.

'Is it about the funeral?' – no response.

'Is it about Janie?' – no response.

'Is it about you?' – he exhales.

'Are you worried?' – he exhales.

'Are you worried this could happen to you?' – he exhales, grunts profusely and his body twists and arches.

Joel has managed to voice the unimaginable question: 'Am I next?'

It was tempting to try to reassure him that there was no reason to expect this would happen to him anytime soon, but my sense in that moment was this would be futile and not what was being asked. Rather, he just needed space to be heard and for me to stay present to his worries.

Supervision is central to allowing the often painful and difficult feelings arise to be present, to be felt and worked with, and not assume that 'thinking' and 'theory' will provide illumination. Sometimes grasping for theory can actually anaesthetise us to basic human concern, perhaps as a way of avoiding unimaginable loss.

One supervisee, Katie, described working with a blind teenager who would always reach for her head and place their foreheads together to connect. Katie found herself pondering the image of heads and brains and thinking, and one time said to her client, 'Yes I've been thinking about you.' Her client responded 'What's thinking?' Under supervision we re-enacted the scenario and again Katie began speaking about the experience – only when I got her to stop talking and thinking could we 'sense' together the client's fear that seemed transmitted through touch.

Another supervisee, Aisha, remarked that she always felt that she was standing behind a closed gate when working with a child who seemed lost and distant. I asked her to describe the gate and we discovered that it had a latch but was not locked. I simply said 'Open the gate!' and she laughed in acknowledgement that she had not in her mind considered this and the idea of playing symbolically with the material opened up a different perspective on the work.

Sometimes supervisees feel empty, helpless and hopeless in the face of overwhelming feelings of sadness and grief. Maria, a Spanish trainee, came to me on placement in tears. She said she simply had no words to describe her experience of working with the children – not in English or Spanish. She couldn't speak, think or feel, describing herself as being like stone. She wanted me to recommend books that would help her.

I encouraged her to work with the stone sensation and the following week she silently entered the supervision space with a handful of stones and a board. She said nothing, but in tears she began to drop the stones, one by one, seemingly at random. She nudged them, pushed them gently until surprisingly they formed a circle. She cried again at the image of their formation and this opened up her world of words to begin to process what lay within her.

In the film *Memoirs of a Geisha* (2005) there is a line: 'At the temple there is a poem called "Loss" carved into the stone. It has three words, but the poet has scratched them out. You cannot read loss, only feel it.'

Loss is a profoundly sensory experience that can leave a deep, bodily felt sense of missing of touch, smell, sound and physical presence. Finding a nonverbal movement language together with our clients to bring the unspoken and unconscious into a shared awareness can allow the unimaginable to be bearable.

In submerging myself in the emotional waters of grief and loss alongside children and young people with profound and complex needs, a wise staff team and numerous trainees and supervisees, I have found myself over the years attempting to become more like the Monkey and 'hear' all they have had to teach me. I am deeply grateful for this learning! If in turn I can teach you something in reading this chapter, it is simply this:

Make the leap!

References

Blackman, N. (2003) *Loss and Learning Disability*. London: Worth Publishing Ltd.
Callahan, A. B. (2011) 'The parent should go first: A dance/movement therapy exploration in child loss'. *American Journal of Dance Therapy*, 33(2): 182–195.

Chadwick, A. (2011) *Talking about Death and Bereavement in School: How to Help Children Aged 4 to 11 to Feel Supported and Understood*. London: Jessica Kingsley.

Cottis, T. (ed.) (2008) *Intellectual Disability, Trauma and Psychotherapy*. London: Routledge.

Doka, K. J. (ed.) (1995) *Children Mourning, Mourning Children*. London: Routledge.

Dyregrov, A. (2008) *Grief in Children: A Handbook for Adults (Second Edition)*. London: Jessica Kingsley.

Endrizzi, C., Bastita, R., Palella, P., Cossino, P. and D'Amico, G. (2014) 'Health workers faced with death: The influence of training language employed in the passage from life to death'. *Body, Movement and Dance in Psychotherapy*, 9(2): 74–81.

Fox, S. (1985) *Good Grief: Helping Groups of Children When a Friend Dies*. Boston: New England Association for the Education of Young Children.

Goldman, L. (2014) *Life and Loss: A Guide to Helping Grieving Children*. New York: Routledge.

Grey, R. (2010) *Bereavement, Loss and Learning Disabilities: A Guide for Professionals and Carers*. London: Jessica Kingsley.

Holland, J. (2016) *Responding to Loss and Bereavement in Schools: A Training Resource to Assess, Evaluate and Improve the School Response*. London: Jessica Kingsley.

Judd, D. (2014) *Give Sorrow Words: Working with a Dying Child (Third Edition)*. Third Edition. London: Karnac.

Kübler-Ross, E. (1980) *On Death and Dying*. London: Tavistock Publications.

Mallon, B. (1998) *Helping Children to Manage Loss: Positive Strategies for Renewal and Growth*. London: Jessica Kingsley.

Nash, P. (2011) *Supporting Dying Children and Their Families*. London: SPCK.

Nepo, M. (2000) *The Book of Awakening*. San Francisco: Conari Press.

Stanford, P. (2011) *The Death of a Child*. London: Bloomsbury.

Sunderland, M. (2003) *The Day the Sea Went Out and Never Came Back*. London: Speechmark Publishing Ltd.

Thompson, B. E. and Neimeyer, R. A.(eds.) (2014) *Grief and the Expressive Arts: Practices for Creating Meaning*. New York: Routledge.

Turner, M. (2006) *Talking with Children and Young People About Death and Dying: A Resource Paperback*. London: Jessica Kingsley.

Webb, N. B. (ed.) (2011) *Helping Bereaved Children: A Handbook for Practitioners (Social Work Practice with Children and Families)*. (Third Edition). New York: Guildford Press.

Worden, J. W. (2009) *Grief Counselling and Grief Therapy: A Handbook for the Mental Health Practitioner*, (Fourth Edition). London: Routledge.

Online resources

Edgette, J. S. (2012) 'Why teens hate therapy: mistakes therapists should avoid, psychotherapy networker'. Available at www.psychotherapynetworker.org (Accessed 13/05/16).

Winston's Wish (1992) 'The Charity for Bereaved Children'. Available at www.winstonswish.org.uk (Accessed 21/10/16).

Film

Children of a Lesser God (1986) Directed by Randa Haines [Motion Picture, DVD]. USA: Burt Sugarman Production.

Memoirs of a Geisha (2005) Directed by Rob Marshall [Motion Picture, DVD]. USA: Amblin Entertainment and Spyglass Entertainment and Red Wagon Entertainment.

Copyright acknowledgement

With thanks for permission to use excerpt from the following previously published work:
The Book of Awakening © by Mark Nepo used with permission from Red Wheel Weiser, LLC, Newburyport, MA, www.redwheelweiser.com.

Chapter 7

Finding a place of collaboration, co-created by clients, staff and therapist

Jacqueline Butler

Is this therapy? The question is often asked of me about working in non-clinical settings with adults with profound and multiple learning disabilities (PMLD).

I have always been certain that the dance movement psychotherapy (DMP) sessions, which I provide in what I am identifying as non-clinical settings, are of value and require a way of working, which I have developed and which has unfolded over a number of years. As a freelance practitioner, I provide sessional work for local government and private care providers and charities, in day centres and residential homes. Starting and running a DMP group in a setting which is not primarily a health care setting, requires a certain amount of flexible thinking for both myself and the setting. This chapter explains my reasoning and experience and offers a practical way of working with clients for whom this way of working can benefit.

My intense reactions and responses to the socio-political themes I encounter as soon as I cross the threshold of the setting have also had an impact on how I choose to work. I find that I cannot ignore the political aspects of working with people with PMLD who mostly cannot change their circumstances for themselves. To satisfy my curiosity, reservations and ethical stance, I have adapted my ways of working to offer what I understand to be the best service possible for the client. As a result, the emphasis of the DMP sessions has the focus of finding that which can be co-created (Parker and Best, 2007) by clients, staff and myself and which is a place where meaningful connections and relations occurs.

All material presented here is an amalgamation of experiences from different settings and does not relate to any particular group or person. The examples that I have used are those which I have witnessed in most or all settings and which are very similar.

Non-clinical settings

In using the term 'non-clinical setting', I am meaning those settings where there is no other psychotherapy or creative arts therapy service provision – where the service is not accustomed to having such practitioners and there is not a remit to work therapeutically. Consequently, there has to be negotiation about having the same private space, regular sessions, having consistent group members and how the work will be evaluated. Who will be responsible for handovers? Will I become involved in the multi-disciplinary team? The settings usually insist on there being members of staff present in the sessions. The settings in all probability will be considering the DMP sessions as an 'activity' and will not be familiar with thinking about gaining consent and contracts for clients who are attending sessions. Confidentiality is taken seriously at settings and it can be difficult for me as a non-team member to have access to personal information about clients.

Adults with profound and multiple learning disabilities

Participants range from those with mild/moderate learning disabilities to those with severe and PMLD. Eighty per cent of participants I have seen over the years have been diagnosed as severe to PMLD. The majority of clients with whom I work in groups are those who present with a combination of being nonverbal or have low ability to verbalise, are 'contact-impaired' (Prouty, 2002: 15) and need support for their physical and personal needs.

When considering assessments, referrals and contracts with service providers, it is evident that people with PMLD are almost never independent of another person for decision making and representation. Clients who have one-to-one support have to be accompanied by their support worker to sessions and so there are many practical considerations when working with a group where there is a range of abilities, medical conditions and behaviours. Staff are encouraged by their managers to attend the sessions; to support the clients because they will be in a new situation and with a new person, and primarily to aid in communication and understanding. All of this was frustrating for me in my role as a DMP during my first encounters in these situations, where I wanted to meet the clients in a safe private space. I have, however, made the conscious decision to persevere and work with what is on offer and with what is being presented. Over time, I have learnt that this scenario reflects the lives of many, if not all of those with learning disabilities – where the person has little control over their life. Practically, it is not always possible for each person to manage and run their lives, in the same way as it is not always possible for one person (i.e. a therapist) to facilitate a group without support.

When working with the clients, I am aware from their reactions that they are responding to me and my body, my nonverbal communication. However, what I feel in my body, my felt sense (Gendlin, 2003), is a feeling of disconnection and emptiness. I wonder about whether I am holding a nascent group (Sandel and Johnson, 1983), a group that is still forming. I now realise that I am meeting with people who are 'hidden' and hiding from themselves and others (Sinason, 1992), yet I have a strong sense that there is potential for connection and expression. I find a resonance with pre-therapy,[1] which is described as being 'used for clients who cannot utilise relationships because they are contact-impaired' (Prouty, 2002:15). The 'contact' which Prouty (2002) describes could be with reality, oneself or others, and being impaired hinders the psychological contact that is essential in the building of the therapeutic relationship. My perception is that there needs to be a stage with this client group, which can lead to the possibility of working psychotherapeutically, from a 'pre-expressive', 'withdrawn and isolated' state to an 'expressive' state (Prouty, 2002: 20). Pre-therapy theory supports my experience and DMP practice with those hard to reach. I find that making contact with my clients requires them being seen beyond their condition, to the point where they are able to begin to see themselves as a person and have a sense of self.

Stern's (1985: 111) notion of '[b]eing with' is vital to this client group as it offers a space and time to be present without expectation or judgement. Having permission for the clients and the group to 'be', and this being good enough, provides 'a potential space in which it is not important who does what; it is a place for relaxation, of freedom, where spontaneity arises' (Fischman, 2009: 40). With some groups, the ability to 'be' is the end result; with others; there is noticeable change in the behaviour and way of relating of the client(s). This is seen, for example, as soon as a happy mask disappears and a genuine expression of feelings is seen, in my witnessing of a genuine body-shaking laugh between people, or in the ambulant client bringing themselves to a session.

My reactions and responses to the environment

Experience in my practice with this client group over a number of years, has evidenced recurring themes of choice, power, survival, equality, boundaries, competition and being seen. These themes emerge at each setting, with their intensity varying over time. They impact on me most intensely outside of the DMP sessions, within each setting where I am embodying the environment and where I am part of the lived experience of the clients.

Examples of my embodied responses include:

My attention is drawn to the homogenous group identity and issues rather than seeing the individuals who make up the group. I may see a group of people sat together in a uniform 'shape', the texture of this shape, two-dimensional, nothing going on?

My reactions as I begin setting up DMP sessions are often very intense and the feelings disproportionate to, for example, the actual negotiations about referrals and assessments. I can have strong feelings of powerlessness as what I have put into place gets changed. Suspicion may arise in me as I wonder whether I am being judged; at times I feel as if I am on trial and have to prove myself (quickly) in order to stay; fear of annihilation, which may range from a mild flutter inside to a feeling as if I may disintegrate and die. All very relevant to the experience of a large percentage of people with learning disabilities. My lived experience and feeling the uncertainty when establishing a group joins with the very strong feelings which I am picking up from the clients and reflects their lived experience.

Most clients are unable to get themselves to the session and so rely on staff to ensure that they get there. I learnt that if I stayed in the DMP space and waited for clients to be brought in, I could find myself in the space with half of the group. I am then unable to leave the space to find the others who are due to attend. Resisting a strong embodied response that this is the way it is or that it does not matter, I spend time before the session gathering and reminding clients and members of staff that they are due to attend the DMP session. My felt sense when gathering the group can feel like going into battle and having to fight to just get the clients into the space. I can feel guilty when I am told that if I take someone into the session, they will miss out on a fun activity, or it might be that some other person may miss out because the staff member will be in the DMP session. I feel that I have to stand my ground and hold the line and not waiver to demonstrate that each client matters. The idea of the group is kept alive and there is a message that no one is forgotten. As I go to each client, reminding them and members of staff that they need to attend the DMP session, I stress how they are a core member of the group and the message is that they belong to and own this group. Those clients who can say a few words and those who are verbal will let me know where some clients are and will remind me to go and check for other clients.

Boundaries

Choosing to interact with clients outside of the DMP-designated group time and space alerted me to how boundaries for the clients and the system are malleable and, in some cases, non-existent. I seemed to be reflecting these 'flexible' boundaries by disclosing more about myself than I would with a different client group or setting. This being my attempt to build relationships between myself and others at the setting, and my modelling 'being seen'. Boundaries were an important subject for exploration in supervision until I realised that although I can stretch boundaries and may appear to be flexible and adaptable, there are certain conditions and practices which are non-negotiable for me, for the clients, for members of staff and the setting. This took time for me to identify, although I would become very indignant when these boundaries were crossed, not acknowledging that they were my non-negotiables, not necessarily that of others. Understanding and establishing my non-negotiables (see Table 7.1), those of the organisation,

Table 7.1 My non-negotiables

My non-negotiables
I will work with staff in the session
I am flexible with the to-ing and fro-ing of both clients and staff during a session
I am adamant that the idea of the group be taken seriously
That the clients can express choice
That there is an attitude of equality and respect in the room
That there is a structure to the session
That the same space is used for the sessions on a regular basis

98 Jacqueline Butler

the clients and members of staff is imperative when providing DMP with this client group at these settings. If the combined non-negotiables can be abided by, the intention demonstrated is that of respect and provides the foundation of trust which is essential for collaborative working, itself conducive of good psychotherapy practice.

Working together

The boundaries and non-negotiables arise from the context and follow social constructionist ideas as outlined by Parker and Best (2007:7) where 'meaning is created in terms of the particular context we privilege in any episode of interaction'. Parker and Best go on to explain how this allows the potential for creating 'new and more empowering contexts'. More recently, Wengrower (2015) wrote about working with the construct of resilience in non-clinical settings; in her writing, she challenges DMPs to widen our lenses in terms of our professional identity and to accept 'shifting the focus from deficit and pathology to health and prevention' (Wengrower, 2015: 165). Affirming the validity of the work in the DMP sessions, as they are forming in these non-clinical settings, allows me to utilise and work with the paradigm shift, which Wengrower (2015) describes, where there is an attitude of respect, an absence of judgement, encouragement of choice, and a place to 'be' rather than 'do'. I had to change my attitude to working with members of staff, let go of control and concentrate on that which was being co-created so that the DMP sessions could become a space where we could all experience being together in a different way.

Power

The DMP session reflects the system within which it exists and where 'relationships are displayed in the interactional movement behaviour' (Dulicai, 2009: 148). The roles and relationships between clients, staff and DMP are tempered by the norms of the system. My preference is for a collaborative way of working. However, this is not always possible, although within all settings I will give the time and effort required to gain the confidence and trust needed to work collaboratively. Can members of staff trust that I, the 'spy' in their midst, will not use any of their unguarded comments during sessions as information for management? Will all their movements be understood and analysed by the DMP who, they say, seems to be using magical powers to understand the clients?

Will I read their inner thoughts and then expose these to others? These are some of the tensions which I must consider.

Where the DMP sessions and I are being attacked by those involved with a setting or a client and there is no respite, difficult decisions have to be considered, such as to stop offering DMP in such a setting. The starting point for trying to understand what the client material and my experience is reflecting, is explored at individual and group supervision sessions which I regularly attend.

As the DMP in these sessions, I have to be courageous and express in words and movement that which I am embodying from the group and from individuals in that session. I mention the need for courage because I have experienced members of staff refuting my observations and felt sense and being thought of as deluded. It can feel unbearable to embody the experience of both the clients and the detractors and to stand by what I am experiencing, especially where I am unable to prove what I am saying, and where those members of staff who are in doubt are yet to appreciate speaking from an experience of what they feel in their body. Also, nonverbal people will not be able to confirm whether or not they identify with my experience. Those clients who can speak may not be able to articulate their experiences or they may not be taken seriously by the person(s) in which they confide. Integral to my DMP practice, I monitor my own state of being – before entering a session, I check in with myself to note my feeling state so that I am clear during a session how much of my thoughts and feelings belong to me rather than the clients or indeed staff. Unfortunately, I have experienced being with clients where I have embodied troubling feelings and so have suspected bad practice at a setting, either as part of the culture or from an individual worker. My suspicions may be denied or I am placated by an authority figure at the setting only to find, at a later date, that I was correct in my concerns as I learn that a member of staff has 'whistle blown'.

The sessions

Roles

The role of the client, member of staff and DMP is defined both by the ethos and culture of the organisation where the work takes place. Meeting each other in DMP sessions requires shifts in our usual ways of being together and consideration of the implications. Once in the session, I feel comfortable, I understand the space, I can be in a familiar role. For clients and members of staff this is a more gradual shift from being in their usual roles.

Quite often, the client enters the DMP session as a passive participant, appearing withdrawn and/or distracted. Over time as it becomes established that the session is theirs to shape and direct, I notice the changes in the individual's behaviour, which suggests to me their ownership and engagement. For example, I observe those clients who become able to stay in the room for an entire session, those who show how competent they are by offering a movement or sound during the sharing of turn-taking movements, or those who initiate an interaction or choose a prop. There is also evidence of participants 'sharing joint attention, sharing intentions and sharing affective states' (Stern, 1985: 128) – what Stern terms as intersubjective relatedness. In these moments, my felt sense detects a range of feelings where previously there had been a neutral and/or a numb felt sense.

Members of staff may find it particularly difficult to switch from their usual role of supporting clients to one of supporting and *engaging* with clients. I suggest to each staff member that they find their own way to be part of the group, and for some, inviting them to take an observer position is preferable to being a participant. I encourage staff to try both participant and observer positions. My intention in suggesting and offering different ways of being in the group is so that they can use skills best suited to them to support clients. Someone who is more comfortable observing will make interesting and insightful comments about individuals or the group. Often, I will see a member of staff who has taken the observer role, trying out some kind of interaction with a client inspired by something that they have noticed. Those who prefer to join in and actively engage and express their experiences can reflect the group process. They are at times, a catalyst for expression and activity. It is made clear that whichever way staff choose to support clients in the group is acceptable. Previously, I had invited members of staff the opportunity to choose how they wanted to attend the group. After a number of people chose to sit and use their mobile phones, I reconsidered the implications of this choice. This kind of ill-timed behaviour does give valuable material for the session and I choose carefully where I reflect on the impact of these behaviours on the clients, myself and the group as a whole, or choose a more directive intervention and simply ask the member of staff to stop using their phone. I am mindful of the impact of my intervention on those attending the group. Will I be modelling a judgemental attitude? Will I alienate the member of staff? Will I be championing self-respect? My intention is to communicate that the member of staff is a member of the group and not an onlooker or outsider.

Structure of the sessions

The structure of the session is something which I instigate and hold for the group. It is one of my non-negotiables and there can be different non-negotiable structures for each group. When initially observing a group, it may be difficult at first to identify the structure, especially where the beginning of the session begins in rhythmic synchrony. Generally, I facilitate a check-in, body awareness and warm-up, use of props and movement, and a check-out, to end the session. During the check-in at the start of sessions, everyone in the room is asked how they are. Sometimes members of staff assume that they are not included or they do not want to say. If they are asked to offer a movement, they can seem embarrassed to do so. These responses offer me the opportunity to wonder out loud how it might be for the clients in this situation and highlight the value of the clients witnessing members of staff adapting to a new and unfamiliar situation alongside them. When I am asking individual, nonverbal clients how they are, and insisting that the person be given their time, there may be remarks from members of staff such as 'they won't be able to say' or 'they don't understand'. In several groups, I have encountered clients who verbalise the same sentiments and attempt to usher me on to the next person in the circle. I find the check-in so important in establishing the principles of inclusion and acceptance. I have experienced many incidences where a person who has been overlooked becomes a valued member of the group and should this person be ignored by, for example, a new member of staff in the session, fellow members of the group will protest.

After the check-in, there is a body awareness warm-up. Clients are very used to being touched by staff when being helped with personal care or being moved, and so there is a familiarity on both sides to allow touch. The type of touch which all are accustomed to is appropriately practical. Using touch to aid body awareness for clients requires a shift in approach and awareness for both staff and clients. Discomfort appears with staff offering light massage to clients or brushing of the skin; questions arise, is it okay? Some members of staff withdraw, not wanting to impose until they find a way to support the client, which does not feel so contact intrusive.

Bridging the gap between being and doing

I have experienced a mismatch between some settings and myself regarding the aims of the groups, and yet the groups are seen to be successful by those at the setting. I think that this reflects the conscious needs of the clients as expressed in the aims of the setting, and the unconscious feelings of the clients as perceived by me. Arriving at these sessions I can notice a sense of relief in my body as I feel like 'the cavalry arriving' and I cannot know for sure what this represents. However, I have my story, which says that when I arrive, there is an opportunity for clients to be seen, heard and received *emotionally*. There could be any number of other reasons for there being a sense of a need for re-enforcements at the setting. Maybe I am picking up on the feelings of members of staff and systemic tensions: another pair of hands or a distraction?

Sessions where members of staff are asked by management to assess whether or not the clients are dancing and enjoying themselves, particularly highlight that which is going on at the surface, and that which is going on underneath. Particularly in the beginning stages of a group, there is a need to exhibit the liveliness expected whilst attending to the themes, feelings and emotions which are in the session. Relating on two different levels is often the only way to keep the sessions running. This actually gives insight into the world of these clients where they are mostly, unintentionally denied the ability to express who they are. With time, I notice that I can begin to define the needs of the setting and how the sessions need to be structured, thus bridging the gap between doing and being.

Choice

During sessions attempts are made to clarify how much choice clients and staff have in attending DMP sessions. Where possible, those clients attending are encouraged to decide where they may want to sit and the kind of contribution they wish to make. Conscious decisions are made about how much engagement in meeting each other is necessary for each person.

One of the decisions that interests members of staff is when a client either refuses to attend or leaves the DMP space. Members of staff say that they really appreciate the sense of freedom in the choice. In several settings, there have been incidences where a client in a wheelchair has either built up the ability to wheel themselves towards the door or where someone who is being helped to walk around the space heads for the door. Encouraging clients to experiment with or decide to leave the session is a risk, as it could be seen that the DMP sessions are not successful. I hold in my body the apprehension that the sessions may not be viewed as successful and so far, the settings have appreciated that the choice not to attend the session is a positive development for the client. Those clients who choose not to attend or who leave the space are given the opportunity each week to attend or re-join the group. I maintain a relationship with them outside of the group in order for them not to feel punished by their decision. Invariably, most will re-join the group when they are ready. How we can determine the needs of a client who cannot verbalise or who is unable to remove themselves from the session is a cause of discussion and concern for members of staff (and me). Expressing this concern in the session with clients and members of staff allows for a discussion and encouragement for noticing the nuances of movement and behaviour of clients.

Staff attending DMP sessions are consenting to be part of the group process because they are required to attend the session. Although I have not experienced members of staff thinking that they are being offered therapy, I do make this clear to those attending the sessions. In my experience, teams do accommodate preferences of activities. It is possible though, that a member of staff will be required to join the DMP group and they may have reservations. I have experienced members of staff who have been disruptive and who have attempted to (what I would describe as) sabotage the DMP sessions. My strategies in these situations vary from attempting to reach and understand the person, to reflecting what I am observing and feeling, as a way of naming that which is present in the space, to asserting my therapeutic authority. The intervention which I choose to use will be in response to the level of attack I perceive and in harmony with the group in that particular moment, as my intention will be to protect the group space.

Attuning

I use what I am feeling, thinking and noticing while I am attuning and embodying what is present in the session. Sometimes the number of members of staff in the session is equal to that of the clients. As I attune to the group and the individuals, it is not always clear whether my resonance is with clients and/or members of staff. As I name what I am sensing, members of staff along with clients can become silent and my wonderings hang in an atmosphere of nothingness; a charged, uncomfortable silence. I may find out during or after the session what is behind the feelings that I am picking up. It is important that in the session I can be seen to be bearing the feelings, whilst naming and moving with and through that which is there and unsaid. If I can be seen to survive the most unbearable feelings, there is hope for clients that their inner world can be witnessed and shared. Due to their level of dependency, clients are extremely sensitive to the mood of their carers. When there is acknowledgement in a session by a member of staff that the tension expressed in the uncomfortable silence in the room is due to a so far unnamed problem in the setting or team, changes in the breathing patterns of clients are witnessed. A feeling of relief for us all as we understand that the tension is a consequence of something external and not a consequence of in-session relationships or the responsibility of a particular individual.

Movement

The different expectations and conscious and unconscious mismatch as referred to earlier surface in relation to the role of dance and movement in the sessions. As I mirror clients' movements and join them in rhythm, my emphasis is on the 'nonverbal synchronisation and inter-corporeal relating' (Samaritter and Payne, 2013: 20), which are about 'establishing and maintaining contact and relationship'. Members of staff will probably be focussed on how to improve the movement skills of the clients and wondering how it is going to be possible for each person to dance.

A seemingly safer and more acceptable way for clients and staff to show themselves and interact with each other is by working with props. Props, as Winnicott asserts (1971), offer a meaningful opportunity for play, something other than each other, which could feel too exposing for the individual. Instead, props help navigate the building of relationship whilst also enabling the connection with a sense of being whole as a person. However, the use of props can also give the illusion that something is being achieved and happening. Waving a ribbon stick whilst looking out of the window and standing over a client in a wheelchair can be interpreted as doing something with the client by the member of staff, however, when I am observing such a duo, it is evident that both the client and staff are dis-engaged bodies in the room at that moment. My hope is that over time they will develop an appreciation for engaging in a meaningful relationship through the use of props. Where the DMP groups develop to a place of trust and spontaneity and where members of staff feel it appropriate to move alongside the clients, movement and play has almost always involved the use of a parachute as a prop. There is a release of energy and a variety of emotions, culminating in dividing into teams to see which is the stronger. Clients have a range of responses and reactions, some encouraging the staff at play, others joining in, some observing from a distance.

I am aware that throughout the sessions I am verbalising that which I am noticing. At the same time, I am having a nonverbal dialogue through movement, which is probably unrelated to what is being verbalised. Does the disconnection between verbal and nonverbal, conscious and unconscious and thought and feeling represent a parallel process to the systemic failings between what is said to be provided and what is actually provided in social care? In the DMP sessions, members of staff are the ones mostly verbalising their thoughts, perhaps a way of distracting and distancing themselves from the unbearable or uncomfortable silence of the verbal void which occurs when working with people whose communication is not through words. There is then a lack of 'affect attunement' (Stern, 1985) as members of staff assisting the sessions do not always have the skills to respond to and reflect the feeling state of the clients. Concannon (2005: 93) writes that verbal communication is concerned with directly conveying information, whilst nonverbal communication is about feelings and attitude. The lack of integration in the client is being reflected in the DMP sessions; so, integrating 'the wholeness of the person' (Dulicai, 2009: 146), the context, community and family system which they are part of, needs to be taken into consideration.

My reflecting on movement interactions and what sense is being made of them is important in the sessions as a way of awakening curiosity and awareness for all who are attending. Certain aspects of the movement dynamic between people at times interest those members of staff who attend the sessions regularly. Moments of connection can be seen where the staff member trusts in the experience without having to have evidence of a skill being learnt in order to justify what has occurred between them and a client. Thus, developing meaningful communication with clients changes how members of staff participate during sessions, and is beneficial for the clients who can then witness another side to staff's interaction with them. Clients and staff can perhaps identify with the emotions being expressed as they interact verbally, nonverbally, through movement and with the use of a shared prop. This only happens once the group is established and there is an understanding that I can and will hold the space for both clients and staff.

Collaboration

As the barriers between people dissolve, those areas which are taboo or disregarded appear. For example, changes to lifestyle, endings and bereavement, areas which are difficult to approach and address for fear of upsetting the clients too much, may be explored. In most settings where I am working, there is concern that certain clients may not be able to manage their feelings and that by acknowledging their bereavement, we are being cruel. When there is collaboration between members of staff and myself, it is possible to find a way in which to approach, for example, the subject of loss, metaphorically in sessions or by staff members talking with clients about *their* experience of loss. This enables staff, who will have to manage any residual feelings from the client after the session has ended, to be able to use their initiative in how to best support the person in their situation and with their feelings.

Members of staff, who are contractually in a supporting role for clients, are given the option in the DMP sessions to relate on a mutual level. This can be very different to what is expected by them on a day-to-day basis where relationships are not equal. Research (Chan and Yau, 2002) into interactions between care staff and people with learning disabilities in residential care shows how care staff are very observant and very aware of the person in their charge. However, being aware of clients' feelings and showing empathy for them may be discouraged by management, or regarded by staff as another task to be added to their workload. Also, staff are wary of offering opinion on what they think a client may want or how they may be feeling, because it is impossible to unequivocally know how a person who cannot verbalise feels or thinks. This is where the skills of a DMP can be employed to model ways of offering an opinion that is not judgemental or definitive. As familiarity and trust develops in the group, members of staff can learn to test out their observations and begin to speak about what they are finding.

Within some settings and staff teams, it can be frowned upon for the staff to join in with the dancing and moving if they seem to be enjoying themselves. Staff chide each other with remarks such as 'who is getting the most benefit'. The same comments are aimed towards me sometimes. I explain to members of staff how important social interaction is in improving the quality of life of clients (Chan and Yau, 2002). I also explain to members of staff the evidence from neuroscience regarding mirror neurons and how witnessing movement in others activates the feeling as if the witness has performed the movement themselves (Berrol, 2006). To further convince members of staff that we are performing an important service for clients, I speak to them about 'mirroring' (Chaiklin and Schmais, 1986) movements and how this can lead to a shared experience where meaningful interactions are created. The resistance in members of staff to moving freely in the sessions is understandable, as 'dancing' as a social activity can be linked to feelings of sensuality, attraction and, for many, dread. Members of staff sometimes say that they are not prepared to 'let themselves go' for fear of doing something inappropriate, as if they have no control over themselves when the moving body is engaged. I am aware that there is little time or space for members of staff to debrief after the sessions and I also hear from members of staff that they think that it may be too confusing for clients when members of staff switch from being playful and sociable back into their carer's role. I notice that when the culture at the setting shifts to acceptance and it being okay for members of staff to engage in social play within the DMP session, positive shifts in interactions and constructive ways of being between clients and members of staff develop in these sessions.

Naming what I am noticing in the sessions about relationships and interactions between people enables the unspeakable to be acknowledged and spoken within an atmosphere of curiosity and trust. This adds to the culture of each person being seen as equal. However, embodying what it means to be equal in the DMP sessions draws out the subtle and sometimes not so subtle reactions in all of us. Thinking about the positive or negative reactions which arise, there is something about competence and/or ability which provokes responses within the session and which questions our equal status. As an example, I may think that I am more in tune with the emotional theme of a group than the others in the group. I may not realise this assumption until others feel confident to offer their views, to question and challenge that which is unintentionally assumed. Paying attention to equality in the relationships between myself and staff, myself and clients, staff and clients, assists in the creation of different ways of being together in the sessions.

Collaboration and equal contribution is most evident when there is a visit from either an authority figure or, for example, a person from an external funding organisation. The group steps up and there are sounds, words, movements on cue during the check-in, dexterity with props, eye contact, focus, movement and postures which suggest alertness. As the outsider leaves, there is a general collapse as a result of the supreme effort expended and we, as a group, congratulate and acknowledge ourselves on showing the best of ourselves and working together. These moments are important to hold on to as they demonstrate the successful collaborations we have worked on as a group.

Conclusion

When I first began working in 'non-clinical' settings I became very aware of the influences of the social, familial and health systems we inhabit as I experienced strong reactions to the socio-political issues surrounding the client group. In this context, I was very aware of the impact of the nonverbal communication of members of staff on clients and decided that I needed to pay attention to both clients and members of staff.

How members of staff embody their working environment and how this impacts on the people with whom they are working was the focus of my Master's in DMP dissertation. Research participants, who were members of staff with whom I was working at the time, expressed feeling physically scared, worrying about being blamed and how they felt they assumed a high level of responsibility (Butler, 2009). What has unfolded for me through twelve years of practice with this client group and insights gained from my research is that we, the clients, members of staff and I, create a space where we can work collaboratively and derive our own meanings and environment, a space which serves us in our differing roles at the setting.

The process of establishing DMP sessions takes a considerable amount of effort on the part of all concerned at a setting. Holding the tension between needing to be flexible and adaptable while maintaining structure and keeping in our roles as we navigate and negotiate what is possible is a challenge. I notice how a commitment towards positive engagement in the sessions marks a turning point in the work. Why and how this occurs cannot be generalised, however, I do believe that respecting my non-negotiable, the 'non-negotiables' of the organisation and those of members of staff and clients provides a solid foundation for the development of trust and collaboration.

As I delve beneath the surface at a setting, I begin to realise that I am not the only one wanting to make connections with others. The stifled interactions and stilted atmosphere, which is often present, reflects how social relationships between clients and staff are not encouraged. What gets lost and is dampened is the colourful, creative and vibrant characters of each individual, of which there is an abundance! The DMP sessions provide a space where permission is given to interact and express individual character, where members of staff appreciate the sense of freedom when clients make choices. I experience this sense of freedom too when we are moving and being together and not shutting out the colour of our relationships with a monochrome filter.

Movement and awareness of how we are using our nonverbal communication creates a language which includes everyone in the room. This expression of what we are embodying is sensed by all and verbalised by me, members of staff and those clients who offer words and sounds. There is a great deal that is unsaid in the setting, which is brought to light and voiced in movement, in the posturing and gesturing of individuals and the group. It is difficult to hide the personalities and characters of those attending the group when relating through creative play. The richness which ensues reminds me of what a privilege it is to be working alongside these clients and members of staff.

Most often members of staff tell me that together with service users they enjoy the DMP space but that they cannot qualify why. They describe the sessions as relaxing, nice, lively, fun and sometimes boring. I think that it is because a space has been created in which the normal constraints of meeting and relating do not exist, and in which I, the DMP, tolerate the celebratory and happy as well as uncomfortable and difficult feelings of both staff and clients. We have managed in some way to 'change our habitual ways of moving' (Sheets-Johnstone 2010), stretched our habitual ways of holding the 'rights' and 'wrongs', and grown more generous and dynamic ways of being together.

Note

1 Pre-Therapy is a client-centred treatment to prepare psychotic persons, often with learning disabilities or organic impairments, for regular psychotherapy. For further information see www.pre-therapy.com.

References

Berrol, C. (2006) 'Neuroscience Meets Dance/Movement Therapy: Mirror Neurons, the Therapeutic Process and Empathy'. *The Arts in Psychotherapy*, 33(4): 302–315.

Butler, J. (2009) *Finding Their Voice: The Role of Embodiment on Non-Verbal Communication Between Care-Staff and Residents with Learning Disabilities.* Unpublished original manuscript, Roehampton University, UK.

Chaiklin, S. and Schmais, D. (1986) 'The Chace Approach to Dance Therapy'. Lewis, P. (ed.) *Theoretical Approaches to Dance/Movement Therapy, Vol. 1. Dubuque* IA: Kendall/Hunt.

Chan, J. S. and Yau, M. K. (2002) 'A study on the nature of interactions between direct-care staff and persons with developmental disabilities in institutional care'. *British Journal of Developmental Disabilities*, 48(94): 3951.

Concannon, L. (2005) *Planning for Life: Involving Adults with Learning Disabilities in Service Planning.* London: Routledge.

Dulicai, D. (2009) 'Family dance/movement therapy: A systems model'. Chaiklin, S. and Wengrower, H. (eds.) *The Art and Science of Dance Movement Therapy: Life Is Dance.* New York: Routledge.

Fischman, D. (2009) 'Therapeutic relationship and kinesthetic empathy'. Chaiklin, S. and Wengrower, H. (eds.) *The Art and Science of Dance Movement Therapy: Life is Dance,* New York: Routledge.

Gendlin, E. T. (2003) *Focusing, How to Gain Direct Access to Your Body's Knowledge.* London: Random House. (First published 1978).

Parker, G. and Best, P. (2007) 'Moving Reflections: The Social Creation of Identities in Communication', *e-motion*, XIV(19): 7–1. (First published 2001).

Prouty, G. (2002) 'The theory of pre-therapy'. Prouty, G., Van Werde, D. and Portner, M. (eds.) *Pre-Therapy: Reaching Contact-Impaired Clients.* Herefordshire, UK: PCCS Books.

Samaritter, R. and Payne, H. (2013) 'Kinaesthetic intersubjectivity: A dance informed contribution to self-other relatedness and shared experience in non-verbal psychotherapy with an example from autism'. *Arts in Psychotherapy*, 40(1): 143–150.

Sandel, S. and Johnson, D. (1983) 'Structure and process of the nascent group: dance therapy with chronic patients'. *Arts in Psychotherapy*, 10: 131–140.

Sheets-Johnstone, M. (2010) 'Kinesthetic experience: Understanding movement inside and out'. *Body, Movement and Dance in Psychotherapy*, 5(2): 111–127.

Sinason, V. (1992) *Mental Handicap and the Human Condition.* London: Free Association Books.

Stern, D. N. (1985) *The Interpersonal World of the Infant: A View from Psychoanalysis and Developmental Psychology.* New York: Basic Books.

Wengrower, H. (2015) 'Widening our lens: The implications of resilience for the professional identity and practice of dance movement therapists'. *Body, Movement and Dance in Psychotherapy*, 10(3): 153–168.

Winnicott, D. W. (1971) *Playing and Reality.* London: Tavistock/Routledge.

Chapter 8

I will dance with you, all that you have been, all that you are, and all that you can become

An exploration of the application of a Person-Centred Dance Movement Psychotherapy approach with nonverbal clients in a group context

Linsey Clark and Victoria Smith

Introduction

We are choosing to co-author this chapter as a symbolic statement of our shared experience, to guarantee the picture of our clients is painted with clarity and the reader gains a sense of the co-creation on which all relationships are based. While our individual paths have obviously been personal, we have danced them side by side since our involvement with one of the most established dance movement psychotherapy (DMP) organisations in the United Kingdom, sixteen years ago as volunteers; learning, growing, becoming established as practitioners in our own right. Our duet sees us living and breathing the person-centred ethos of the organisation, becoming ambassadors of the DMP approach championed in our practice setting, with a particular commitment to providing a voice for the voiceless.

Over the years of establishing itself as an active and instrumental DMP and education centre, the organisation has developed its own approach to the facilitation of DMP. The approach embodies the belief that we all have something worth saying and everyone deserves the chance to experience the feeling of empowerment. We aim to achieve this by looking beyond labels and diagnosis and by developing unique therapeutic relationships with each individual as they present themselves within the DMP space.

Every one of us deserves the opportunity to journey towards reaching our potential. Integrating DMP with the person-centred approach (Rogers, 2004) allows for an environment in which the person with the most profound learning difficulty has the space to grow and become a valued member of our community. For this to be fully established and embodied by the DMP, to create a non-judgemental environment in which we can all flourish must be a desire that resonates professionally and personally. We have noticed that this is established most profoundly when the DMP lives and breathes this value system rather than maybe restricting it to the professional domain.

One of the strengths of our organisation is that among the work we deliver, we facilitate five ongoing closed DMP sessions a week for people with a variety of learning and physical difficulties. These sessions include support workers, volunteers and Master's in DMP placement students. This enriches a sense of social integration and inclusivity. Due to having an average of sixteen clients, and therefore complex group dynamics during these sessions, three registered and experienced DMPs facilitate each session.

We work with a range of clients with degenerative diseases, congenital disabilities, acquired brain injury and with those on the autistic spectrum. This non-exclusive list only refers to the learning difficulty and does not encapsulate the psychological needs that clients experience and present, not to mention the emotional narrative each person brings. While knowledge of diagnosis is informative, it paints a one-dimensional picture of a unique and complex person.

For the purpose of this chapter we are referring to the dancers we work with as 'adults with learning difficulties'; this descriptor immediately places people in a category and under a label and evokes a particular picture of how this group of dancers might appear (Chesner, 1995; Hawkins, 2014). However, we see this as a broad term, as the dancers that join our DMP sessions have a range of needs or challenges: physical, cognitive, emotional and behavioural. A group can consist of dancers with profound differences, from someone who is wheelchair bound with minimal movement to someone who is verbal and ambulant.

The Person-Centred approach

Rogers (2004) discusses the phenomena of true understanding leading to the potential for change and growth. To understand another person in this capacity, certain conditions need to be in place: empathy, unconditional positive regard, congruence, willingness of the client to enter a process and the ability for the therapist to make these conditions tangible and felt. These are the core-conditions or stepping stones to the person-centred approach.

Two unique human beings meeting in a shared space, one the client, one the therapist; two narratives combine to create one inner world (Mearns and Thorne, 2013; Rogers, 2011, 2003). A deep understanding and mutual respect develops as the therapist opens herself up to her own knowing, prepared for what she might meet in the world of the client. Within a space that aims to be free of judgement the client finds strength in expressing their true selves. Together the dance takes shape; the dance movement psychotherapist immerses him- or herself within the creative process. All becomes visible: symbolism and metaphors are laid out across the dance floor; the body feels its meaning. The sequence begins, 'I trust you, all that you have been and all that you can become'; in mirrored reflection, 'I begin to trust myself and all that I can be'. The dance has moments of true intimacy and togetherness. From this holding springs forth a new energy, a leap into the freedom of possibility, the spiralling of growth.

As DMP practitioners, we have discovered that the reasons of *how* or *why* the client is different can become a barrier to meeting the client in the here and now and influence our assumptions and expectations. For this reason, we endeavour to create a culture of acceptance and empowerment with no preconceived ideas of how someone should be. Working within a professional climate that accepts its clinical and ethical responsibilities, we become tightrope walkers: balancing the acknowledgement of the *how* and *why* through delving into our clients' clinical records with the ability to store the information within ourselves, only to retrieve it when necessary, so as not to interfere with the *here* and *now*.

> If I accept the other person as something fixed … already shaped by his past, then I am doing my part to confirm this limited hypothesis. If I accept him as a process of becoming, then I am doing what I can to confirm or make real his potentialities.
>
> (Rogers 2004: 55)

Rogers's (2003) original development of the 'core-conditions' (as mentioned previously) was created with the concept of the person-centred therapist meeting with a client who has the capacity to make psychological connection. This feeds into the socio-cultural debate of the possible depth of psychotherapy with people with learning difficulties, and whether the person-centred approach would be enough to enable change for those who may be deemed unable to provide psychological contact. For the person-centred approach to become accessible, inclusive and deemed appropriate for those diagnosed with severe learning difficulties, Prouty (1994) posited a psychotherapeutic concept enabling those who are considered hard to reach to enter a psychotherapy framework: pre-therapy. Pre-therapy provides the therapist with techniques to form a bridge to the client's reality to draw them into the present and into the relationship; thus establishing 'contact reflections' (Sanders, 2012).

This is where we (as DMPs) sigh a breath of relief, as we recognise that the immediacy of working with the body provides such a portal, thus enabling us to make contact with the most severely learning disabled person by offering 'literal reflections of the client's verbal as well as nonverbal behaviour and of the concrete reality surrounding client and therapist in any given moment' (Sommerbeck, 2016: 2). The embodiment of the person-centred approach automatically allows for a therapeutic foundation to be built, based on felt sense, somatic transference (Bloom, 2012), kinaesthetic empathy and attunement (Fischman, 2009; Hayes, 2013). With an open mind, an open heart and a moving body we reach into the world of our clients, simultaneously providing a loving pathway to mutuality and back to self. Empathic reflection becomes the dance and the sharing of worlds taking place in the creative process. Creativity is established with permissiveness and a freedom for expression; it provides a bedrock for symbolic gestures and symbolic meaning; therefore providing a platform for us to establish an understanding of the world of the client, however psychologically distant they may appear.

From within our model, DMP provides a framework that allows the therapeutic relationship to develop from the moment the learning difficulty client and therapist meet. With elements of pre-therapy naturally occurring in the nonverbal movement of DMP there is no need to differentiate stages of therapy or to

112   Linsey Clark and Victoria Smith

question with whom person-centred DMP can work. In our experience, there is no doubt that the learning difficulty adult can access therapy, establish a more meaningful sense of self and develop in-depth relationships that have a profound effect on themselves and others. The creative medium of DMP provides endless opportunities for nonverbal exploration, expression and communication, bringing the client and DMP onto a level playing field.

My name is George

Throughout this chapter, we will introduce and invite you into George's world. His story and identity is an amalgamation of information, observations and experiences gathered from the variety of clients we have danced with over many years of practice. George is being presented as a case study, as a way of inviting you into our world of DMP. By presenting George's DMP story we simultaneously present our story as DMPs; a shared narrative.

The group sessions that George attends are always facilitated by three DMPs. Throughout the following case study, our two voices and perspectives combine to represent the united strength of our underpinning belief system.

George first accessed DMP at the age of thirty-five. He had lived in the family home until he was thirty years old, at which point he moved into a residential home, housing six men with a variety of learning difficulties. The move had a profound effect on his emotional well-being and self-confidence; he became withdrawn and isolated from other members of the house. George had very little verbal communication skills, which made it very difficult for him to express his feelings verbally or be understood by others. At times of heightened anxiety, George had been known to hit himself or others, pull hair and on occasions bite. After attempting different activities to no avail, the house manager noticed George's physical animation and relaxation when listening to music and referred him to DMP.

When initially meeting George and observing his movement, we were able to get a sense of how he related to his own body. A slight scoliosis of the spine limited the mobility of his spine and the range of movement on the left side of his body and had an impact on his kinaesphere (his personal space). However, George had the potential to access low- and medium-level movement and to extend his movement range on the right side of his body. Through our observations it became apparent that his movement range was significantly influenced by his emotions. When anxious and frustrated, George's movement would become more bound and restricted, causing his kinaesphere to become smaller.

Vignette 1: DMP Session 1

George arrives accompanied by two members of support staff who stay close to his side; he makes the short distance from his car to the front door of the building with ease. At the point of entrance, there is hesitation, a holding of the breath and tension in his body. On this threshold, the essence of the therapeutic alliance begins. I step outside and simultaneously enter George's frame of reference, meeting him in his physicality; I sense his anxiety, his uncertainty, and offer my presence.

I stand side by side with George affirming his arrival, keeping distance but being tangibly close, breathing in synchrony while verbally and nonverbally encouraging a step forward. By my allowing George the time he needs, setting his own pace and taking direction (Hawkins, 2014), by being sensitive to the shifting of positions and altered breath, George takes his first step. For today this is enough: George has added his contribution to the group. He will be welcomed back every week, however long it takes for the next step to come.

Through the referral procedure, the DMP team learnt about George's case history, read a risk assessment and his diagnosis. With all this information, it would have been easy for the team to make assumptions about how George would present, behaviours he would exhibit, and therefore how to be in relationship with him. However, it was essential to our practice that we were able to put this information aside and meet George with minimal expectations or assumptions. As Hawkins (2014) suggests, 'challenging behaviour' is often labelled as such, as it creates a challenge for those interacting with the person; it is not deemed a challenge to the individual, but is rather a form of their communication.

With this premise in mind we always take the time needed to learn each person's individual form of communication, to understand the fine detail of the nonverbal cues. By taking the position of non-expert (Mearns and Thorne, 2013; Rogers, 2003; Sanders, 2012), we give ourselves the space to learn everything we need to know directly from the client; such learning has no boundary. If we can let go of the need to be an expert and instead become ready to learn, to observe, to truly listen on a felt sense (Hayes, 2013; Rogers, 2003), our clients automatically relax into the mutuality of the relationship, and become empowered to take the lead. It is important that we try to understand our clients and really connect to what they are physically and emotionally communicating (Hawkins, 2014). To empower them we must open ourselves up, heart and mind, soul and spirit.

Vignette 2: DMP Session 2

I meet George at the entrance with reassurance and familiarity: I attune to his breath and body posture, gently letting my presence be known. There is a significant shift in his body tension, a release. In letting go of the tension, his anxiety seems to soften. He also stands taller: his upper body is more open and expansive, decreasing the restriction to his breath and enabling him to breathe more easily. Eye contact is present and exchanged with playfulness. George is acknowledging and recognising us; we respond with warmth and encouragement. George has become more engaged with his surroundings; There are no signs of uncertainty in his movement. Instead he is curious about the space and the therapist and he lets his body lead him in this new state of exploration: he takes a step into the building.

> *I notice George's curiosity; he responds to the music with a slight rhythmic pulsation through his upper body. In response, I attune to George's rhythm, taking his pulsation and translating it into my movement: I reach out into the periphery and make connections to the environment, making physical connection to the floor, walls, chairs and table, my intention is to demonstrate permissiveness to explore the environment. In attuning to George, I embody his pulsation; I resonate with a small movement that is locked within his upper body, sense it through my whole body and let it out into the space. This seems to enable George to connect to this new environment. A smile from George is a cue for me to open the doors into the DMP studio; in doing so George arrives to the group and is welcomed into his therapy.*

George's experience echoes that of the early infant: he is discovering a 'secure base' (Bowlby, 1988) from which he can explore his potential. It is through providing the adequate conditions for emotional, physical and relational development and growth that a holding environment (Winnicott, 2002) with potential for growth is being created. Thus, in the quality of her presence, the DMP creates a context for reciprocal relating akin to that which the mother creates with her infant.

Through recognising the subtle differences that arise at a physical level when working with someone who has little or no verbal communication, we hone into a deeper sense of connection with our own body and that of our client and step into the physicality of the communication with them. Hayes (2013) compares this embodied experience of connecting with a client with the dyadic relationship of the mother with her baby, where the early interpersonal world of the child is affirmed (Stern, 2003). This is not to suggest that the adults we work with are children; it is more that these important relational experiences are not always fully formed in an adult with learning difficulties. As therapists, we respond at a kinaesthetic level in order to understand our client's unique means of communication. Kinaesthetic empathy is a shared construct that requires our sensing and attuning to the subtleties and intricate detail of body, tension, shape or movement. Thus, we are able to reflect back to our client that we have heard them and understood them on a somatic level. Through this physical connection, we gain a greater understanding and awareness of the client (Leijssen, 2010).

Through this process of kinaesthetic empathy, we echoed George's movement with our own bodies. A movement dialogue was created, accessing all available sensorimotor channels (Fischman, 2009), thus providing George with the reassurance and understanding needed to engage in a movement dialogue.

Vignette 3: DMP Session 6

> *George is fully integrated into the DMP group, has made friends with other group members and built relationships with the whole DMP team. When he is most relaxed, George is able to access his full kinaesphere and move in close proximity to other dancers.*

># Person-Centred DMP – nonverbal clients 115

> *George is in the process of making a music choice when another client moving close by becomes unpredictable. George's body tension suddenly changes: moving from relaxed and expansive to bound. He moves his right arm impulsively towards me and tries to grab my hair. Immediately, I recognise the need to counter any of my own 'fight–flight' response: I release my body tension, allowing George to experience my calmness and steady breathing. I hope to reassure him and foster a sense of safety. In this moment, my full attention is on holding George unconditionally. I understand his impulsive movement as a communication of his anxiety and uncertainty about his environment. I believe that attempting to grab my hair is George's only way of asking 'Am I safe, will you hold me?'*

> *In this moment, I embrace my empathy for George's situation, my unconditional holding of all of who he is; I do not judge his actions but hear what he is saying and respond with compassion. I release my tension through the breath, maintain eye contact with George and reach my hands out to him. In doing so, saying 'I'm okay, you're okay'. George makes fingertip contact, steadies his breath and releases a small amount of tension.*

In order to hold George unconditionally in this situation, it was essential that I engaged both emotionally and physically in the 'here and now', thus enabling George to experience my intention at a somatic level. In this embodied process, I am multi-tasking on a felt sense: I check-in intuitively, emotionally and psychologically with myself (Brown, 2012). What is my congruent response to this moment (Mearns and Thorne, 2013)? What are my levels of fear and need for safety? What in this moment will aid or hinder the therapeutic relationship?

Decisions need to be made in a split second to diffuse difficult situations and support the clients. With the awareness that George's intention is not to hurt anyone, but rather to communicate his anxiety and need to be reassured, I find my way to accept his behaviour. Being accepting of behaviour that challenges, such as this, does not need to replace the acknowledgement of boundaries or an awareness of a congruent sense of fear. I remain grounded in my response by physically and consciously feeling my feet on the floor, allowing the breath to connect me to the support of the earth. The reaching out to George and use of steady eye contact informs him that we are both ok; this in turn enables George to relax. I aim to connect verbally and nonverbally with George, to enclose him in the safe boundary of the DMP relationship, to trust that on a visceral level, George will feel my embodied expression of unconditional warmth.

The creative space can be unpredictable, especially when clients are invited to share embodied expression. It is impossible to prescribe which emotions and responses are acceptable and which are not. This is especially poignant in the learning difficulty community due to limitations of processing and understanding of emotional expression. If we invite our clients into an embodied state of being, we are opening the door to all forms of expression, including their aggressive feelings and responses. Within the DMP sessions, the energy or expression presented by clients is not responded to as right or wrong, but is always acknowledged. Through creative exploration, we discover possibilities with our clients, ways in which to enable them to release or express their feelings safely whilst creating a safe context for all. For a safe environment to be immediately felt by clients, we have to simultaneously engage our felt and authentic selves, while assessing our clients' experience at a psychological and somatic level. This is experienced symbolically in movement and dance, often supported through the use of music and props. Accessing the creative process provides opportunities for any extreme energy such as aggression to be re-directed away from an individual and enter the space as symbolic expression. As Rogers stipulates: 'The therapist (or facilitator) is willing for the client to be with whatever immediate feeling is going on – confusion, resentment, fear, anger, courage, love or pride' (2011: 59). As person-centred DMPs, we have a responsibility to hold the full range of expression 'unconditionally' (Mearns and Thorne, 2013; Rogers, 2011, 2003).

To be unconditional is to provide an environment free of *conditions of worth*, allowing the clients the freedom to be truly themselves, to express themselves fully in the knowledge that they will still be held and *prized* (Rogers, 2003). The unconditional holding of the DMP space is often a unique or new experience for the client with a learning difficulty who could have suffered a lifetime of conditional worth, rejection and limited expectations (Miller, 2004). With an 'acceptant attitude' in place, the client will be more willing to take risks, therefore, 'therapeutic movement or change is more likely to occur' (Rogers, 2011: 59).

Vignette 4: Six months into DMP

George enters the DMP session with a sense of belonging: he moves directly to his preferred space within the room. From here he can acknowledge the group and choose to stay on the periphery, accept people into his space or move out into the wider surroundings to initiate contact and shift his perspective.

I recognise George's need to maintain his sense of spatial boundaries and the importance for us to continuously look for his nonverbal cues as to when to be with him and when to give him space.

In order to respect George's need for maintaining his personal kinaesphere, I offer him a piece of lycra. At first he is reluctant, but then he observes intensely. I remain close by, moving with the lycra, I offer eye contact with the hope that George will connect.

I maintain an openness and acceptance within this interaction to ensure that George feels the freedom to initiate on his terms. After a short while, George picks up one corner of the lycra and gives it a tug while laughing. In response, I mirror the efforts of his movement. This movement interaction develops into a playful tug of war, where we are giving and receiving each other's weight and gradually moving closer to one another. The music ends and we find ourselves standing shoulder to shoulder. I offer George my hand; at that moment, the lycra is dropped and the next dance begins, moving hand in hand.

Through the safety of the therapeutic alliance, George is more able to take the risk of moving away from his 'secure base' and becomes more integrated within the group.

We are respectful at all times of George's wishes and aims, developing a relationship in which he is empowered to initiate the sharing of space. In turn, we are invited into his world.

> When functioning best, the therapist is so much inside the private world of the other that he or she can clarify not only the meanings of which the client is aware but even those just below the level of awareness.
>
> (Rogers, 2011: 59)

When working with George, we hold onto the value of choice making, adding to his sense of empowerment, achievement and ownership. If there is a limited expectation from society of the individual's potential then they become accustomed to things being done for them; subsequently, this negatively affects levels of self-worth and reduces their personal world (Chesner, 1995: 47). Institutionalisation within care/nursing homes or within the community can be suppressive, causing physical and psychological limitations. Therefore, it is essential that the DMP process be empowering, contrasting with and compensating for the disempowering experience that often occurs within the learning difficulty world.

Connecting with George through mirroring, somatic attunement/resonance (Hayes 2013; Rand 2002) and the use of props allowed for a co-created relationship that doesn't rely on speech. Chesner (1995: 46) describes this as an opportunity for the client to find 'new spontaneity, validity and freedom'. The exploration through DMP and use of physical communication skills can enable the client to gain a sense of success, focusing on their abilities as opposed to disability or failure.

As part of our approach, we hold an annual performance, where we transpose the creative process of DMP from the therapy space onto a public stage. This transition into a public arena is an empowering statement for our clients to be heard and seen as active members of the local community. Every year we enter a debate about the appropriateness of therapy to performance and whether the safe and growth-enhancing environment we strive to create is transferable.

Vignette 5: A year into DMP

George has been invited to take part in the performance alongside the other dancers who attend DMP sessions; the invites are open to all, so as not to cause pressure or unnecessary anxiety. As with all of our dancers, we hope that George will arrive at the theatre and be able to make his way onto the stage and dance with his group.

We are in luck and George arrives with his support. He has been very excited all day, making dance shapes at home. When George first arrives, he enters the auditorium, a new and uncertain space. His excitement starts to transform into anxiety, but he is soon met by the familiarity and comforting presence of his DMP team. One takes his hand and gently strokes his skin, while the other affirms his arrival and expresses her joy in sharing this experience with him. The three of us slowly make our way to an empty stage where the third member of the DMP team waits. To a silent and empty auditorium George dances his dance in the trusting and safe presence of his DMPs; the only difference is the external environment, internally he feels held, met and free to be, in a similar way as in the DMP space that is familiar to him. An hour later, costume on and an auditorium full, George is amongst the rest of his DMP group. Noisily, nervously and with excitement they make their way to the stage.

George and his peers are each met with a familiar face, either a DMP, trainee DMP or volunteer. As this is George's first performance he is partnered with one of the DMPs. Similarly, to that of his first day at the centre, I attune to George's breath; I am aware of his subtle tremor and of the strength of his grip. I listen in, close my eyes to still the sound and focus on the body next to me, to be as one as we enter the stage. In turn, the grip loosens, the tremor lessens and the breath slows down. We are ready.

The lights are bright, the music loud and people are watching – can the safety of the DMP space be replicated in such an atmosphere? George freezes for just a moment. I remain completely focused on him, and then the dance begins. George smiles, laughs and moves quicker, more expansively and confidently than seen before; he relishes every moment. The audience applauds, an unfamiliar sound, but George recognises it is for him: he is being applauded by 350 people. Gripping my hand, he bows and bows again, he feels the sense of affirmation, achievement, acceptance wash over him – a pivotal moment in his self-confidence and sense of self.

Conclusion

Our DMP practice works with a theory of existence that every human being deserves the opportunity for growth, acceptance and recognition, delivered through the embodiment of the person-centred approach within a creative process. George's story demonstrates why the performance continues to remain a pivotal moment in enabling our clients with learning difficulties to move closer to their *self-actualising tendency*: in person-centred terms seen as the authentic element of self, 'which despite every kind of opposition or hindrance, would ensure that an individual continued to strive to grow towards the best possible fulfilment of their potential' (Mearns and Thorne, 2013: 9).

Looking beyond the label and diagnosis of those we dance with allows for assumptions and limitations to disperse and in their place comes possibility, potential, wonderment and humility. Within the mutuality of the co-created relationship, we are constantly learning, humbled and inspired by our dancing companions.

References

Bloom, K. (2012) *The Embodied Self: Movement and Psychoanalysis.* London: Karnac.

Bowlby, J. (1988) *A Secure Base.* London: Routledge.

Brown, D. (2012) 'Person-centred expressive arts therapies'. Sanders, P. (ed.) *The Tribes of the Person-Centred Nation. An Introduction to the Schools of Therapy Related to the Person-Centred Approach.* Ross-on-Wye, UK: PCCS Books.

Chesner, A. (1995) *Dramatherapy for People with Learning Disabilities. A World of Difference.* London: Jessica Kingsley.

Fischman, D. (2009) 'Therapeutic relationships and kinesthetic empathy'. Chaiklin, S. and Wengrower, H. (eds.) *The Art and Science of Dance Movement Therapy. Life Is Dance.* London: Routledge.

Hawkins, J. (2014) 'Person-centred therapy with people with learning disabilities: Happy people wear hats'. Pearce, P. and Sommerbeck, L. (eds.) *Person-Centred Practice at the Difficult Edge.* Ross-on-Wye, UK: PCCS Books.

Hayes, J. (2013) *Soul and Spirit in Dance Movement Psychotherapy. A Transpersonal Approach.* London: Jessica Kingsley.

Leijssen, M. (2010) 'Caring for the Soul as the Keystone in Health Care'. Leonardi, J. (ed.) *The Human Being Fully Alive. Writings in Celebration of Brian Thorne.* Ross-on-Wye, UK: PCCS Books.

Mearns, D., Thorne, B. and McLeod, J. (2013) *Person-Centred Counselling in Action* (Fourth Edition). London: Sage Publications.

Miller, L. (2004) 'Adolescents with learning disabilities: psychic structures that are not conducive to learning'. Simpson, D. and Miller, L. (eds.) *Unexpected Gains: Psychotherapy with People with Learning Disabilities.* London: Karnac.

Prouty, G. (1994) 'Theoretical Evolutions in Person-Centred/Experiential Therapy'. *Applications to Schizophrenic and Retarded Psychosis.* Westport, CT: Praeger Publishers.

Rogers, C. (2003) *Client-Centered Therapy.* London: Constable & Robinson Ltd.

Rogers, C. (2004) *On Becoming a Person: A Therapist's View of Psychotherapy.* London: Constable & Robinson Ltd.

Rogers, N. (2011) *The Creative Connection for Groups Person-Centred Expressive Arts for Healing and Social Change.* Palo Alto, CA: Science & Behaviour Books, Inc.

Sanders, P. (2012) 'New developments – pre-therapy and contact work'. Sanders, P. and Cooper, M., Merry, T., Purton, C., Baker, N. and Worsley, R. (eds.) *The Tribes of the Person-Centred Nation.* Ross-on-Wye, UK: PCCS Books.

Sommerbeck, L. (2003) *The Client-Centred Therapist in Psychiatric Contexts.* Ross-on-Wye, UK: PCCS Books.

Stern, D. N. (2003) *The Interpersonal World of the Infant. A View from Psychoanalysis and Developmental Psychology.* New York: Basic Books.

Winnicott, D. W. (2002) *Playing and Reality.* London: Brunner-Routledge. First published 1971.

Online resources

Rand, M. (2002) 'What is somatic attunement? (somatic resonance)'. First published in *American Psychotherapy Association Journal*, (5): 6. Available at www.biomedsearch.com (Accessed 03/11/2016).

Sommerbeck, L. (2006) 'Beyond psychotherapeutic reach? An introduction to Pre-Therapy'. First published as 'Udenfor terapeutisk raekevidde? Introduktion til Prae-Terapi.' *Psycholog Nyt* 60(8): 12–20, translated and revised for the World Association for Person Centered and Experiential Psychotherapy and Counselling. Available at www.pce-world.org (Accessed 31/10/16).

Chapter 9

Men shaping men

Gender discoveries in a Dance Movement Psychotherapy men's group

Geoffery Unkovich

This study is shaped around a group of men whose identities are impacted by a context where the biggest daily focus can be high physical and practical support needs, in preference to supporting individuality within a broader socio-cultural and sexually constructive framework (Wilson *et al.*, 2011). From my experience this socially oppressive context reflects a broader socio-political context, where society continues to struggle with acceptance of difference by not managing to offer equality of service for those less able to protest.

Following seven years of practice in a learning disability day service, my research affirmed my concern that there was limited provision for men and women with a learning disability to speak about their gender and sexual identity (Wheeler, 2007). Literature confirmed that topics of sexuality and/or sexual orientation of men and women with a learning disability can be marginalised aspects of their lives that remain unrecognised and undefined by the individuals themselves (Hollins and Sinason, 2000; Leutar and Mihokovic, 2007). Negative attitudes towards sexual expression and uncertainty about gender and sexuality (Bedard *et al.*, 2010; Noonan and Gomez, 2010) from the wider population mean that the human rights of people with a learning disability are being denied (McCarthy *et al.*, 2012; Wilson *et al.*, 2011). Speaking about gender identity and sexuality can still be taboo in many contexts and even more so when talking about people with a disability who may be infantilised, asexualised and/or denied their gender identity (McCarthy *et al.*, 2012; Rembis, 2010; Swango-Wilson, 2010; Wheeler, 2007).

Service users' different levels of knowledge, experience, attitudes and feelings about sexuality and gender (Yacoub and Hall, 2009) led me to support clients in knowing more about their self-identity, so they are more able to consider informed and acceptable risks (McCarthy *et al.*, 2012; Sinason, 1992) in their search for intimate and/or interpersonal relationships. Greater understanding of informed and acceptable risk includes awareness that the possibility of sexual exploitation and abuse exists (Cuskelly and Bryde, 2004; McCarthy *et al.*, 2012; Swango-Wilson, 2010; Yacoub and Hall, 2009). It is important to note that, while affirming the positive elements of clients' masculinity (Wilson *et al.*, 2010), it is also essential to acknowledge behaviour that may damage or challenge relationships. My experience with society's struggles to accept my gendered sexual orientation, and power struggles in personal relationships, have made me believe that it is essential to provide focused therapeutic support for those who find themselves facing similar challenges. Integrating this focused therapeutic support with guidance, related to experiences of power in relationships, empowers individuals to explore and safely express their gender identity and sexual issues in the wider context.

Some of the feelings experienced by the men who shared their stories with me are echoed in Shuttleworth's (2000) life-history interviews with men with cerebral palsy. These men have experienced personal frustration, rage and hopelessness that block their enthusiasm to develop interpersonal relationships. These blocks can be a consequence of having idealised images of what it means to be a man (McVittie *et al.*, 2008; Rembis, 2010; Shakespeare, 1999; Siebers, 2008).

My clinical practice at the day centre has shown me that the lived experience of clients is affected by tensions in the relationship between social models of disability and clients' personal perceptions of their learning disabilities relative to the disabilities of those they see and know (Hoffman *et al.*, 2008; McVittie *et al.*, 2008; Samaritter, 2009; Sinason, 1992). These men have varied experiences of other people's perceptions of their gender and sexual identity due to age differences and living with either parents or in supported accommodation (Cuskelly and Bryde, 2004). This interplay of social and personal constructs brings self-perpetuated meanings and/or societal pressures that can lead those with a learning disability to feeling immobilised and to withdraw from intimate relationships, or to take further risks and hence trigger further rejection (Milligan and Neufeldt, 2001; Shuttleworth, 2000).

This dance movement psychotherapy (DMP) group work provided a space for clients and me to explore embodied and undeveloped nuances of our sexual and gender identities (Allegranti, 2009). Bringing attention to the body's experience is vital for us all as embodied understanding provides a direct experiential link to our felt sense and encourages an awareness of intuitive feelings we experience in our bodies (Simmons and Watson, 2015).

Generally speaking, men who attended the DMP group had mild to moderate learning disability, some developmental delay, a neurological degenerative condition and autism. This choice of mine not to foreground a diagnostic label is my preference in practice and in life, as my intention always is to foreground the person. I have wondered if, by not foregrounding the label, do I deny the disability? Am I shutting the disability out of the room? No, I am not. From a young age, I had a brother with Williams syndrome[1] so in my familial life the person and loving relationship is ever present regardless of ability. 'Seeing the disability' as foreground has, therefore, never been my experience.

My hope with this study is to raise awareness of the continued need for greater appreciation of men's differences and understanding of gender and sexual identities. If sexual knowledge and understanding of people with a learning disability are ignored or denied (Wheeler, 2007) then they are likely to experience unsafe behaviour on their part or on the part of another. Socio-politically, the male voice and male perspective from their experience is much needed in this work and in society where the necessary voice and rights of women have been championed over the last few decades. There is a need to now develop a greater appreciation for differences in male gender and sexual expression, so that the behaviours of those men (and women) with learning disabilities are not misconstrued or seen as the same as the abuser. In my experience, as a male therapist, I too can 'suffer' being seen as the same as the abuser. I believe the psychotherapy and health care professions will benefit from greater appreciation of the male perspective in therapeutic work with male and female clients in all contexts, particularly in learning disability contexts where men and women continue to be denied a right to authentically express their gender and sexual diversity.

Shaping the therapeutic relationship

My worldview on intersubjective relating (Behrends, 2012; Berrol, 2006) in movement relationships informs my work as a DMP. I am interested in and curious about the shapes we create through movement and the way we shape the personal space we inhabit, at a cellular to a fully embodied inter-relational and cerebral level (Allegranti, 2011). My use of the word 'shape' also relates to expansion and contraction on a cellular and interpersonal level, as discussed in formative psychology (Keleman, 2007); I attend to the interactional shaping that occurs in the expression between self and others, the space between self, the environment and or others (Best, 2003) and the impact of open and closed postures on emotions (Rossberg-Gempton and Poole, 1993).

I have found in shaping my work with this particular group that it has been most beneficial to work with movement we incorporate in our conversations and interpersonal spatial relationships in preference to improvised dance movement. These postural and gestural conversational shifts are the dance of communication in our spontaneous responsive relationships (Shotter, 2004) where meaning is realised in the amplification of posture and gesture. The group's exploration and recurring use of posture and gesture has led to their embodied amplification of thoughts and personal statements. The experiential nature of this DMP work has magnified meaning of the lived experience, where my intention has been for a topic under discussion to be understood from an embodied sense of our sexual and gendered being. Long-term experiential processing is particularly important to people with learning disabilities who may struggle with complex verbal communication and cognitive processing. This ongoing embodied experience is a bridge from unprocessed emotional or intellectual experience to more individual appreciation of emotional effect on self and others.

Embodying a client's movement expression is integral to work as a DMP, where attunement to a client's processes from my felt and somatic sense (Hartley, 2004; Winters, 2008) allows me to remain curious about what that movement feels like to me (Fischman, 2009). My intention when working with people who do not use improvised movement the way I do is to support our empathic movement relationships through movement shaping (Best, 2003; Loman and Sossin, 2009) and verbal reflections that resonate with each other (Sheets-Johnstone, 2010) via our neural pathways (Winters, 2008). In this way, we do not have to grasp the concept cognitively or conceptually but experience it through our somatic experience and empathic connection (McGarry and Russo, 2011). For example, I might notice that Basil,[2] while seated in a chair, is making many changes to his leg and feet positions. As a group, we have developed a use of humour in our interactions, so I echo Basil's movement and make changes to my leg and feet positions. Basil and I make eye contact as he notices we are doing similar movements; he begins to exaggerate what I am doing and the shared movement becomes more and more playful until we both stop with feet on the floor. I amplify an exhalation and sit back. Basil says 'Oh that feels better Geoffery'. Without words we have shared a somatic movement exchange that has allowed Basil to settle in the present moment. After the movement, which the rest of the group have watched, John laughs, Michael says 'You're mad', and Roger says 'Do you feel better Basil'?

Such explicit consideration of the impact of emotions on posture (Rossberg-Gempton and Poole, 1993) is important with this client group, as so much of the lived emotional, somatic and physiological experience is manifest in the posture and gesture of people with learning disabilities and complex needs who may struggle with or have no verbal expression.

The group

Consultation with the arts therapies team led to the following criteria for referral to the group:

- Thoughts of loneliness due to being single.
- Frustration around sexual expression.
- Difficult feelings due to not having a physical relationship with another person.
- Confused feelings about intimacy, sexuality or love.
- Self-esteem issues related to sexual orientation.

All group members were initially referred by their keyworker within the day service; subsequent referrals came from within the arts therapies team and from the mental health team for people with a learning disability. All group participants had a one-to-one meeting to discuss their reasons for referral and to ask if they thought they would benefit from the group. All were informed that I wished to research the group, which was explained with a user-friendly information sheet on 'what is research'. Following this meeting each client agreed to be a research participant, with one client saying no to any photography or video being used. I have not used any film or photography throughout the life of this group.

The closed group ran for four years, with four participants being members throughout. Participants were aged between twenty-nine and sixty-three. An initial member left after the first year due to leaving the service and two members

Men shaping men 125

joined in the second year. Therefore, the same six members attended from year two to year four. Most group members attended the day service on the day of the session, so there was a regular attendance of five members. One participant was an external client who attended less often. Unfortunately, the work ended due to financial cuts in the arts therapies service and my consequent redundancy.

Session notes

I have included examples of early session notes to set the context for my observations and discussion of the group movement process. These illustrations highlight shape and movement observations with the thematic content of some early sessions.

Session one

Presented group rationale and consent forms. John, Michael and Roger agreed to all, Basil began by agreeing then when completing the form filled in all yes and no sections, which suggested indecision/ambivalence. Craig did not agree to any film or photography.

Significant themes

Being men, safety, respect. Lots of laughter and joking, camaraderie? Can we talk about sex?

Movement/shaping

Group sat quite close together on chairs. Legs are predominant – out and crossed, one crossed over at knee, or spread with feet flat on floor. All gives a sense of weight and posturing.

Group all agreed to stand and look at the group in the mirror. 'Here is the group, here is a group of men, see how different we all are' were words I shared. They responded with laughter and affirmation. John stood back from the mirror and did not make direct eye contact or look in the mirror.

Group explored props and space. Basil took charge of props and fabric, giving fabric to others and draping self in fabric; also-threw balls and beanbags to group then sat on various beanbags. He stretched out on large one to relax for last fifteen minutes. John stayed seated near GU with occasional direct eye contact. Some talk of girlfriends – when asked what having a girlfriend meant there was no reply.

Shapes

Very solid shapes in the space that are not consciously formed, a sense of finding oneself shaped in the space by coincidence! These shapes appear as

Session Four

Collaboration via the group rules with John holding the paper and handing it to GU to pin up – Basil took paper down at end and began to fold it. When encouraged asked John to help – who declined at first, though with encouragement from GU folded it up and left it in group folder. Sexual orientation – Craig asked GU direct question re orientation and GU answered honestly. Craig then apologised for asking – GU affirmed that it is okay to ask and okay to be who we are. Brief talk about having a partner or not led to John saying Elton John was married and they have a baby. Brief explanation of artificial insemination, egg donors and surrogate motherhood. Some talk of other people giving distasteful looks on way to the day centre, reiteration of difference and to be aware of using prejudicial language. Girlfriends and wanting one, or the possibility that it might be a boyfriend. Discussion with all stating how many brothers or sisters they have and where they live.

Shapes

Basil held big posture leaning forward on knees with one hand on forehead and the other arm resting across knee. GU asked group what this posture might say. Michael said headache, John said thinking and Craig said depression. Much more individual shapes this week with all taking more of their own space by sitting further away from each other – making choices.

John still very curious and taking more flexible posture, shifting shape that suggested some softening. Basil folding and unfolding – trying to find a shape that fits? Craig some rigidity through tensions in body structure – tensions in self and what is and is not allowed? Michael quite upright, very attentive posture – alert and ready – hands seem prominent in their shaping of the space.

Session Fourteen

Group sat throughout speaking of the recent death of a service user. All shared thoughts re what happens when we die: where do we go, heaven and earth, what is spirit, disease, resuscitation, burial, cremation, funeral services. All were very attentive to other people's words and feelings. John left and returned to share letter re service info with the group, Michael left early to go to bathroom, John and Craig left early, Basil and Roger stayed until end.

Movement/Shaping

Lots of stillness/calm in the group – maybe group theme invited calm and gentle reflection? John joined group discussion rather than moving self away as in previous sessions. Sense of a very supportive circle – staying in the circle to feel the support – to feel safe enough to share personal thoughts – and to own, appreciate and acknowledge one's feelings to the group. Movement qualities were quite gentle and constant throughout – this sustainability was also reflected in the group's thematic process that was also constant throughout – sense of the vertical in conversations on what happens after death – gestures skyward to heaven, the moon, another planet, and some conversation on differences in personal belief systems. John stood in centre for several minutes to focus and take in words of mine related to owning feelings (processing of emotional affect?).

Embodied amplification of personal process

During sessions, I continued to playfully model the amplification of posture and gesture to support the men's awareness of shapes they inhabit in their conversation. This mode of practice (intervention) came about through my initial observations of the men in the group and of other men in the setting. What I observed is (what I experience as) a stereotypical hetero-normative male camaraderie, with back slapping and joking (taking the mickey) as a demonstration of empathy. This was brought into the group by the men and incorporated into our initial shared movement repertoire with ongoing discussion on the impact of these actions on each other. This style of jocular intervention is not something I would automatically do with a group. Through my initial embodied expression of statements the men make in their nonverbal communication, and in the animated punctuation of their verbal communication, they were able to observe in me how their nonverbal communication is experienced by another person. A simple example is someone saying 'no' and using a stopping gesture, I echoed that gesture and amplified it several times while inviting the individual and/or the group to join me in amplifying the gesture of 'no'. We also amplified the verbal expression as well, ending with us all standing in a broad stance with strong arm gestures and loudly shouting 'NO'. We were then able to explore a range of movement, vocal and spatial levels to say 'No' while seeing and experiencing how that feels to self and others in relationship.

My ongoing amplification of the men's posture and gesture in this way supported the group in embodying their own self-expression. It may be that in this process the clients' mirror neurons (Berrol, 2006; McGarry and Russo, 2011) come into play as something of their intrapersonal experience recognises or resonates with the posture, gesture or movement they have seen. I remain mindful that even though similar neurological systems are at work, I cannot be prescriptive and definitively state that we all feel the same emotion when we see or experience the same movement (Winters, 2008).

Amplifying one another's posture and gesture requires that we trust each other in the moment of interaction (Butté and Unkovich, 2009). This trust is reliant on adjustments we make in relationships so developing an empathic connection (Fischman, 2009) means I can attune to tensions in the body and respond to changes in clients' use of breath and body shaping (Best, 2003, 2009). I have found that the use of breath in movement expression supports the release of vocal sounds and the spoken word (Butté, Unkovich and Whelan, 2012) for some clients who are selectively mute, or for those who struggle to let their voice be heard. Expanding and contracting as we breathe (Keleman, 1985, 2007) are like ebb-and-flow motions (Loman and Foley, 1996) that we experience in our nonverbal relationships. For example, John moved his chair right next to mine when he needed to feel safe or much further away when he felt our closeness was too intimate. This shared forming of our interpersonal experience results in the mutual reshaping of our relationships and so impacts on the way in which we are perceived in and experience our social environment (Butté and Unkovich, 2009).

When sharing the content of this study with the group I asked, 'What shapes do we make in this group?' The group responses were that 'our shapes say what we feel, our shapes are our emotions, when we get upset we get emotional, when our mind is restless our body is restless, you can't sit still you have to keep moving'. These reflections demonstrate their new awareness of the body in space and the potential impact that their emotions have on the body and vice versa.

It is important to remember that these relationships and our personal identities need not be fixed. We can shift the shapes of our relationships in response to the time, space and context of the sensorial and improvisatory experience (Allegranti, 2011). These relational movement experiences lead clients to experience their self as a person who has the potential to manage their intersubjective experience (Allegranti, 2013; Berrol, 2006; Samaritter and Payne, 2013).

Different styles of bodily expression incorporate a varied use of interpersonal space and as we move close together or further apart we make contact through the use of sight, sound and touch that stimulates nerve, muscle, and thought pathways (Fischman, 2009). This sensorial experience encourages a broader range of movement expression on biological, psychological and emotional levels. In the tactile movement exchange where the senses are stimulated the exploration and use of safe and *appropriate* touch is an important element of the work.

Touch

When working with people with complex physical and communication needs, the direct engagement of gross and fine motor skills and consideration of sensory processing related to the impact of touch on emotional experience is vital. The interplay of touch and subsequent sensorial experiences raises awareness of new possibilities in movement relationships, in proprioception and in the development of new or different motor skills that shape our interpersonal relationships. The use of touch (Leutar and Mihokovic, 2007; Popa and Best, 2010; Stötter *et al.*, 2013) was very quickly a topic of exploration as some group members' referral highlighted an inappropriate use of touch in interpersonal relationships. However, I make here an important distinction between incongruous and inappropriate touch, as I would argue that these men had not had enough learning opportunities to consolidate their understanding and experience of the use of touch in adult-to-adult relationships; for this reason, I view their use of touch as incongruous to social contexts, not inappropriate.

An integral element of shaping our interpersonal relationships is the use of safe touch in greetings, friendship and intimacy, so it was important for the group to explore touch through interactional movement and words in a safe context. Creative exploration of role play, shared observation of touch interactions, experimenting with personal boundaries and physical strength supported the discovery of safe and respectful touch to shape our interspatial relationships. Consequently, the group's increased movement awareness has led to better self-regulation of the appropriate use of self-touch in a public space, more congruent use of touch with another person and greater awareness of the use of personal strength in interactions. This better self-regulation was highlighted by the men's key-workers, who in client reviews mentioned obvious change in Basil's interpersonal touch and John's self-touch, for example. The use of touch can also stimulate, coerce, seduce or block interpersonal movement relationships (Best, 2009; Butté and Unkovich, 2009), so as a therapist it is vital to sense, respond, observe and interact with the very subtle nuances of touch (Popa and Best, 2010; Winters, 2008) to inform interventions and group members' interactions. This explicit tactile experience has provided the group and me with the opportunity to speak of and safely explore congruent and safe uses of touch in the wider context. For example, Basil, who is over six feet tall, initially presented with big hugs and close face-to-face greetings, which were experienced as overwhelming by others as he stooped to greet or show people affection. Through our movement improvisations and reflections on the impact of his stature and personal greeting style he has developed an appreciation of his impact on others. Consequently, he is now welcomed with ease by others as he offers a handshake that is pleasing for all and can be openly accepted and welcomed in numerous situations. He can of course still offer a hug and now seeks permission to do this.

My disclosure

My earlier session notes make specific mention of the group's curiosity about my sexual orientation and this highlights considerations of therapist disclosure. While preparing for the group, I had in-depth discussions with colleagues and in supervision regarding explicit transparency of my homosexuality to the group. This was because I experienced this setting as a hetero-normative environment and hence my awareness over time of a lack of openness to other gendered possibilities in this setting. This discussion and research led me to believe that if my intent was to support greater understanding and confidence in our different ways of being men, then I would need to be an authentic role model. My work and life experience has taught me that environments which restrict and/or persecute harmless sexual expression and diversity in sexual orientation can lead to damaging sexual behaviour, so we need to strive for greater appreciation of difference in our relationships. I also considered in this setting the potential impact of clients discussing my sexual orientation in the wider context.

130   Geoffery Unkovich

Within the group, I was surprised how quickly I was asked about my sexual orientation and in week three I diverted the conversation rather than answer directly as this was the first session that all participants were present. In week four I was asked the question again and answered openly, as avoidance or dishonesty went against my intention to be an authentic role model on what it means to be a man: this meant confirming to the group that I am a gay man. There were a range of responses from the group with Craig who asked the question saying, 'Ooh I am sorry for asking you'. Roger said, 'Geoffery I am sorry for you, it must be hard' and Basil asked 'Are you sad?' This set the scene for my regulated transparency in support of the men's process and led to many constructive conversations with greater understanding and acceptance of difference.

These are conversations these men had never had and have empowered them to speak of their own sexual identity and hopes of relationship while acknowledging that their needs and desires may be different to each other's.

An important consideration when working in a learning disability setting is the need for the contextualised holding of therapeutic boundaries as the therapy work advocates the support of social and communicative skills outside of the therapy space. For example, soon after the group began John, who has a strong voice, spoke with me excitedly in a busy corridor about my partner and me being homosexual and married. In this instance, I encouraged conversation in a soft voice in preference to postponing the conversation to the next therapy session. This was an important intervention for John as it supported his conversation and did not suggest excluding discussion on gendered relationships in the wider context. Through repetition of this interaction on other occasions, he was more able to appreciate and implement soft speaking when addressing personal matters in a public space. In following sessions, the group were also able to discuss and appreciate the significance of sharing personal information in a public space, while not denying that sensitive discussions on gender and sexuality need to be undertaken. Through this work we have all become more able to experience fluidity in our gender and sexual identities (Sherry, 2004) where we do not need to fit an either/or belief system or social model. When asked what they have learnt about gender and sexuality from the group, some responses were 'being gay or straight is quite normal, this is a space to talk about men's personal habits and safe sex'.

Benefits and outcomes

When reviewing our time together, we discussed group and individual experiences. The men said that the group is a place to

- learn different things about being a man;
- get your frustrations out;
- find a way to be happy;
- learn about self-control;
- listen to others and hear each other;
- talk about problems;

- express your feelings;
- learn to take turns;
- speak honestly with other men;
- take care of each other and yourself.

Over time group members experienced movement as part of their inter-relational experience more often and became more comfortable with embodied amplification as an intervention. Movement also brought much laughter to the group, which was a release of tension when discussing sensitive topics or due to the group being energised by an individual's verbal and nonverbal expression. Their greater physical awareness led to discussions on different types of abuse, self-care, intimacy, physical disabilities, fitness, weight, drugs, alcohol and the impact of medication on bodily processes such as energy and libido. Other significant themes were the loss of family members and friends, ways of grieving, remembering others, remembering our earlier lives, the impact of war and violence perpetrated by men, the qualities of being a man and acceptance of difference.

Some members of this group have difficulties expressing their feelings (Wilson *et al.*, 2010) and have had habitual ways of thinking and being to divert attention away from personal feelings; this has previously led them to always responding in the same manner (McClure *et al.*, 2009). For example, always speaking of transport issues or public holiday dates as a distraction from the anxiety of speaking about personal experience. As a consequence of the depth of embodied experience in their nonverbal (and verbal) expression, the group have developed much greater self-regulation of their emotional processes (Todd *et al.*, 2012). The embodied process and greater movement awareness has led group members to become much more capable of experiencing what it is like to pause, inhale, think (McClure *et al.*, 2009), exhale and embody letting go of anxiety, so they are now more able to notice their emotional experience. For example, by the end of the group John was able to acknowledge that when he spoke of sports fixtures or calendar social events it was because a conversation was too close to his feelings. He was then able to say 'I don't want to talk about it now'.

Conclusion

Through this DMP work, I have been able to explore with the men a range of emotional experiences and differences that has allowed them to become more able to self-manage sharing the space and time together, to listen more earnestly to one another, to respect each other's personal space, and to consider developing a different opinion through informed discussion. Due to several years of developing awareness of their personal movement preferences (Sheets-Johnstone, 2010) in their posture and gesture, the men's movement direction and path are now more clarified with much less chance of the incidental collisions I initially experienced. These inter-relational and interspatial skills have led to enhanced collaborations, appreciation of cooperation to support each other, and greater capacity to self-regulate anxiety in contexts outside of the group.

Reshaping our relationships has included remembering life stories and experiences that have arisen in the embodied shaping of our shared movement dialogue (Samaritter, 2009). This has enhanced our gender perceptions that are experienced in the body and in the physical, emotional and psychological interspatial shaping of our body. Explicit embodiment of and use of the word 'shape' is a construct that these men grasped well; so explicitly incorporating the use of shapes into this DMP work has provided something concrete to be visualised and embodied. After four years, the men's shapes are now more malleable with greater conscious formation and fluidity in their use of space. They are now less likely to find themselves shaped in the space by coincidence as they have much better awareness of the shapes they make and the impression that their shape has on others (Sheets-Johnstone, 2010). The group now has a greater appreciation of their differences and know that we do not all need to be the same type of man. Being men in this therapy and social context has raised our understanding of different ways of being, of speaking and acting with respect for those who are not the same as ourselves, and of being genuinely supportive of each other in our differences. Most importantly this group has given these men a chance to be seen, heard and respected for their now amplified individuality.

These men have given me a much greater appreciation of my own gender, sexuality and sexual orientation in a men's group context. Like them, I am more malleable in my interpersonal shaping and so am much more conscious of the impact of my shaping in a range of circumstances.

The significant personal realisation in this writing is about my brother, Richard.[3] While assessing why and what I am writing about these men with learning disabilities, I have remembered that my ease and interest in the shaping of posture and gesture is because I know this so well; this was integral to Richard's way of being. His arms and hands that folded, unfolded, twisted, turned, wrapped, unravelled and reached out to others are integral to my own familial and interpersonal shaping. I thank him for inadvertently teaching me how to consider being shaped as a man.

Notes

1   Williams syndrome is a genetic condition that includes developmental delays, learning disabilities and medical problems such as cardiovascular disease,
2   In this chapter, I use pseudonyms to protect client confidentiality. I used GU for myself in the original session notes. This is intentional as it helps to place me as a group member.
3   My three living brothers enthusiastically support using Richard's real name in this context.

References

Allegranti, B. (2009) 'Embodied performances of sexuality and gender: A feminist approach to dance movement psychotherapy and performance practice'. *Body, Movement and Dance in Psychotherapy*, 4(1): 17–31.

Allegranti, B. (2011) 'Ethics and body politics: Interdisciplinary possibilities for embodied psychotherapeutic practice and research'. *British Journal of Guidance and Counselling*, 39(5): 487–500.

Allegranti, B. (2013) 'The politics of becoming bodies: Sex, gender and intersubjectivity in motion'. *The Arts in Psychotherapy*, 40: 394–403.

Bedard, C., Zhang, H. L. and Zucker, K. (2010) 'Gender identity and sexual orientation in people with developmental disabilities'. *Sexuality and Disability*, 28(3): 165–175.

Behrends, A., Müller, S. and Dziobek, I. (2012) 'Moving in and out of synchrony: A concept for a new intervention fostering empathy through interactional movement and dance'. *The Arts in Psychotherapy*, 39(2): 107–116.

Berrol, C. (2006) 'Neuroscience meets dance/movement therapy: Mirror neurons, the therapeutic process and empathy'. *The Arts in Psychotherapy*, 33(4): 302–315.

Best, P. (2003) 'Interactional shaping within therapeutic encounters: Three dimensional dialogues'. *The USA Body Psychotherapy Journal*, 2(1): 3–11.

Best, P. (2009) 'Swim alongside, block and then seduce: Building blocks of relationship'. Scoble, S., Ross, M. and Lapoujade, C. (eds.) *Arts in Arts Therapies: A European Perspective.* Plymouth, UK: University of Plymouth Press.

Butté, C., Unkovich, G. and Whelan, D. (2012) 'Turning, listening, moving closer, as you speak, when you dance. Arts Therapies for adults with profound and complex needs'. *PMLD Link*, 24(1)71: 22–25.

Cuskelly, M. and Bryde, R. (2004) 'Attitudes towards the sexuality of adults with an intellectual disability: parents, support staff, and a community sample'. *Journal of Intellectual & Developmental Disability*, 29(3): 255–264.

Fischman, D. (2009) 'Therapeutic relationships and kinesthetic empathy'. Chaiklin, S. and Wengrower, H. (eds.) *The Art and Science of Dance/Movement Therapy.* London: Routledge.

Hartley, L. (2004) *Somatic Psychology.* London: Whurr Publishers.

Hoffman, R., Hattie, J. and Borders, L. (2008) 'Personal definitions of masculinity and femininity as an aspect of gender self-concept'. *Journal of Humanistic Counseling, Education and Development*, 44(1): 66–83.

Hollins, S. and Sinason, V. (2000) 'Psychotherapy, learning disabilities and trauma: New perspectives'. *British Journal of Psychiatry*, 176(1): 32–36.

Keleman, S. (1985) *Emotional Anatomy.* Berkeley, CA: Center Press.

Keleman, S. (2007) 'A biological vision'. *The USA Body Psychotherapy Journal*, 6(1): 9–14.

Leutar, Z. and Mihokovic, M. (2007) 'Level of knowledge about sexuality of people with mental disabilities'. *Sexuality and Disability*, 25(3): 93–109.

Loman, S.. and Foley, L. (1996) 'Models for understanding the nonverbal process in relationships'. *The Arts in Psychotherapy*, 23(4): 341–350.

Loman, S. and Sossin, K. M. (2009) 'Applying Kestenberg Movement Profile in dance/movement therapy'. Chaiklin, S. and Wengrower, H. (eds.) *The Art and Science of Dance/Movement Therapy.* London: Routledge.

McCarthy, J., Sinason, V. and Hollins, S. (2012) 'Intellectually disabled in Britain: Sexuality and procreation'. Chichester, UK: eLS. John Wiley & Sons, Ltd.

McClure, K., Halpern, J., Wolper, P. and Donahue, J. (2009) 'Emotion regulation and intellectual disability'. *Journal on Developmental Disabilities*, 15(2): 38–44.

McGarry, L. and Russo, F. (2011) 'Mirroring in dance/movement therapy: Potential mechanisms behind empathy enhancement'. *The Arts in Psychotherapy*, 38(3): 178–184.

McVittie, C., Goodall, K. and McKinlay, A. (2008) 'Resisting having learning disabilities by managing relative abilities'. *British Journal of Learning Disabilities*, 36(4): 256–262.

Milligan, S. and Neufeldt, A. (2001) 'The myth of asexuality: A survey of social and empirical evidence'. *Sexuality and Disability*, 19(2): 91–109.

Noonan, A. and Taylor Gomez, M. (2010) 'Who's missing? Awareness of lesbian, gay, bisexual and transgender people with intellectual disability. *Sexuality and Disability*, 29(2): 175–180.

Popa, M. and Best, P. (2010) 'Making sense of touch in dance movement therapy: A trainee's perspective'. *Body, Movement and Dance in Psychotherapy*, 5(1): 31–44.

Rembis, M. (2010) 'Beyond the binary: Rethinking the social model of disabled sexuality'. *Sexuality and Disability*, 28(1): 51–60.

Rossberg-Gempton, I. and Poole, G. (1993) 'The effect of open and closed postures on pleasant and unpleasant emotions'. *The Arts in Psychotherapy*, 20(1): 75–82.

Samaritter, R. (2009) 'The use of metaphors in dance movement therapy'. *Body, Movement and Dance in Psychotherapy*, 4(1): 33–43.

Samaritter, R. and Payne, H. (2013) 'Kinaesthetic intersubjectivity: A dance informed contribution to self-other relatedness and shared experience in non-verbal psychotherapy with an example from autism'. *The Arts in Psychotherapy*, 40(1): 143–150.

Shakespeare, T. (1999) The sexual politics of disabled masculinity'. *Sexuality and Disability*, 17(1): 53–64.

Sheets-Johnstone, M. (2010) 'Kinesthetic experience: Understanding movement inside and out'. *Body, Movement and Dance in Psychotherapy*, 5(2): 111–127.

Sherry, M. (2004) 'Overlaps and contradictions between queer theory and disability studies'. *Disability & Society*, 19(7): 769–783.

Shuttleworth, R. (2000) 'The search for sexual intimacy for men with cerebral palsy'. *Sexuality and Disability*, 18(4): 263–282.

Shotter, J. (2004) 'Responsive expression in living bodies. The power of invisible "real presences" within our everyday lives together'. *Cultural Studies*, 18(2/3): 443–460.

Siebers, T. (2008) *Disability Theory*. Ann Arbor, MI: University of Michigan Press.

Sinason, V. (1992) *Mental Handicap and the Human Condition*. London: Free Association Books.

Stötter, A., Mitsche, M., Endler, P., Olesky, P., Kamenschek, D., Mosgoeller, W. and Haring, C. (2013) 'Mindfulness-based touch therapy and mindfulness practice in persons with moderate depression'. *Body, Movement and Dance in Psychotherapy*, 8(3): 183–198.

Swango-Wilson, A. (2010) 'Systems theory and the development of sexual identity for individuals with intellectual/developmental'. *Sexuality and Disability*, 28(3): 157–164.

Todd, R., Cunningham, W., Anderson, A. and Thompson, E. (2012) 'Affect-biased attention as emotion regulation'. *Trends in Cognitive Sciences*, 16(7): 365–372.

Wheeler, P. (2007) "I count myself as normal, well, not normal, but normal enough." Men with learning disabilities tell their stories about sexuality and sexual identity'. *Learning Disability Review*, 12(1): 16–27.

Wilson, N., Parmenter, T., Stancliffe, R. and Shuttleworth, R. (2011) 'Conditionally sexual: Men and teenage boys with moderate to profound intellectual disability'. *Sexuality and Disability*, 29(3): 275–289.

Wilson, N., Parmenter, T., Stancliffe, R., Shuttleworth, R. and Parker, D. (2010) 'A masculine perspective of gendered topics in the research literature on males and females with intellectual disability'. *Journal of Intellectual & Developmental Disability*, 35(1): 1–8.

Winters, F. (2008) 'Emotion, embodiment, and mirror neurons in dance/movement therapy: A connection across disciplines'. *American Journal of Dance Therapy*, 30(2): 84–105.

Yacoub, E. and Hall, I. (2009) 'The sexual lives of men with mild learning disability: A qualitative study'. *British Journal of Learning Disabilities*, 3(1): 5–11.

Online resources

Butté, C. and Unkovich, G. (2009) 'When disabilities disappear. Foundations of dance movement psychotherapy practice in profound and multiple learning disabilities'. *e-motion*, 14(2): 29–33. Available at admp.org.uk (Accessed 01/05/14).

Chapter 10

How can I meet Syon where he is today?

Céline Butté

Introduction

In this chapter, I present my reflections on how dance movement psychotherapy (DMP) offered a psychotherapeutic intervention that attended to Syon's experience of chronic pain, loss of mobility and increased dependence on others to perform activities of daily life. I share vignettes that illustrate my interventions; reflect on the challenges I faced through working with this vulnerable middle-aged man, week after week, until his passing; and address how this piece of work pushed me to the edges of meaning making and stretched my understanding of DMP.

Syon had Down's syndrome, which tells us little about him really, as people with Down's syndrome have all degrees of learning disabilities and have more in common with their families than with each other (Down's Syndrome Association, 2016). He had a gentle nature and a warm contagious smile; his friends, family, good food and singing at his local church were the most important things in his life. He lived at home with his mother and sister for many years and, following his mother's ill health a few years ago, had moved into a modern, warm and homely care home. His family visited him every weekend and were lovingly attentive to his well-being, to the point that throughout Syon's several hospital stays, they always took it in turn to stay with him, day and night.

Dramatic changes to his physical independence and sense of self brought on by myelopathy[1] prompted a referral to a DMP. Syon had been affected by myelopathy for many years. However, when he lost the ability to feed himself and carry out his personal care independently, started to experience acute bouts of pain and became wheelchair bound, staff at the day centre requested one-to-one DMP to provide him with a reliable and safe space to process these dramatic changes. At the time of referral, Syon's good comprehension and ability to express himself verbally with two- to three-word sentences were not affected by myelopathy; it was only in the very last stage of his condition that Syon stopped communicating verbally.

Syon and I knew one another quite well as he had previously attended a weekly music and movement therapy group I co-ran with a colleague music therapist at the day centre where the arts therapies service is based. During these sessions, he had found joy and excitement using arm and leg movements as well as his voice. Lifting his arms up in the air and wafting a scarf he delicately held with his fingers, for example, would often bring him much joy; on other occasions, he would apply himself with focus, and exude pride when succeeding to place, on his own, both his hands underneath his legs to lift and gently shake them, one at a time. Or he would project his voice with confidence when singing the hello and goodbye songs. Syon was a committed member of these sessions that offered him a creative and reflective space every week (Butté and Whelan, in press).

Looking back through Syon's DMP journey, it is possible to recognise five significantly different phases in our work together, each brought on by changes triggered by the progression of the myelopathy.

Arriving: Engaging in a shared dance-movement-sound-word story

Syon and I spent many earlier sessions creating stories that expressed what he was willing and able to convey about his experience. For the first couple of months of our one-to-one work at the day centre, Syon was engaged and forthcoming with verbal communication, using words such as 'story', 'movement', 'Syon', Céline', 'Elia' (his sister), 'yes', 'no' and 'body'. We embodied these words. At times, I weaved my words with Syon's and created sentences and stories, checking with him what he wanted and adapting the movement and story accordingly. This was a to-and-fro creative process with a verbal and embodied storyline that unfolded organically between us as the session progressed.

My focus during this time was on encouraging independent creative movement and verbal and sound expression as well as some release through movement and sounds. *Why?* I knew through my previous work with Syon (as described) that singing, engaging his arms and legs in creative movement and inviting a gentle attention to his body brought him joy and satisfaction; during those moments of shared dance-movement-story-sound-making that engaged his abilities and skills, Syon's face would light up. Sensorimotor psychotherapy (SP), a prominent embodied approach to working with trauma, would describe these as some of his resources (Ogden *et al.*, 2006) as they tapped into the memory of events and activities that made Syon happy. Neurologically speaking, these activities triggered the release of 'happy hormones' (endorphins, serotonin, dopamine and oxytocin). Knowing how to support Syon in connecting to feeling pleasure in life offered a safe ground to which we and, most importantly, he could return in difficult times. SP describes how, in trauma work, reconnecting to our resources enables us to modulate and even deactivate debilitating anxiety-laden experiences, fuelling instead pathways that nurture resilience and self-healing processes. It was evident that my work with Syon focused on the trauma he was going through within himself and the way it rippled into all aspects of his life. Therefore, finding, recognising and capitalising on these resources was essential to our work. Tapping into our shared history also fostered the establishment of a comfortable, playful and inquisitive dialogue between us.

In a discussion with his sister, during this early stage of Syon's therapy, we realised that it was not clear whether Syon had been informed of his diagnosis. Sadly, research tells us that communication about their diagnosis with people with learning disabilities is poor (Heslop *et al.*, 2013). There is no record either of patients with learning disabilities being involved in end-of-life decision making (Bekkema *et al.*, 2014) and little record of research into palliative care for people with learning disabilities (Tuffrey-Winje *et al.*, 2016).

This conversation with Syon's sister felt like a pause in a whirlwind of activities and professional interventions that, while well intentioned, deny the person with learning disabilities the opportunity to be included in his own life and, more to the point here, in his own death. *Why?* To spare him the pain of knowing because we think that he 'will not be able to cope' or that 'he will not understand'? Or are these excuses and clichés that cover a much starker and broader truth: our desperate attempt at sparing ourselves the pain of feeling helpless in letting someone know that they are dying (De Hennezel, 1997), whether they have a learning disability or not?

I needed to be clear that Syon knew what was happening to him, physically and neurologically, if I was to carry out any meaningful body-oriented psychotherapeutic work with him. Through my conversation with Syon's sister, we agreed that I would speak to him about his diagnosis and prognosis. So, when I met with him over the subsequent weeks, I used words, eye contact, exploring where to position myself and tuning in to his subtle nonverbal communication cues to share with him what I knew about his condition. I held some silent pauses between all that I wanted to say to allow for his response. I felt awkward many times; sharing this information verbally and knowing that Syon did not have the words to respond and ask questions triggered an unease in me about not only what I was sharing but also the discrepancy in our ways of communicating. *How much to share? What words to use?* Sometimes I told Syon about these uncomfortable feelings and sometimes I held them in our silence. I took my whole being – body, heart, senses and soul – to our encounters and reflected with him on his experience. Besides sharing feelings I knew were mine, I shared with him possible feelings that he might be experiencing.

In my work with clients whose communication is predominantly nonverbal, I share my own feelings; feelings that I believe are theirs which I am intuitively, somatically or emotionally resonating with; and the feelings that would be natural for many of us in a given situation – those that are part of our collective human experience. I do this in order to let my clients know that we indeed all have feelings and that no feelings are taboo. My aim is to hold the truth of each person's experience and acknowledge that someone's experience is important for what it is. It is also my way of inviting my clients to recognise their own feelings more clearly in order to soften the powerful grip of unconscious resistance to or denial of all that we find uncomfortable and unknown. I let Syon know that there was no map for the territory we were navigating together, but that we would figure it out as we went along. My intention was to support him in allowing his experience simply to be and in trusting himself. I invited us to be present to and curious about the changes, seeking to create a context in which he could feel met, as well as free to reject what I was offering (Butté and Unkovich, 2009).

During these moments of sharing his diagnosis and prognosis with Syon, there was a palpable sense of relief in the room as our eyes met with intensity; it felt as if Syon was thanking me through his gaze. And as his condition progressed, every time we looked his situation in the face, we continued to meet through eye contact, a constant marker of our relationship. Such profound moments of arriving and accepting resonated all the way to the core of my being. During those moments, I experienced a deep sense of peace. *Did Syon also feel this deep peace?* I believe so as these were the times when he would utter my name with much warmth, or breathe out a deep sigh and smile his most heart-warming, wise man's smile. It was through verbally and nonverbally attuning to each other at those times when I felt most hopeless, that Syon and I experienced the most powerful moments of connection, not only to each other but also to something much greater than ourselves.

Pain!

During the subsequent two months, Syon's experience of physical pain increased significantly and his spasms became more frequent. Whilst this was being medically addressed, Syon brought to my attention his burning need to have his back massaged, to have his legs touched and stretched, and to have his shoes and socks removed. Being touched or having clothes on can at times be painful for someone with myelopathy (*NHS choices,*, 2014). Syon's expression of relief when resting his legs on a beanbag without shoes or socks let me know how essential it was to attend to the positioning of his body as his legs and back tightened under the grip of myelopathy.

This was a time of urgency and action, a time during which I desperately sought to answer Syon's pleading commands so as to offer him as much relief from the pain as possible. These sessions were charged with intense emotions as Syon and I faced the stormy waters of his experience: from agony, despair and hopelessness to frustration, anger and exhaustion, with moments of blissful relief.

Immobility, loss, grief and acceptance

Five months into our work, Syon stopped attending the centre due to a pressure sore wound that would not heal. A temporary measure at the time, this non-attendance was recognised as permanent a year later. With hindsight one might wonder why it took a year for a whole multidisciplinary team (MDT) and a caring family to realise this. But the progression of an illness is vicious and invisible when one is caught up in it, and we were all caught up in it, to varying degrees. The hope that things would return to 'normal' (i.e. Syon returning to the centre) was so compelling that it took us all time and courage to recognise and accept that temporary had become permanent. But finally, I too understood: I stopped waiting in the movement studio and made it to Syon's bedside in his home. The beginning of this period was difficult as we had to learn how to undertake DMP whilst he was lying in bed and wearing far fewer clothes than he had at the day centre, often only a tee-shirt, an incontinence pad and a duvet over his bare legs.

What could we do? How to be together? How to be Syon's therapist? Aware of how much more intimate the sessions had become due to taking place in his bedroom and anxious about how my work might be perceived by anyone at his home, I stopped offering Syon touch. In this more intimate context, I did not feel equipped enough professionally to use touch with him, despite his requests for me to do so. So, I held back from touching him and preferred to focus on the use of upper body movement and creative sounds. We continued creating stories and inviting movement with the words he shared. During that time, I also brought attention to the weather and the outside world, offering us some relief or, perhaps, escape. From then on, opening Syon's curtains or a window and moving his bed so that he could see outside became part of the sessions. It felt so intense with the two of us in his bedroom that I needed to bring the outside in, or maybe to allow a bit of the intensity of the inside to slip out. Most of the time, Syon would open his eyes, utter my name and our eyes would meet. We had arrived, he from the confines of solitude in his bedroom and I from my hectic commute to his place.

Spending all his time in bed precipitated further significant losses in Syon's mobility. He became unable to lift his arms as high, the movement in his legs disappeared completely, his joints became stiff and he lost his grip. At that point, the MDT recognised that due to his evolving prognosis our input should follow a palliative approach to care, aiming to make Syon's life as comfortable as possible by managing his pain and other distressing symptoms. The National Council for Palliative Care (*Palliative Care Explained*, 2015) and the NHS (*End of Life Care*, 2015) stress that palliative care is a holistic approach that involves psychological, social and spiritual support for the individual concerned as well as for their family or carers. This informed and supported my intuitive sense of how to work with Syon as I directed my intentions to meeting his physical, psychological, social and spiritual self. I liaised more spontaneously with his family, carers and the MDT and attended with renewed curiosity to our time together to make sure embodied creative interventions and verbal and nonverbal communication continued to provide Syon with a reliable and meaningful context in which he could be seen, heard and held.

In Figure 10.1, I illustrate how I understand DMP provided a holistic container to various aspects of Syon's life.

During this phase, Syon closed his eyes for extended periods of time, sometimes clearly asleep but at other times probably not. I would stay with him, regardless; it did not feel right to consider his closing his eyes as a cue for me to leave. During those moments, I wondered whether Syon was dreaming, whether he was cutting himself off from a world he struggled to engage with, or whether he was opening up to something else: from awake to asleep, from engagement with

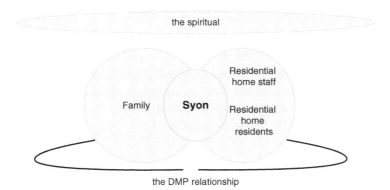

Figure 10.1 DMP holistic container.

life to withdrawal from life (Coaten and Houston, 2016). Seated next to Syon, I wondered about my role as DMP in those moments. Reading palliative care psychologist De Hennezel (1997) reassured my intuitive sense that staying with him in those moments was an important clinical intervention. When Syon had his eyes shut, I turned my attention inwards, attending to my feelings, senses and posture and tuning into my needs, cultivating a self-caring presence. When Syon opened his eyes again, I would speak from this place of noticing, asking him whether he too had been on an inner journey and expressing my curiosity about what he had found behind the veil of his closed eyes. On many occasions, Syon's expression on opening his eyes showed his joy at my still being there with him. He would call my name with a kind, gentle tone of voice or simply meet my eyes and smile.

Syon's smiles were a significant part of his therapeutic journey. At times, they were broad and relaxed and conveyed joy, even a sense of peace. At other times, however, Syon's smiles were tight and seemed forced. They conveyed unease. On these occasions, I reminded him that during his therapy, he did not have to put on a smile to make me more comfortable with the situation. If he was in pain, I could be with this; if he was angry, frustrated, fed up, disappointed, we could be with these feelings together. On several occasions, Syon made direct eye contact and sighed, a sigh of relief, I believe, in being allowed to simply be himself. Robbin Higgins talks of 'authentic and healing sadness' and contrasts it with the sustained atmosphere of 'hysterical merriment' imposed on residents in care homes (in Waller, 2002: xiii). Although he describes dementia care, his words resonate with my work with Syon.

Whilst Syon's movement range significantly reduced during this third phase, our work continued. During this time, it felt important to acknowledge both the changed or lost functions in Syon's body and to focus on and celebrate what worked, such as the rotation in his shoulders, a little rise of the arms, his breath and gentle sounds. This, I believe, offered him an opportunity to experience 'a sense of constancy, stability and continuity not only of [his] body but of [himself], as a

142 Céline Butté

person [...] providing him with a sense of dependability and solidity' (Papadopoulos, 2015: 4; Coaten and Houston, 2016), whilst I bore the losses with him too.

Embodied listening, tactile presence

One year into our work together and following recurring debilitating episodes of aspiration pneumonias leading to hospitalisation, Syon was fitted with a PEG.[2] During this period, the work took place at the hospital on and off and in Syon's bedroom when back home. With the PEG, Syon faced yet another loss, that of not being able to use his mouth to drink or eat anymore, something he enjoyed so much. The slower rhythm of his digestion also impacted on our work as at times just digesting his breakfast required all of his energy. Syon was not experiencing such acute pain anymore, however, and his spasms were less frequent. Still uncomfortable about offering direct physical contact, I introduced a silk scarf into our work, to create a bridge between us. The scarf also enabled me to gently offer him some relief from being in the same position for extended periods of time and a way to connect to body parts he often indicated, such as his back. I would slide the scarf behind his shoulders and under his arms, and gently pull. As he experienced his slightly changed posture, Syon would often ask for 'more'.

One day, following my attendance at a Body Mind Centering® training (BMC),[3] I reintroduced the use of touch, in response to Syon's repeated requests that I massage his legs. I applied gentle touch on his legs and feet, placing my hands over his duvet. Syon opened his eyes, apparently encouraging me to continue. The quality of touch I was offering invites a conscious, tactile presence to the muscular and nervous systems – a form of hands-on 'listening' with no intention to 'do' anything. What I learned in this training supported what I already knew about holding a deeply attuned presence with the other and gave me the confidence to reintroduce touch into the work with Syon. As I held my hands lightly on his legs, I explained to Syon what I was doing. This refined understanding of touch supported my trust in deeply attuned presence through our hands, and reminded me of the importance of being fully awake to the flow of life, to the aliveness of my own body in order to fully come into relationship with the flow of life in Syon. This quality of attuned presence through touch was in fact similar to my way of being with Syon in all aspects of our relationship, including those moments when he had his eyes shut. During this experience of my tactile presence, Syon found an enjoyable connection with his legs, as if able to recognise parts of him through my touch. He seemed surprised by this, as he made inquisitive and warm eye contact. This tactile connection became part of many of Syon's sessions from then on.

As he had lost the pleasure of taste, one of the senses that animated him the most, it was significant to be able to offer Syon the possibility to feel alive through the sense of touch. Syon's spasms would also ease or even stop when I used this form of hands-on attunement with him. This form of embodied presence nourished my practice and enabled us to continue the therapeutic dialogue (Dymoke, 2014) at a time when I could have let Syon's frequently closed eyes and shutting down body push me away.

Letting go

This last phase of my work with Syon lasted about a month (i.e. four visits to his home) and was marked by his consistent refusal of any intervention; he would either be asleep when I arrived and not respond to my gentle calling of his name (an invitation he had never failed to respond to in previous sessions) or he would turn his head away from me.

One day, on finding out that Syon was in hospital, I had a conversation with his home manager and key staff, and told them that I thought it was time we prepared to let Syon go. It was my way of being present to what I had been witnessing for the past few weeks and of acknowledging with those around him that Syon was turning away from us all and perhaps towards something else. Later that day, I sent an email to his sister as I wanted to share with her what I had shared at his home. In my email, I only told her that it would be good to speak. The following week when I returned to work, I learned that Syon had passed away at the weekend. Later, when discussing the week prior to Syon's passing with his sister, I told her that my intention in that email had been to share with her what I had shared with staff at Syon's home. She remarked that my email (which only contained an invitation for us to speak) had somehow helped her trust her own intuitive sense that it was time to let Syon go when the medical team was desperately trying to resuscitate him. She had then found the courage to discuss letting Syon go with everyone else around him so as to support him as best they could with breathing his last breath.

Reflections

In my clinical work the therapeutic dialogue evolves around my clients' expression – verbal and nonverbal, creative and embodied – and around their physical experience of sensations and emotions. It is not a context in which my clients come with a verbally articulated problem that we investigate together through DMP. I have come to understand that relying primarily on the verbal to guide the focus of our work may be good as a starting point, but that it is in the body that we find what really needs attending to. How the work evolves may depart significantly from the original reason for referral. The territory we navigate together relies on ancestral modes of communication: somatic, intuitive and spiritual. My work with Syon was shaped around single words he uttered; my story making around these words; attention to our breath, to the intention to move, to the direction of his gaze and to the movement within and around us. I slipped readily into a predominantly nonverbal realm, while not completely relinquishing my own familiar verbal mode of expression (Butté and Unkovich, 2009). My intention was to avoid cluttering our shared space and time with my words, my experience and my world view.

In a society that is both goal oriented and fearful of the use of touch as a psychotherapeutic intervention, it is a challenge to the therapist to trust in the profound importance of sitting in silence with a client and to trust that touch is a natural and vital aspect of human dialogue. I grappled with the themes of 'doing nothing' and 'uselessness' on numerous occasions, at times doubting in the efficacy of my work with Syon. I was often challenged, in this largely nonverbal realm, to stay steady in my own trust that somehow what was happening between us was correct and necessary. Drawing on my practice of being present with my own experience of silence, I faced my own helplessness and looked into Syon's eyes. I met his smiles, his head turning away, his voice begging me to stay and asking me to leave. I drew on my dance background, informed by somatic movement practices such as BMC (Bainbridge Cohen, 2008; Hartley, 2004), as well as on my mindfulness in movement practice inspired by movement artist and DMP Sandra Reeve in particular (Bloom *et al.*, 2014; Reeve, 2011). I was reminded, in the core of my being, of the value of 'listening' fully and deeply to our experiences, mine and Syon's. BMC empowered me to use my hands again and offered us an exquisitely sensitive means of attending to him. These practices gave me tools to work in a way that I intuitively understood was necessary: an intuitive knowing that is in my own deep feeling for relationship; a knowing that is in my body and soul, where my own experience of the value of connecting with such a quality of presence, whether with another or with myself, safely rests.

Again and again, I stood alongside his family and carers, 'bearing witness to the slow dissolution of a loved one' (Waller, 2002: xiii). I held questions such as 'Why me?', 'Why so much pain?', 'Why so little movement?', 'Is this really life?', and then I asked myself, 'Are these questions mine or Syon's?' I, not he, was having these thoughts. However, in the DMP relationship with a nonverbal client, we always hold the possibility that the many questions that arise within us might perhaps be arising, unspoken, in our client. As the therapist, we attend closely to the possibility that anything we are experiencing – somatically, emotionally, intuitively – might be resonating with the experience of our client.

Conclusion

'Start with where the patient is', the famous phrase of pioneer DMP, Marian Chace (cited in Feldman, 2016,107), was repeated throughout my DMP training and has become a mantra in my practice. In my work with Syon, this translated into: *How can I meet Syon where he is today?* My dance background, both rigorous and theoretically generous DMP training and long-time practice with adults with learning disabilities (over fifteen years) enabled me to be receptive and to work creatively with his nonverbal expression and his soulful sounding and moving in the early stages of our work, giving Syon the opportunity to dance his dance. An in-depth understanding of trauma work, from a Sensorimotor Psychotherapy perspective in particular, helped me recognise the importance of 'good memories' and activities that gave Syon pleasure. Gradually, as Syon's ability to direct his limbs diminished and as he frequently kept his eyes shut during sessions, our focus turned towards the much subtler dance of life. In those moments, it was the ability to offer deeply attuned touch that enabled me to *meet Syon where he was*. Through touch, we discovered that there was another realm still to be explored: the life and dance within. Movement was always central in our relationship, initially as intentional, self-directed movement, then, as Syon's nervous system progressively shut down, as internal movement. There was life, therefore there was movement, visible initially and later palpable through touch. During our weekly meetings, I invited Syon to be whole, to be who he was. Together we found a place of deep connection. I believe that it is through staying with Syon's dance – always adjusting the quality of my presence, always attuning in order to meet him where he was – that I was ultimately able to recognise when Syon was ready to die. As Lear (2008: 153) aptly tells us: 'It is one thing to dance as if nothing has happened; it is another to acknowledge that something singularly awful has happened [...] and then decide to dance.'

Initially, the work with Syon felt like a descent. The most difficult step for me was to stop resisting this descent and to accept the direction of the work. Supervision offered a much-needed reflective space. In supervision, I recognised my resistance, my collusion with others around him in not facing Syon's impending death, my anger, my helplessness, my doubt that I had anything helpful to offer, and consequent behaviours such as repeatedly arriving late for sessions. Acknowledgement of the pain as well as the beauty in this journey together helped me to find my way back to his bedside.

> ... When everything is fluid
> And nothing can be known for certainty
> Hold your own
> Hold it 'til you feel it there
> As dark and dense and wet as earth
> As vast and bright and sweet as air
> When all there is
> Is knowing that you feel what you are feeling
> Hold your own ...
>
> (Tempest, 2015)

This poignant poem that Kate Tempest shared with passion as she closed the 2015 Glastonbury Festival evokes perfectly the necessity in this work to fully meet myself, to recognise and 'hold my own'. It was essential that I come into conscious relationship with the distressing feelings evoked in me to avoid acting in ways destructive to Syon's therapy.

In this DMP intervention, facilitating greater awareness of his condition enabled Syon and me to differentiate his degenerative condition from who he was, so that he did not lose a sense of self, so that he – indeed, both of us – were not lost in hopelessness. I believe that our work enabled him to stay engaged with his life and to return, again and again, to the experience of his changing body (Coaten and Houston, 2016, Papadopoulos 2015).

There is something simply human about the journey Syon and I went through together and I believe and hope that I have demonstrated here that DMP is a profession particularly well equipped to accompany individuals through changes, losses and ultimately death. Not only because we have the means to offer a connection that engages mind, body, heart and soul, but also because we are practitioners located within the artistic, the medical and the social worlds, thus offering opportunities for translation and connection amongst different dimensions of human experience. We hold together many different strands of our clients' lives, and offer interventions that are responsive to the reality in which they live and to the changes that they face. We are committed to fully and consciously meeting ourselves to enable fully 'meeting our clients where they are'.

Notes

1 Myelopathy is a common neurological degenerative disease often mistaken for normal ageing, a condition that will likely affect most of us if we live long enough (Myelopathy, 2015). In the most extreme cases such as in Syon's, myelopathy leads to a gradual loss of mobility and progressive impairment of most bodily functions. A lot of physical pain is experienced in the process.
2 Percutaneous endoscopic gastrostomy feeding tubes: a tube that is inserted in the stomach area and used to feed individuals instead of them taking food in via the mouth, thus avoiding recurrent episodes of aspiration pneumonia, for example.
3 Body Mind Centering® is an 'integrated and embodied approach to movement, body and consciousness' (About BMC, 2016) that changed my life, strongly informed my professional dance training and led (together with other somatic movement practices) me to train as a dance movement psychotherapist.

References

Bainbridge Cohen (2008) *Sensing, Feeling, and Action: The Experiential Anatomy of Body-Mind Centering* (Second Edition). Northampton, MA: Contact Editions.
Bekkema, N., de Veer, A. J. E., Wagemans, A. M. A., Hertogh, C. M. P. M. and Francke, A. L. (2014) 'Decision making about medical interventions in the end-of-life care of people with intellectual disabilities: A national survey of the considerations and beliefs of GPs, ID physicians and care staff'. *Patient Education and Counseling.* 96: 204–209.
Bloom, K., Galanter, M. and Reeve, S. (eds.) (2014) *Embodied Lives: Reflections on the Influence of Suprapto Suryodarmo and Amerta Movement.* Axminster, UK: Triarchy Press.
Butté, C. & Whelan, D. (in press) 'Ambivalence, boundaries, edges and expansion: Relatedness and collaboration in a Dance Movement Psychotherapy and Music Therapy group with adults with learning disabilities. Colbert, T. & Bent, C. (eds.) *Working Across Modalities in the Arts Therapies: Creative Collaborations.* London: Routledge.
De Hennezel, M. (1997). *Intimate Death: How the Dying Teach Us How to Live.* New York: Random House.
Dymoke, K. (2014) 'Contact improvisation, the non-eroticizing touch in an "art-sport"'. *Journal of Dance and Somatic Practices*, 6(2): 205–218.
Feldman, Y. (2016) 'How body psychotherapy influenced me to become a dance movement psychotherapist'. *Body Movement and Dance in Psychotherapy*, 11(2–3): 103–113.

Hartley, L. (2004) Touch, boundaries, and bonding in L. Hartley. *Somatic Psychology: Body, Mind and Meaning.* London: Whurr Publishers.

Heslop, P., Blair, P. S., Fleming, P. J., Hoghton, M. A., Marriott, A. M. and Russ, L. S. (2013) 'Confidential Inquiry into premature deaths of people with learning disabilities (CIPOLD)'. Final Report, Norah Fry Research Centre.

Lear, J. (2008) *Radical Hope: Ethics in the Face of Cultural Devastation.* Cambridge, MA, UK: Harvard University Press.

Ogden, P. Minton, K. and Pain, C. (2006) *Trauma and the Body: A Sensorimotor Approach to Psychotherapy.* New York: W. W. Norton and Company.

Reeve, S. (2011) *Nine Ways of Seeing a Body.* Axminster, UK: Triarchy Press.

Tuffrey-Wijne, I., Wikki, M., Heslop, M., McCarron, M., Todd, S., Oliver, D., de Veer, A., Ahstrom, G., Schaper, S., Hynes, G., O'Farrell, J., Adler, A., Riese, F. and Curfs, L. (2016) 'Developing research priorities for palliative care for people with intellectual disabilities in Europe: A consultation process using nominal group technique'. *BMC Palliative Care*, 15: 36.

Waller, D. (ed.) (2002) *Arts Therapies and Progressive Illness. Nameless Dread.* London: Routledge.

Online resources

Body Mind Centering. An Embodied Approach to Movement, Body and Consciousness. (2016) *About BMC.* Available at www.bodymindcentering.com (Accessed 30/09/16).

Butté, C. and Unkovich, G. (2009) 'Foundations of dance movement psychotherapy practice in profound and multiple learning disabilities: When disabilities disappear', *e-motion*, 14(2): 25–33. Available at admp.org.uk (Accessed 04/02/15).

Down's Syndrome Association (2016) *For Professionals: Health & Medical.* Available at www.downs-syndrome.org.uk (Accessed 15/06/15).

Myelopathy. (2015) *What Is Cervical (Spondylotic) Myelopathy?* Available at www.myelopathy.org (Accessed 12/03/15).

NHS choices. Your health, your choices. (2015) *End of Life Care. What End of Life Care Involves.* Available at www.nhs.uk (accessed 10/08/15).

NHS choices. Your health, your choices. (2014) *Cervical Spondylosis – Symptoms.* Available at www.nhs.uk (Accessed 11/07/15).

The National Council for Palliative Care. (2015) *Palliative Care Explained.* Available at www.ncpc.org.uk (Accessed 10/08/15).

Papadopoulos, N. (2015) 'The body as home'. *e-motion*, 25(3): 4–7. Available at admp.org.uk (Accessed 25/07/16).

Webinar

Coaten, R. and Houston, S. (2016) Interviewed by Julian C. Hughes. *Arts, Health and Wellbeing Webinar: Movement, Dance and the Neurodegenerative Condition* [Webinar]. Available at www.rsph.org.uk (Accessed 09/07/16).

Copyright acknowledgement

'Hold Your Own', written by Kate Tempest, used by permission of Domino Publishing Company Ltd.

Closing reflections

Our body stories are real

Geoffery Unkovich, Céline Butté and Jacqueline Butler

To conclude, we reflect on the eclectic and precious themes that this book offers. Each chapter has spoken of the lived dance movement psychotherapy (DMP) experience, and presented practice-based evidence to demonstrate how movement and embodiment nurture animated encounters in DMP with people with learning disabilities. It has been our goal to shine the light on this particular area of DMP work, so we are delighted that a group of us found the courage and circumstances to say something of our practice. In so doing, we have brought something that has felt silenced out of the shadows.

We asked authors to define, argue and present concrete examples that explain their interventions and social–cultural–political perspective in order to clarify how and why we do what we do. Our intention has been truthfully represented by them in this area of psychotherapy, where there is often an overriding theme and reality of a need for more. Subsequently, there are many more practice-based stories still to be told. The practitioners in this book have demonstrated their generosity, flexibility and spontaneity in providing the best practice possible. Through their writings we are reminded that there are as many similarities as differences in the ways in which DMPs find their way, and this exemplifies how we utilise our body, mind and soul to offer responsible interventions that contribute something very concrete and relevant for the client. The result in this book is complex, rich and real, with each chapter being the root of new, established, vigorous, tentative or innovative practice.

We are challenged by words and labels in our work, where words such as learning disability, learning difficulty, intellectual disability, learning disabled, appropriate, inappropriate, sexual, sexuality, sexual orientation, sensual, adult, man, woman, boy, girl, verbal, nonverbal and vocal have an impact on the way people are perceived by themselves and others. We have particularly discussed the use of the word 'flexibility' in regards to therapeutic boundaries and approaches, as this might suggest a softening of boundaries, or ease with theoretical perspective. For this reason, we have come to appreciate the term 'contextualised facilitation', which supports the essential malleability needed in 'fitting' a model of therapy to best suit the needs of the person with a learning disability, within any given context.

Our most nonverbal clients teach us to be in a wordless, sensory landscape and not to be frightened. They ask us, in their own way: 'Are you prepared to meet me here, and all that it will bring?' The significance of trusting the body of the clients and of the therapists is integral to the work as we shape our interpersonal relationships. We are all bodies that might hold, flop, reach, jump, retract, lengthen or expand; we might open an arm or keep it close to our stomach; actions that are all ways of communicating with the world, ways of being with each other in relationship. All of these possibilities continue to raise our curiosity as DMPs working with adults with mild, moderate, profound and complex learning disabilities, and in the wider context.

Someone with a mild learning disability may be able to express themselves verbally and find a 'fit' with what their local community has to offer. At the other end of the learning disabilities spectrum are individuals with a myriad of medical diagnoses which make life complex. Some people need others to support them with everyday tasks such as eating, drinking or getting dressed. These tasks become a key part of life for a person with severe learning disabilities where families, carers and other professionals need lots of time to provide the support that will enable an individual to sustain life in a dignified manner. For these individuals (people with learning disabilities and their carers) intimacy has a particular quality. The positive and negative aspects of bodies moving together closely, of repeated physical proximity and of intimacy are often themes integral to the DMP process with children and adults in this client group.

The practitioners in this book have provided rich accounts of meeting their clients where they are; of being 'in sympathetic union with the moods of the [client]' (Chace, 1945: 53). What has it been like for you the reader to share in this experience with each author?

Authors have reminded us of some of the fundamental principles of psychotherapy. For example, the very beginning, the first moments and first few sessions with our clients, which may tell us something of their own beginning, of their arrival into this world as a person with a learning disability. Movement, voice, words and sounds all provide essential information, even the information we gather in the corridors (however brief) in passing conversations with clients or colleagues is as important as that which we observe during sessions. Being sometimes overwhelmed through experiencing powerful emotions are common features of psychotherapeutic practice in this field, so the processing of the material in supervision as well as within the confines of a healthy multidisciplinary team is vital to our ability to return afresh to the psychotherapeutic relationship.

Held in all our bodies are the anxieties, depressions, traumas, fears, delights, thrills, joys and revelations of our lived experience. Through the embodied expression of psychological processes, we are able to share clients' good and bad times that they courageously express in movement and in sound. Giving space and attention to this corporeal experience is what we offer clients. The exploration of emotion, sensation, images and movement preferences enhances self-expression via responsive interactions between therapist, individual clients and group members, interactions that are based on attunement, empathy, compassion and the embodied experience of all involved. Working from a felt sense we are able to share what our movements feel like to each other. This is not to make an interpretation of the personal material, but to speak, move and vocalise from an authentic understanding of our lived experience in the movement interaction. Part of this exploration is the therapist's modelling of new or different vocal, verbal and movement possibilities, a dialogue in movement and sound, which posits new modes of expression for us all and which best suits our needs and those of our clients. Together we shape and reshape, form and transform, opening up possibilities in ourselves and each other that welcome, celebrate and hold sensitively the uniqueness of each of us. With curiosity, we open up to the breadth of what being alive and of interacting safely with each other actually means, looks like and sounds like.

Let us not be mistaken here: DMP is not all soft and gentle, fluid and permissive. Negotiating safety within a context where the interpersonal–physical interactions are given full and primordial attention as communication per se, requires that therapists be aptly on their toes. At times, an intervention will indeed appear soft and welcoming, yet at others it might come across as bold, blunt and non-negotiable. Context, intention and experience are key in how practitioners hold their embodied responses to what their clients present; always returning to being of service to the self-actualisation of each individual they work with, fostering an empowered, enlivened and responsible dialogue that ultimately will benefit all.

Clients' expression must be experienced as not right or wrong, but as real; an authentic expression to be welcomed as constructive interaction in our relationships. Coming from the body, we view movement and postural positioning as a vital form of self-expression. It is very possible that habitual postural positioning is a result of neglect, lack of social engagement, or a representation of shutting oneself away from the world. So, as we sense our clients' story through our attention to the body and movement, we recognise the importance of being an advocate for our clients whose bodies may seem unreadable and whose voices cannot be heard. With individuals for whom words are not predominantly reliable as a means to communicate the details of their needs, preferences and story, we as DMPs say 'Yes' to their movement and 'Yes' to their bodies, we say 'Yes' to them as a whole person. This book gives voice to those bodies and minds that may have been marginalised or silenced in other contexts. We thank our clients for the extraordinary journeys they have shared with us and for the life lessons they have taught us along the way.

Reference

Chace, M. (1945), Rhythm in movement as used in Saint Elizabeth's Hospital'. Reprinted in Chaiklin, H. (ed.) (1975) *Marian Chace: Her Papers*. Columbia, MD: American Dance Therapy Association.

Index

Allison, C. 54
'affect attunement', lack of 104; *see also* attunement
Asperger syndrome 22, 24, 32
assessments *see* DMP assessments for children and young people with learning disabilities and special needs
Association for Dance Movement Psychotherapy UK 45, 56
attachment theories 29–30; *see also* autism
attention deficit disorder (ADD) 24
attention deficit hyperactivity disorder (ADHD) 54
attunement 66–7, 111, 117, 123, 142, 150; video and 70, 72; attuning 16, 19, 32–3, 52, 102–3; *see also* video interaction guidance (VIG)
Authentic Movement 58
autism: attachment difficulties and 29–30; autism spectrum condition (ASC) 2, 54; autism spectrum disorder (ASD) 2, 54, 67; benefits of DMP 22, 25, 31–3, 37–8; children and 45–7, 67, 75; main psychological theories 27; services 31; social awareness 31; 'supported living' 22, 27

Baron-Cohen, S. 27, 54
Barratt, H. 3
Bastita, R. 88
Bayne, R. 39
becoming a dance movement psychotherapist (DMP) 22–3, 2–30, 32
Beebe, B. 73
beginnings with learning disabled clients: complexity of 9–19; 'disability transference' 16–17; embodied awareness 16–17; importance of 9–10; inclusion 19; language 9; subjectivity 15–16; symbolic themes 18; working in the transference 16–19
Belsky, J. 73
Best, P. 98
Blackman, N. 84
Body Mind Centering® training (BMC) 142
body stories: contextualised facilitation 148; habitual postural positioning 150
Bolton P. 54
Brayne, C. 54
Butler, J. 1, 6, 94, 148
Butté, C. 1, 7, 136, 148

Callahan, A. B. 89
Care Act 4
Chadwick, A. 84
Chesner, A. 117
Child and Adolescent Mental Health Services (CAMHS) 24, 61, 66, 69–73
Children Act 45
The Children and Families Act 63
Clark, L. 6, 109
collaboration: between group members 126, 131; between members of staff 104–6; boundaries 97–8; non-clinical settings 94–5; non-negotiables 97; working together 98
Concannon, L. 104
'contextualised facilitation' 148
Corbett, A. 16, 43
Cossino, P. 88
countertransference 42; somatic 43; VIG and 75

'Coventry grid' 30; *see also* Moran
Cross, J. 70, 74
Cruz, R. F. 43
Curtis, Sue 5, 81

D'Amico, G. 88
Dance Voice 25
Dayanim, S. 43
death of a client 81–93; bereavement team
  82, 86; fear of losing job 83; four-
  task model of grief 84; school-wide
  training on loss and bereavement 81;
  supervision 90; unresolved grief 84;
  unsupported staff 83; *see also* 'Memory
  Time'
De Hennezel, M. 141
diagnosis of learning disability: autism and
  24, 27; communication with patient 138;
  Down's Syndrome and 15; impact on
  parent and child 15; loss of the imagined
  child 14–15; shame 15
Disability Living Allowance (DLA) 4, 25
DMP assessments for children and young
  people with learning disabilities and
  special needs: assessment meeting 42;
  case example 46–8; DMP assessment
  framework 45–8; ecosystemic approach
  38–41; ethics and confidentiality 45;
  'Every Child Matters Policy' 40;
  information gathered 39; integrative
  approach to dance movement
  psychotherapy 36–7; multi-agency
  work 40; nonverbal communication 38;
  process of assessment 41–3; referral
  source, information from 41; somatic
  countertransference 43; special
  education needs coordinator 40;
  special education needs and disability
  classifications 37; team around the child
  40; terminology debate 37; therapist
  adaptations 44–5; transferences 41;
  using movement observation 43–4;
  see also Laban Movement Analysis;
  'Ways of Seeing' approach
Down's syndrome 9, 13, 15, 136; *see also*
  diagnosis
DSM – IV 27
Dyregrov, A. 83
dyslexia 24

East, V. 55–6
Edgette, J. S. 87

Education Act 24, 29
Education and Health Care Plan
  (EHCP) 63
Education, Health and Social Care plans
  (0–25) 31
Edwards, J. 5, 22
embodied awareness 16
Endrizzi, C. 88
Evans, L. 55–6
'Every Child Matters Policy' 40

'fight–flight' response 115
'Five Part Session™' 54, 57
Fox, S. 84
Frizell, C. 5, 9
'Future in Mind' 67

gender discoveries and DMP 121–35;
  authentic role model 130; benefits and
  outcomes 130–1; bodily expression 128;
  disclosure 129–30; group 124–5; human
  rights 121; jocular intervention 127;
  long-term experiential processing 123;
  negative attitudes 121; personal
  realisation 132; role play 129; safe
  touch 129; session notes 125–7;
  sexuality 121; therapeutic relationship
  123–4; touch 128–9
Goldman, L. 84
Goodwill, S. 43
Grey, R. 83–4, 86, 89
grief *see* death of a client

Hawkins, J. 113
Hayes, J. 114
Herman, J. 70, 73
Hickey-Moody, A. 15
holistic intervention team *see* SEND
  (Special Educational Needs and
  Disabilities School
Holland, J. 83
Hoo, F. 5, 36
Horton, I. 39
Hurley, A. D. 44–5

inclusive education 24; *see also*
  Education Act
'intercultural dialogue' 54–5

Kennedy, H. 70, 74
kinaesthetic empathy 111, 114
Kubler-Ross, E. 84

Laban Centre 4
Laban Movement Analysis (LMA) 43, 58
Lear, J. 145
Leventhal, M. 54, 57
Lewis, C. 43
low registration 31

Makaton sign language 22
Mallon, B. 83
Manford, Bethan 6, 66
Manners, Paula 1
Mathews, F. E. 54
Meekums, B. 43
Meier, W. 54–6
Meldreth Manor School 3
'Memory Time' 88–9
men's group *see* gender discoveries in
  a dance movement psychotherapy
  men's group
Mental Capacity Act 15
Mental Health Act (1989) 31
Merry, T. 29
Mieir, W. 3
moderate learning difficulties (MLD) 53
Moran, H. 30
multi-agency work (MAW) 40
multidisciplinary team (MDT) 139
myelopathy 136–7, 139

National Health Service and Community
  Care Act 30
National Society for the Prevention of
  Cruelty to Children (NSPCC) 76
Neuro-Physiological Psychology (NPP)
  intervention 28
nonverbal communication 25, 32, 38, 42,
  44, 66–8, 72–3, 75–6, 95, 104, 106–7,
  127, 138, 140
Nordoff Robbins Music Therapy Centre 3
Noyes, E. 29
NVQ level 3 qualification 26

The Office for Standards in Education,
  Children's Services and Skills (Ofsted)
  53, 55, 58, 62–3
Orbach, S. 43

Palella, P. 88
palliative care 138, 140–1
parental embodied mentalizing (PEM) 73
Parker, G. 98
Personalised Independent Payment (PIP) 4

person-centred dance movement
  psychotherapy approach 109–19;
  'challenging behaviour' 113; combining
  of narratives 110; creativity 111, 116;
  'fight–flight' response 115; kinaesthetic
  empathy 111, 114; non-judgemental
  environment 109; range of clients 110;
  referral procedure 113; safety of
  therapeutic alliance 117; 'secure
  base' 114
Pfadt, A. G. 44–5
place of collaboration *see* collaboration
Powell, M. A. 43
profound and multiple learning disabilities
  (PMLD) 5; adults with 94–6
Prouty, G. 95, 111

Quagliata, E. 42

Rhode, M. 43
Rogers, C. 28, 110–11
Rogers, N. 116
Rustin, M. 42

Scott, F. J. 54
self-actualising tendency 118
SEND (Special Educational Needs and
  Disabilities) School: associate teacher,
  role of 53; 'classroom monitor'
  software 59; DMP journey form 62;
  holistic intervention documents 58–63;
  holistic intervention team 52–64;
  'intercultural dialogue' 54–5; moderate
  learning difficulties, pupils with 53;
  Ofsted visit 53; session confidentiality
  53; setting 53–4; shift in approach
  to teaching 56; Special Educational
  Needs Coordinator 55; teacher/therapist
  54–6; 'Ways of Seeing' programme 57;
  weekly DMP log 59–60; *see also*
  attention deficit hyperactivity disorder;
  Authentic Movement; autistic spectrum
  condition; autistic spectrum disorder;
  'Five Part Session™'
sensorimotor psychotherapy (SP) 137
Shai, D. 73
Sherborne, V. 3
Shuttleworth, R. 122
Sinason, V. 10
Smith, V. 6, 109
Smith-Autard, J. M. 55
Solihull Approach 72

somatic transference 111
special educational needs (SEN) 54
special education needs coordinator
(SenCo) 40, 55
special education needs and disability
(SEND) classifications 37; *see also*
SEND (Special Educational Needs and
Disabilities) School
'Standard Assessment Tasks' (SATs)
tests 29
'steps to eating hierarchy' 72
Stern, D. 9–10, 16, 73, 96
Sunderland, M. 85
'symptom bearers' 67

team around the child (TAC) 40
Tempest, K. 145
Tomasulo, D. J. 44–45
Tortora, S. 43–4, 54, 56–7, 68
transference: 'disability'17; enactment
in relationship with therapist 41;

somatic 111; VIG and 75; working in
16–19; *see also* countertransference
'Transforming Care' agenda 31
Trevarthen, C. 73

Unkovich, G. 1, 6, 121, 148
using video to increase sensitivity and
attunement with caregivers 66–77; *see
also* video interaction guidance (VIG)

video interaction guidance (VIG) 66, 73–6

Ware, M. 30
'Ways of Seeing' approach 44, 57
Wengrower, H. 54, 56, 98
Williams, J. 54
Wilson, J. 5, 52
Winnicott, D. W. 103
Woods, A. 1
Worden, J. W. 84
working together *see* collaboration